IMAGES
of America

WAVE-SWEPT
LIGHTHOUSES OF
NEW ENGLAND

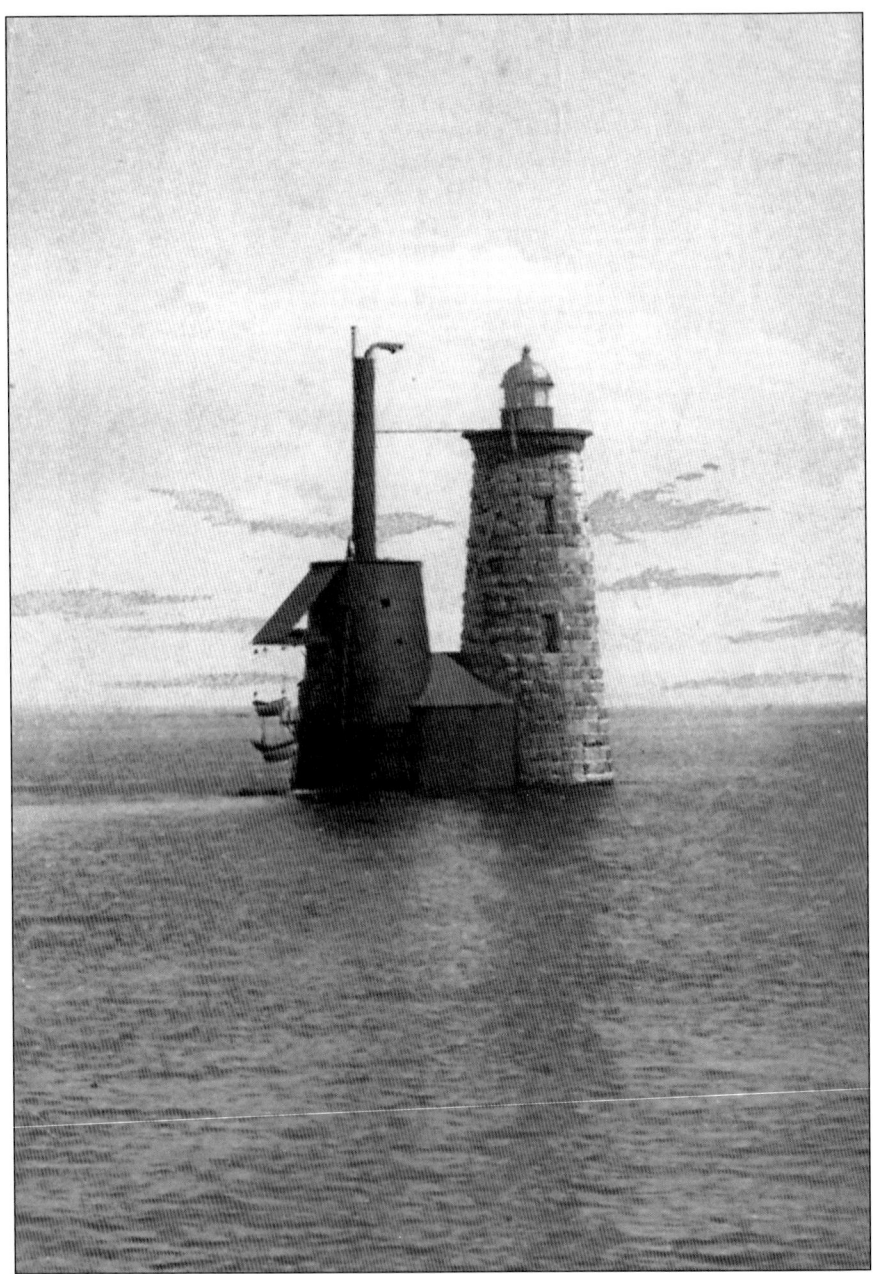

From 1878 to 1969, an unusual cast-iron fog signal tower stood next to Whaleback Lighthouse at the mouth of the Piscataqua River in Kittery, Maine. It was reported in the 1950s that the Coast Guard keepers frequently had to work on the air compressors inside the tower, where temperatures could reach 145 degrees and the noise was deafening. (Author's collection.)

On the Cover: Halfway Rock Light, far out in Maine's Casco Bay, is built on a rocky ledge that is largely exposed at low tide but mostly submerged at high tide. Keeper George Toothaker lived at Halfway Rock between 1872 and 1885. "Me, it affected mentally," he once said of life at the remote outpost. "Others it affects physically, and I have known of one case where it has driven a man insane." (US Coast Guard.)

IMAGES
of America

WAVE-SWEPT LIGHTHOUSES OF NEW ENGLAND

Jeremy D'Entremont

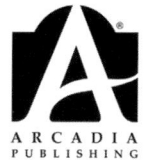

Copyright © 2018 by Jeremy D'Entremont
ISBN 978-1-4671-2897-1

Published by Arcadia Publishing
Charleston, South Carolina

Printed in the United States of America

Library of Congress Control Number: 2017958767

For all general information, please contact Arcadia Publishing:
Telephone 843-853-2070
Fax 843-853-0044
E-mail sales@arcadiapublishing.com
For customer service and orders:
Toll-Free 1-888-313-2665

Visit us on the Internet at www.arcadiapublishing.com

*To the courageous builders and keepers of the wave-swept lights,
and to my wife, Charlotte, my beacon through variable seas.*

CONTENTS

Acknowledgments		6
Introduction		7
1.	The World's First Wave-Swept Lighthouses	9
2.	Whaleback	17
3.	Saddleback	29
4.	Minot's Ledge	37
5.	Halfway Rock	63
6.	Graves	75
7.	Ram Island Ledge	95
8.	"Sparkplug" Lighthouses, Lightships, and Other Remote Stations	107
Bibliography		126
About the Organizations		127

Acknowledgments

I am deeply indebted to many who have provided valuable assistance in my three decades of lighthouse research. Fellow historians Candace Clifford, Elinor DeWire, Jane Molloy Porter, and James W. Claflin have always shared their resources and time generously, and I am very grateful.

The American Lighthouse Foundation and its executive director, Bob Trapani Jr., have been an important source of support, and so have the US Lighthouse Society and its director Jeff Gales. I also wish to thank the US Coast Guard Historian's Office and the Coast Guard at large for providing so many historic images and being so helpful over the years. Many images from the National Archives and the Library of Congress appear in this book, and I am grateful for their assistance over the years.

Lighthouse owners Ford Reiche, Dave Waller, and Nick Korstad are a joy and inspiration to know, and I thank them for their kind assistance.

In no particular order, I also wish to thank William O. Thomson, Dave Gamage, Brian Tague, Janice Jensen, and Tom Tag. And a very special thank-you goes to my friend Dolly Bicknell, whose generosity knows no bounds. Dolly's father, the late historian Edward Rowe Snow, was one of the primary inspirations for my interest in lighthouses, and in many ways, his lifetime of devotion to maritime history laid the groundwork for books like this.

Thank you, to all the others who have provided photographs for use in this book. And many thanks also go to Caitrin Cunningham and everyone with Arcadia Publishing for their support, expertise, and encouragement.

INTRODUCTION

Wave-swept lighthouses, also known as sea-swept or sea rock lighthouses, are perched on exposed rocks and ledges and are subject to the full fury of the mighty ocean. Typically, wave-swept lighthouses are built of granite, and they contain living quarters inside the lighthouse tower itself rather than in a separate dwelling. Bell Rock, Skerryvore, Wolf Rock, and Eddystone are among the most famous lighthouses in the world, and they all fit the definition of a wave-swept tower.

Lighthouses date back to ancient times; in fact, two of the Seven Wonders of the Ancient World (the Colossus of Rhodes and the Pharos of Alexandria) are believed to have served as lighthouses. The Pharos of Alexandria, built on an island in the Nile delta in the third century BC, is often cited as the first significant lighthouse in the world.

In the United States, most of the lighthouses—beginning with Boston Light in 1716—have been built on the mainland or on relatively substantial islands. But when the average person conjures an image of a lighthouse in his or her mind's eye, it is likely to be the type that most stirs the imagination—a remote tower, far offshore, standing steadfast and resolute in the face of towering waves.

Perhaps the most famous photograph ever taken of a lighthouse, Jean Guichard's capture of a massive wave wrapping around the lower part of France's La Jument Lighthouse with a frighteningly vulnerable-looking keeper standing in the doorway, has helped to cement the public's idea of these rugged and dangerous locations. The wave-swept lighthouse tower is one of the ultimate symbols of humanity's ongoing—and often futile—war with the forces of nature.

The first attempt—in 1698—to erect a lighthouse on the treacherous Eddystone Rocks, located south of Plymouth, England, on the western approach to the English Channel, was met with spectacular failure when the initial structure was toppled in a storm in 1703, claiming the lives of the designer and five other men.

The third tower built at Eddystone, known as the Smeaton Tower, marked a major advancement in lighthouse construction. The lighthouse tower built between 1756 and 1759 at Eddystone Rocks was designed by celebrated engineer John Smeaton and was the first to be constructed of granite blocks connected to each other with dovetail joints. Dovetailing was a method often used in carpentry but not in masonry. Each stone in Smeaton's tower was joined to its horizontal neighbors using tabs and notches. In addition, Smeaton famously cited the strength of the oak tree, which is widest at the bottom. He mimicked nature in the design for his tower at Eddystone, making the lighthouse wider at the bottom and tapered toward the top.

The 1759 lighthouse at Eddystone served for more than a century, and it would have lasted longer if the rock beneath it had not been undermined. It was dismantled and moved to shore, and it remains a tourist attraction on dry land in Plymouth, England.

The treelike shape and dovetailed granite blocks of Smeaton's lighthouse were adopted as standard elements in wave-swept towers everywhere. Les Hanois Lighthouse, built between 1860 and 1862 off the coast of Guernsey, England, further advanced the science. Designed by James Douglass, the tower's granite blocks were dovetailed together both laterally and vertically. Coupled with strong cement mortar, the result was a lighthouse with walls that essentially were a solid mass; the stones could not be separated without being broken.

The challenges inherent in the design and construction of wave-swept lighthouses provide plenty of drama, but there is another aspect of these structures that is equally fascinating—the chronicles of the lives of their resident keepers. While lighthouse keepers on the mainland and on larger islands lived in comfortable houses, often with their families, the construction of separate houses on wave-swept ledges was often impractical or impossible. Thus, the keepers at the wave-swept locations usually lived inside the towers themselves. The contrast between mainland lighthouses and wave-swept lighthouses is summed up by the phrase *enfer et paradis* ("hell and heaven"), which was traditionally used in the French lighthouse service.

The beginnings of wave-swept lighthouses in the United States can be traced to the first stone tower built in 1830 on Whaleback (or Whale's Back) Ledge at the mouth of the Piscataqua River in Kittery, Maine. An inadequate budget—along with inexperienced designers and builders—contributed to a lighthouse that was shaky and precarious, but the first Whaleback Lighthouse stood for more than 40 years and can accurately be called the nation's first successful wave-swept lighthouse.

Saddleback Ledge Light, built in 1839 in East Penobscot Bay, Maine, is shorter, at 43 feet tall, than most in this class, but it is cited as the oldest standing wave-swept tower in the United States. The lighthouse was designed so well by famed architect Alexander Parris that it is still standing strong today despite the onslaught of nearly two centuries of the ocean's fury.

Like the first tower at Whaleback Ledge, the first lighthouse at Minot's Ledge, off the South Shore of Boston, Massachusetts, was built in 1850 for far too little money, and two young assistant keepers paid for its defects with their lives when the tower toppled in a spring storm in 1851.

The formation of an efficient new US Lighthouse Board in 1852 brought many positive changes in the construction and management of lighthouses. Most of the country's great wave-swept lighthouses were built during the time period from the 1850s into the early 1900s, with the pinnacle perhaps being the second tower at Minot's Ledge, completed in 1860.

The era of resident keepers at wave-swept lighthouses ended in the 1970s as the last stations were automated. Today, a new breed of keeper—the preservationist—works to maintain these historic monuments, while, in most cases, the navigational lights are still managed by the US Coast Guard. Modern-day preservationists face many of the same daunting challenges that were bravely met by the designers, builders, and keepers of the past. Weather and sea conditions frequently make access dangerous or impossible, and those same forces of nature mercilessly punish offshore lighthouses, rendering restoration an ongoing, perpetual process.

Most of the country's lighthouses continue to function as active—and important—aids to navigation, with solar-powered LED-type optics at most locations. Perhaps even more importantly, our wave-swept lighthouses stand as compelling historical monuments to centuries of human innovation and courage.

One
THE WORLD'S FIRST WAVE-SWEPT LIGHTHOUSES

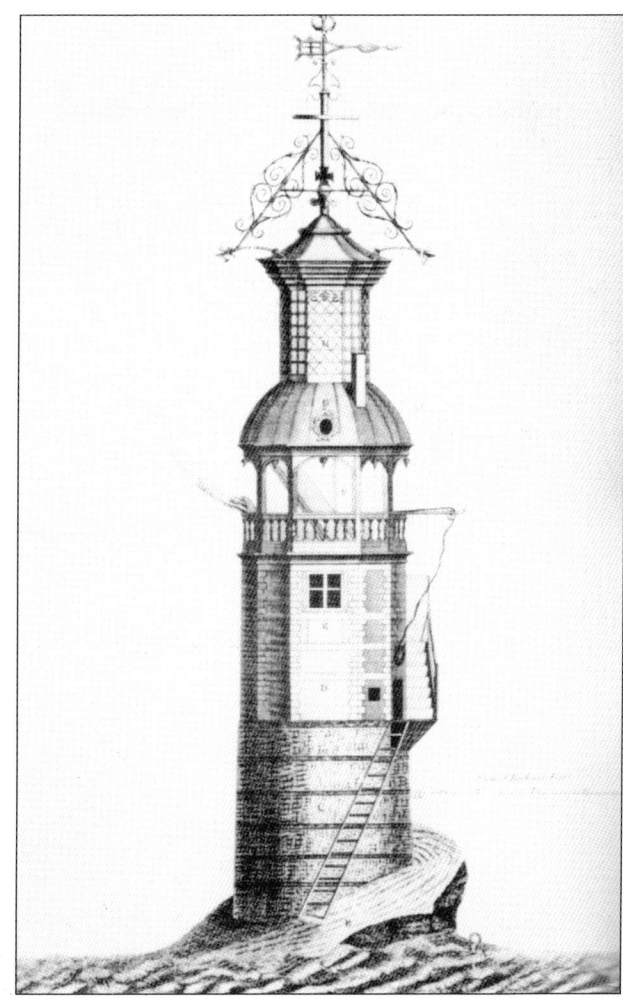

Henry Winstanley, an English engineer and merchant, owned two ships that were wrecked on the Eddystone Rocks off the south coast of England. In response, Winstanley designed a lighthouse that was built on the rocks. The octagonal tower, built of Cornish granite and wood, was erected between 1696 and 1698. (Author's collection.)

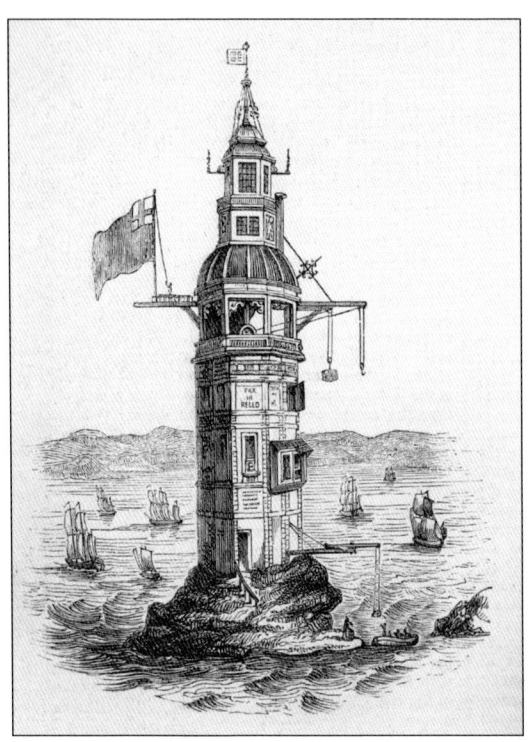

After some damage, the tower was improved and enlarged; this drawing shows it as it looked in 1699. Winstanley was in the lighthouse with five other men on November 27, 1703, when the Great Storm of 1703 swept into the region. The ferocious storm took as many as 15,000 lives. The lighthouse at Eddystone was toppled; Winstanley and the other men were never found. (Author's collection.)

John Rudyard (or Rudyerd), a London silk merchant, designed the second lighthouse on the Eddystone Rocks. The tower, about 70 feet tall, was constructed of alternate courses of oak timbers and granite blocks surrounding an oak mast. It was more successful than its predecessor, standing for 46 years (from 1709 to 1755). (Author's collection.)

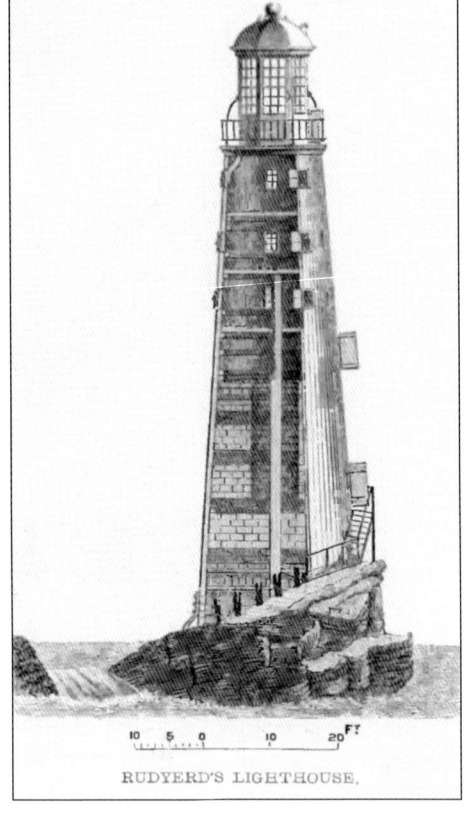

On December 2, 1755, the lantern of Eddystone Lighthouse caught fire. Keeper Henry Hall, 94 years old at the time, valiantly fought the fire with two other keepers. As he looked up, he was showered with molten lead. The lighthouse burned for five days, leaving just rubble. Hall died 12 days after the fire, and a seven-ounce hunk of lead was found in his stomach. (US Lighthouse Society.)

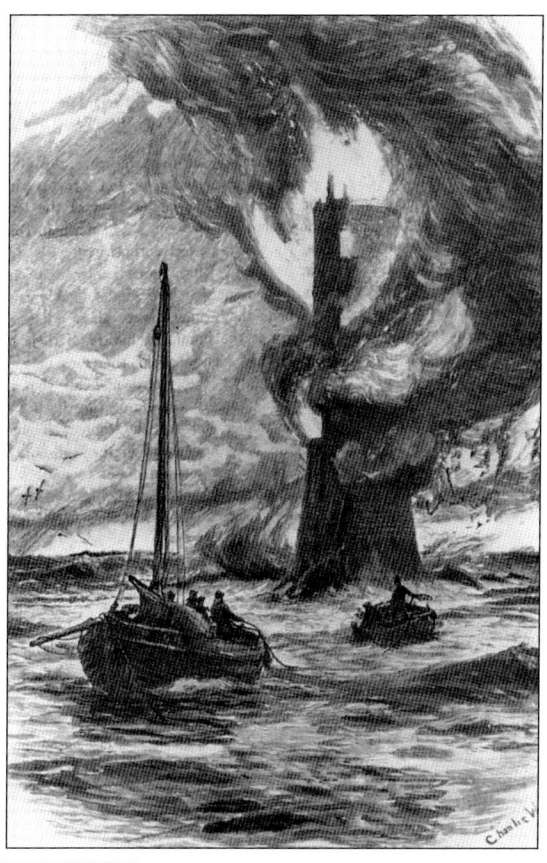

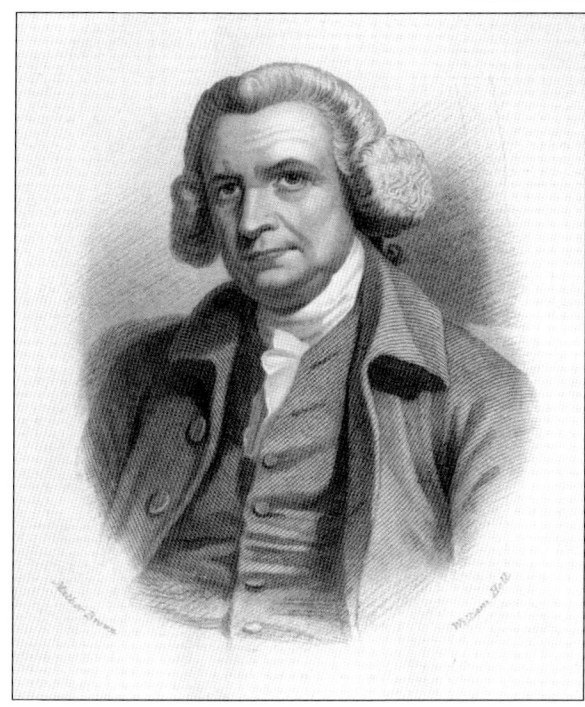

John Smeaton, a Yorkshireman, was an instrument maker, millwright, and canal engineer. Hired to build the third lighthouse tower on the Eddystone Rocks, Smeaton revolutionized lighthouse construction. His 72-foot tower was built of granite blocks that were dovetailed together horizontally, with each course pegged to the ones above and below. (Institution of Civil Engineers.)

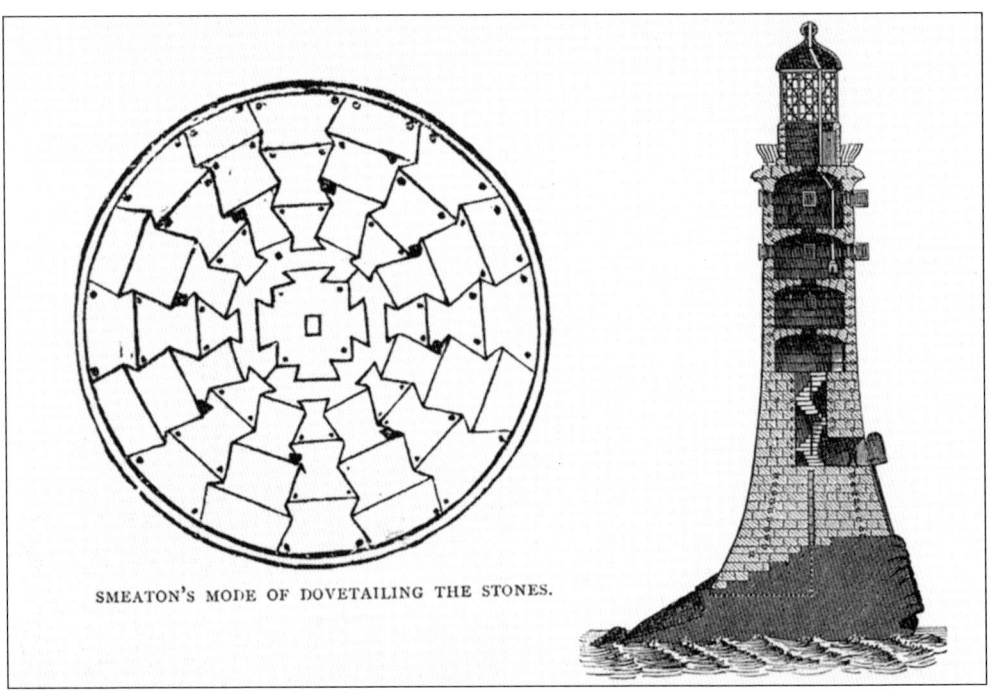

This diagram shows John Smeaton's method of dovetailing granite blocks together in the third tower built at Eddystone. Smeaton also pioneered the use of a new quick-drying cement for the project. When his lighthouse began service in October 1759, its light was produced by 24 candles. Smeaton remarked, "It is very strong and bright to the naked eye, much like a star in the fourth magnitude." (Trinity House.)

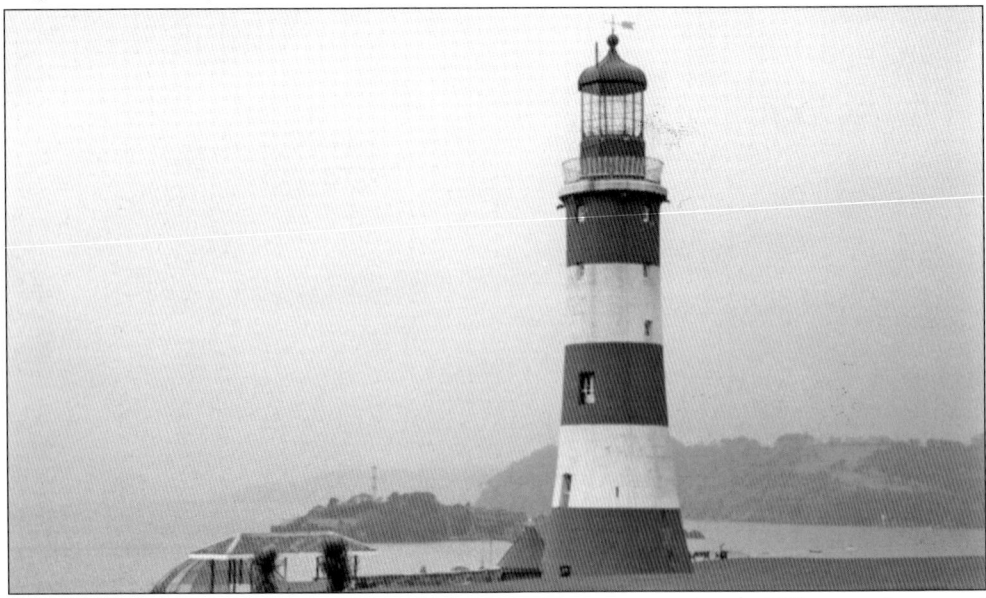

Smeaton's tower at Eddystone held up well for more than a century, but in 1877, it was discovered that the rocks beneath it were rapidly eroding. A fourth Eddystone Lighthouse was built on an adjacent rock, and Smeaton's tower was dismantled and reassembled on shore at Plymouth Hoe, where it now stands as a tourist attraction and a monument to John Smeaton. (Thomas Tag.)

The fourth lighthouse built on the Eddystone Rocks was designed by civil engineer James Nicholas Douglass and located next to the base of John Smeaton's tower. Built of dovetailed granite blocks in similar fashion to Smeaton's tower, Douglass's lighthouse went into service in 1882, and it remains an active aid to navigation today. (Photograph by Darlene Chisholm; US Lighthouse Society.)

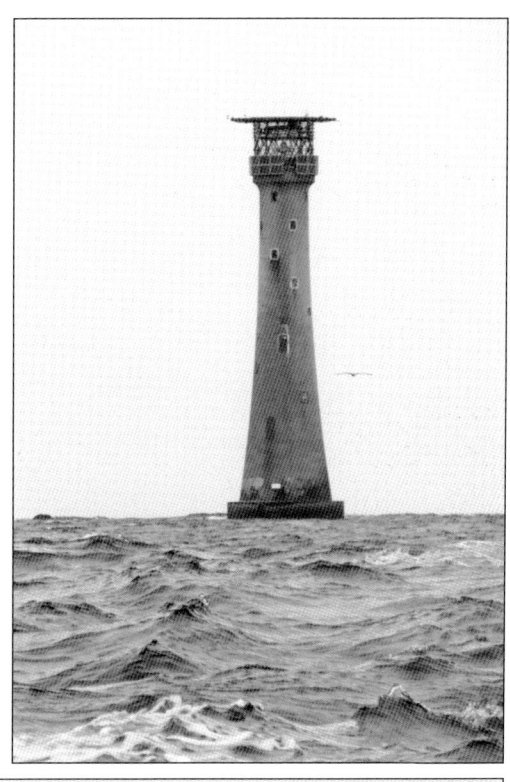

One of the ancestors of modern wave-swept lighthouses was the Cordouan Lighthouse in France. Located on an islet at the mouth of the Gironde estuary, the lighthouse was built between 1584 and 1611, replacing an earlier structure. It is the oldest lighthouse in France and one of the tallest (223 feet) lighthouse towers in the world. It is now a major tourist attraction. (Thomas Tag.)

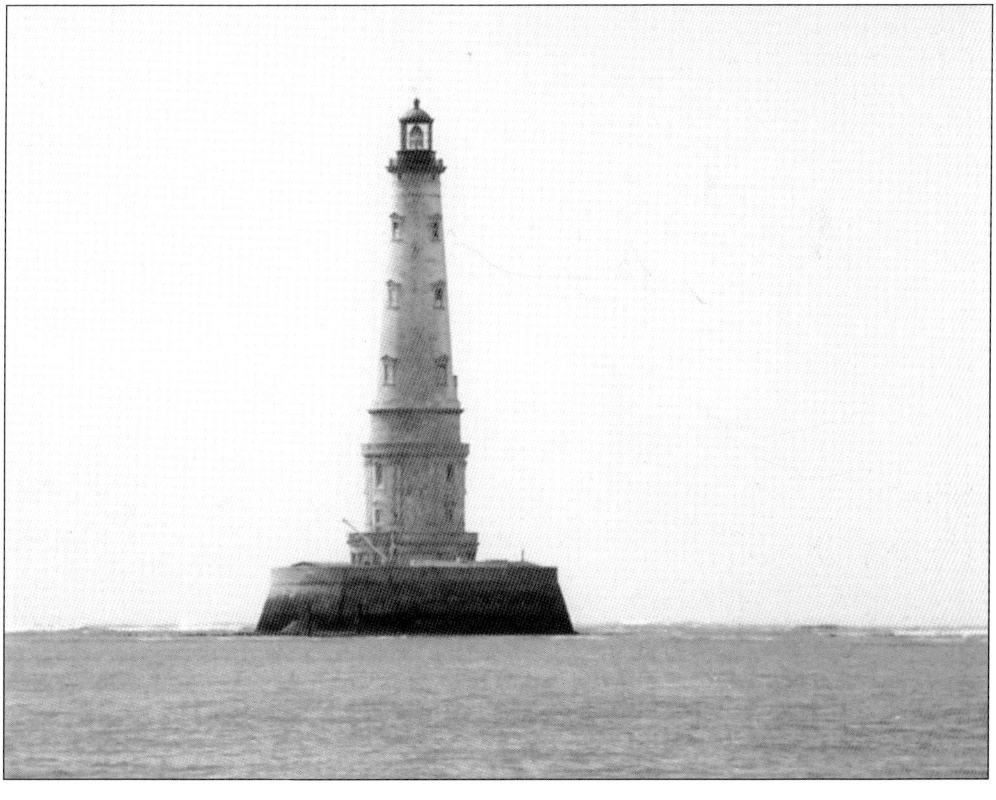

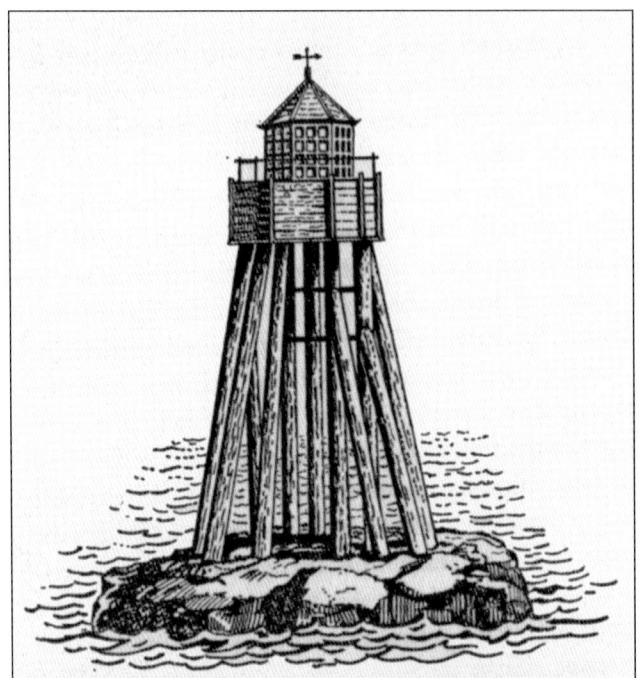

The Smalls are a cluster of rocks in the Irish Sea about 20 miles off the coast of Wales. The first Smalls Lighthouse, built in 1776, consisted of oak pillars surmounted by living quarters and a lantern. It was replaced by a more substantial granite tower built between 1857 and 1861. (Author's collection.)

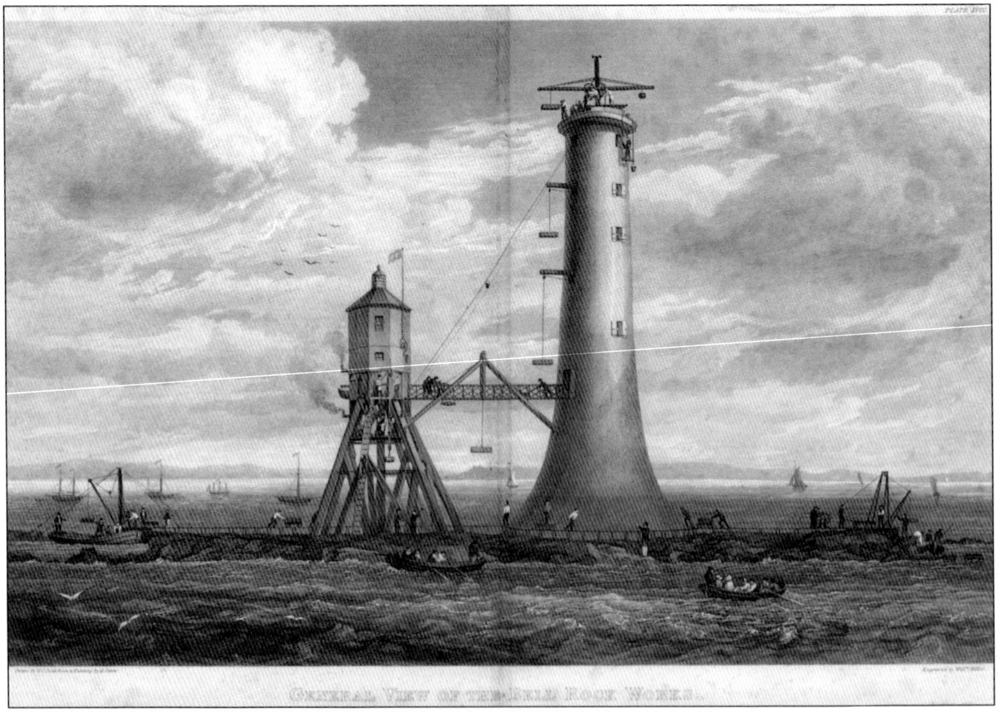

The first lighthouse built at Bell Rock, off the southeast coast of Scotland, still stands today as the granddaddy of the world's wave-swept granite lighthouses. It was built between 1807 and 1810 and was designed by engineer Robert Stevenson, grandfather of author Robert Louis Stevenson. A "beacon house" was built at the construction site to serve as living quarters for the builders. (Author's collection.)

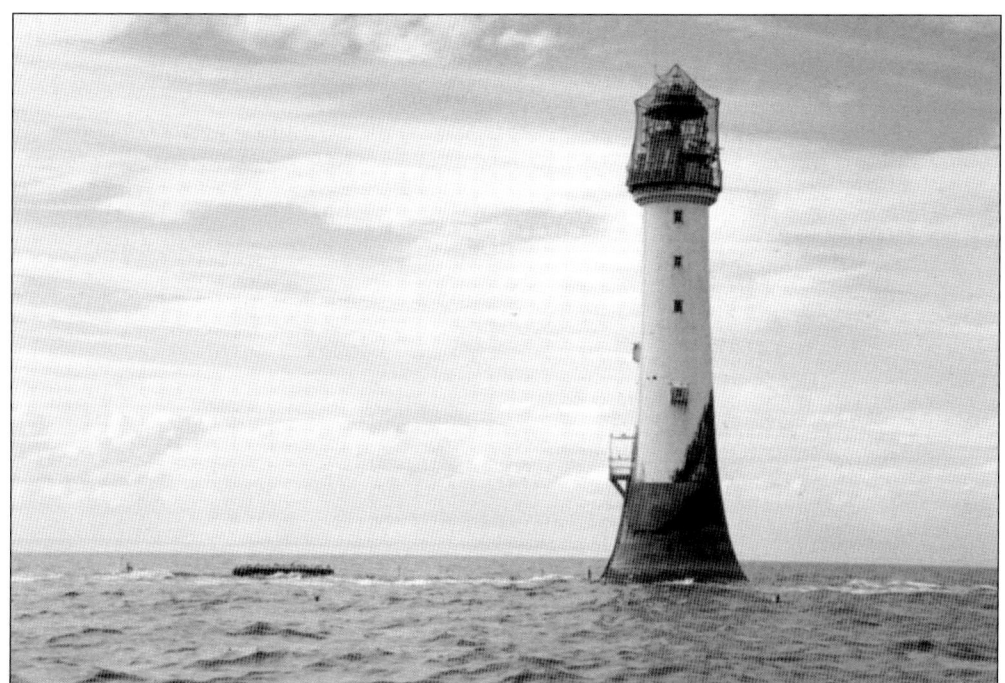

The granite tower at Bell Rock is 92 feet tall and has withstood countless storms and high seas. In December 1955, an RAF helicopter hit the lighthouse, killing two pilots. The lighthouse was damaged, but the keepers were unhurt. The light was automated in 1988, but it continues to serve as an aid to navigation. (Thomas Tag.)

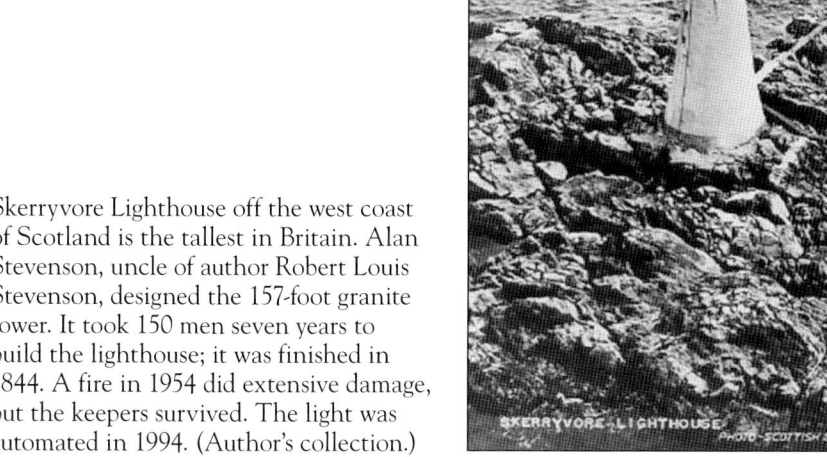

Skerryvore Lighthouse off the west coast of Scotland is the tallest in Britain. Alan Stevenson, uncle of author Robert Louis Stevenson, designed the 157-foot granite tower. It took 150 men seven years to build the lighthouse; it was finished in 1844. A fire in 1954 did extensive damage, but the keepers survived. The light was automated in 1994. (Author's collection.)

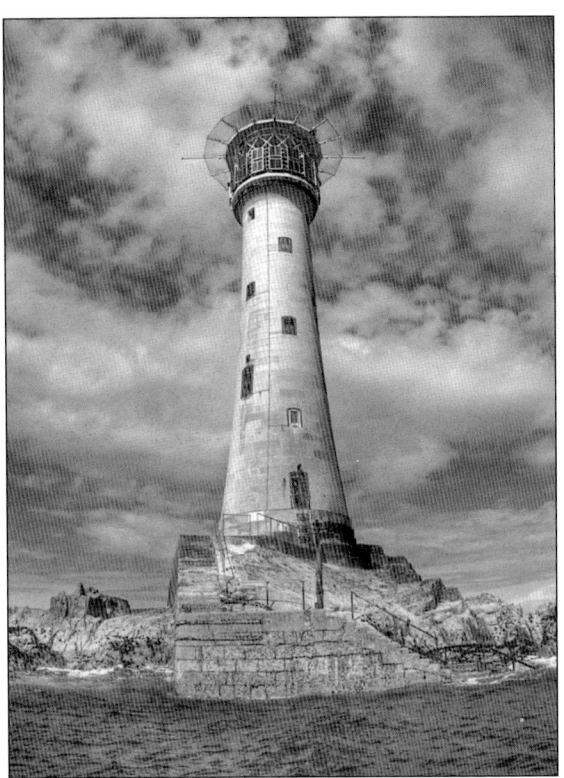

Les Hanois Lighthouse, built between 1860 and 1862 and designed by James Douglass, stands 118 feet tall on a rock off the west coast of Guernsey in the English Channel. The lighthouse marked an important advance in engineering—the granite blocks were dovetailed together both laterally and vertically. (Kevin Lajoie.)

Les Hanois Lighthouse's lens was damaged by gunfire in World War II, and German forces occupied the lighthouse for a time. It was relit after the war in September 1945. Still operated by Trinity House, the flashing light of the Les Hanois Lighthouse can be seen at a distance of 20 miles. (Peter Norman.)

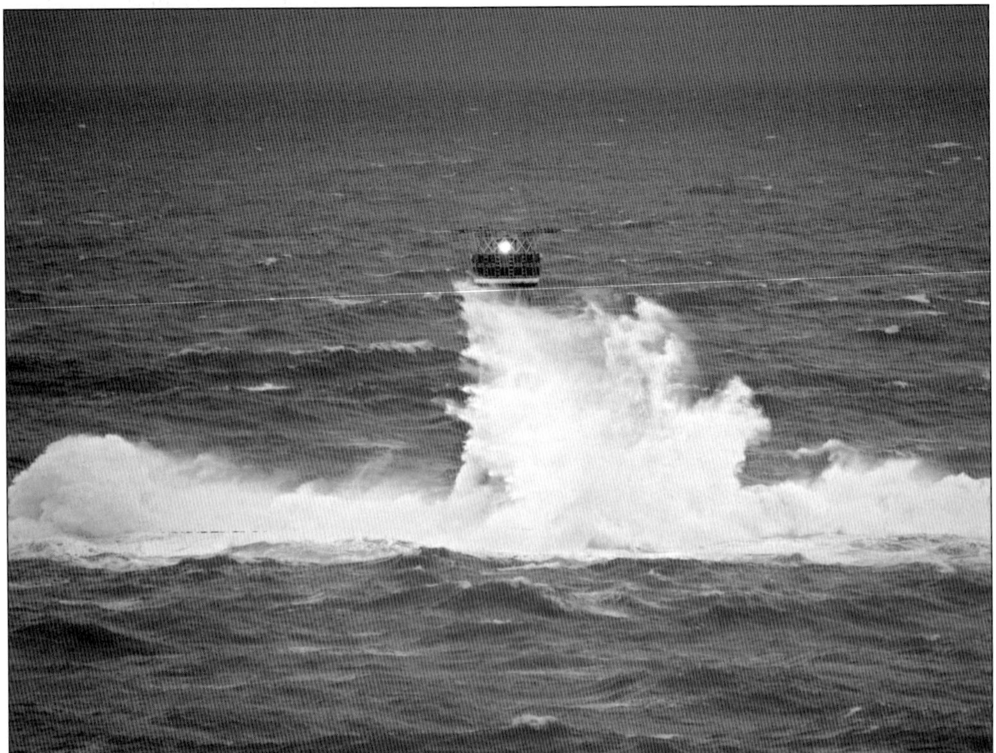

Two

WHALEBACK

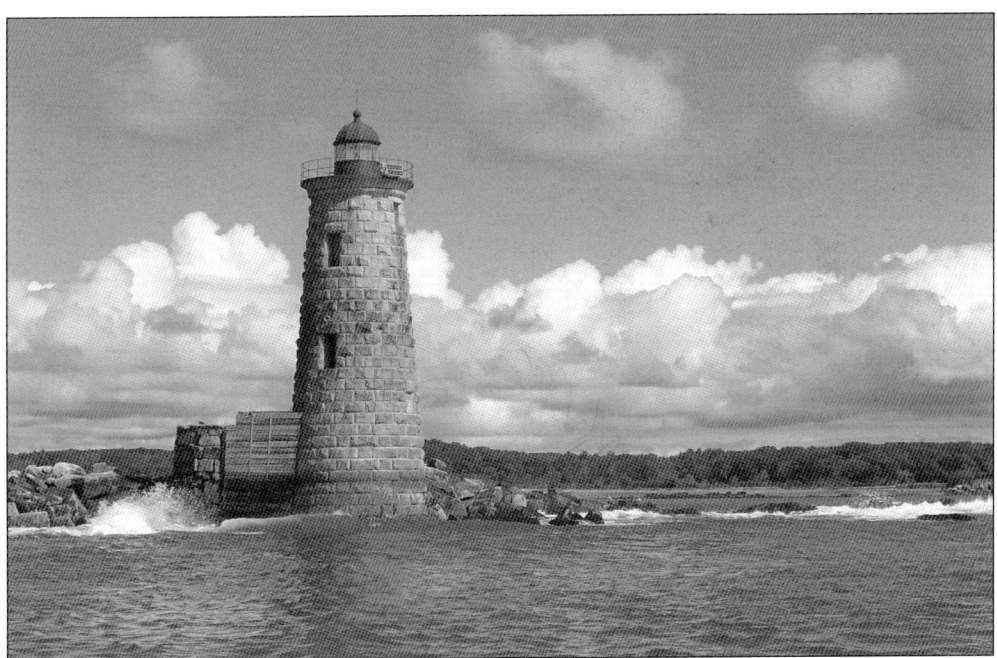

Portsmouth, New Hampshire, with its harbor on the Piscataqua River, was established as an important port for shipbuilding and trade before the American Revolution. Before the establishment of a lighthouse, shipwrecks regularly occurred around the ledges at the mouth of the river. Whaleback Ledge is in southern Maine, just several hundred feet from the border with New Hampshire. (Photograph by the author.)

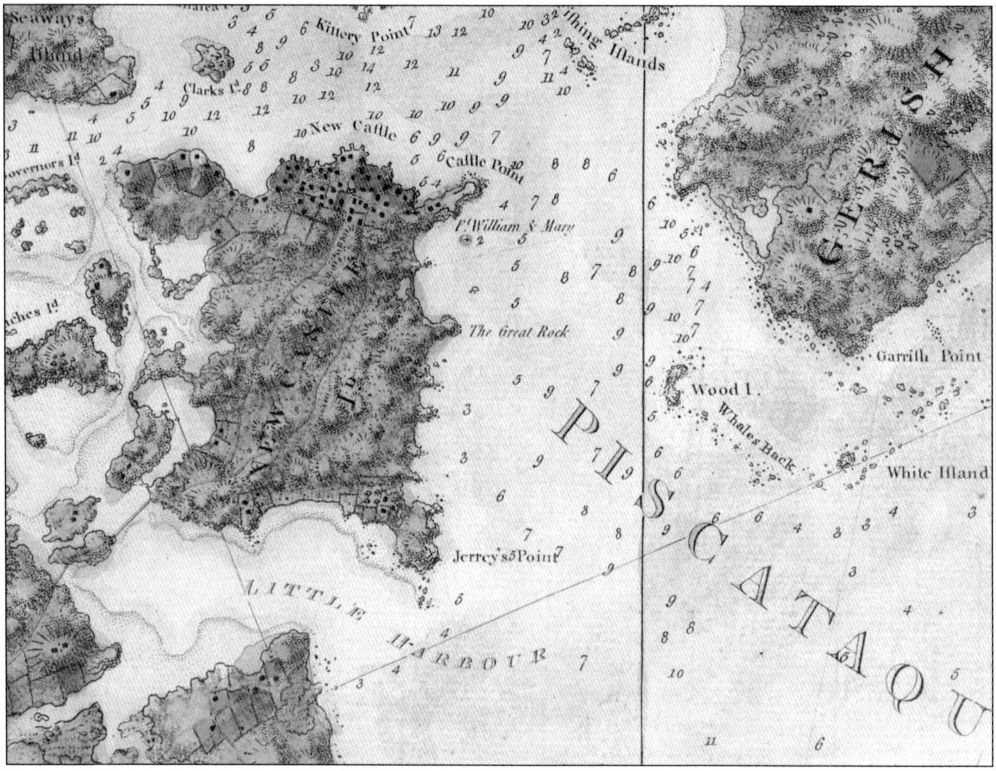

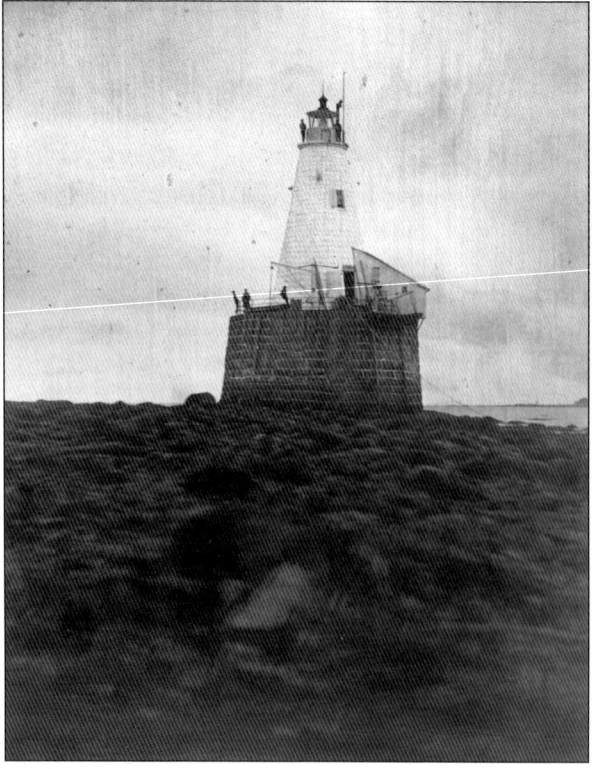

In April 1821, a schooner struck Whaleback Ledge. Several boats of soldiers arrived from Fort Constitution in New Castle, New Hampshire. Cpl. George McAuley asked his crew, "Shall we save them or perish in the attempt?" The response was unanimously yes, and seven people were rescued from the wrecked vessel. More wrecks followed, resulting in an outcry for a lighthouse on the ledge. This chart is from 1779. (Author's collection.)

After three appropriations totaling $20,000, the first Whaleback Lighthouse was constructed in 1829–1830. The stone lighthouse was erected on a conical granite pier. Inside the tower were four rooms of living space on two levels, plus a cellar. The first keeper, Samuel E. Hascall, was paid $500 yearly, and the lighthouse went into service on September 16, 1830. (National Archives.)

The original tower leaked badly during storms and heavy seas. The addition of wooden sheathing helped the leak problem, but in one great storm on July 7, 1837, the vibrations were so violent that "some of the small stones of the tower were shaken out and fell upon the floors of the rooms, and articles of furniture were displaced by the motion of the tower." Alexander Parris, a famed Boston architect and engineer, was brought in as a consultant. Parris advised that a new lighthouse be built for $75,000. He recommended a substantial masonry tower similar to the wave-swept lighthouses in the British Isles. Parris's design ideas from the late 1830s, shown here, were strikingly similar to Smeaton's 1759 tower at Eddystone. (Both, National Archives.)

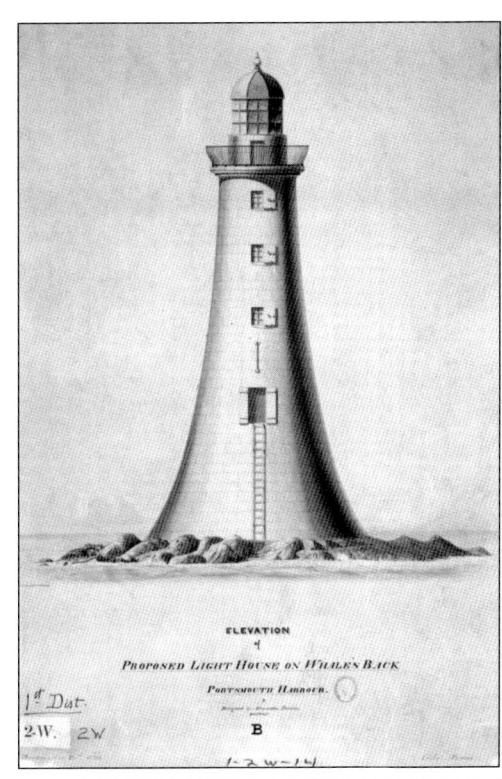

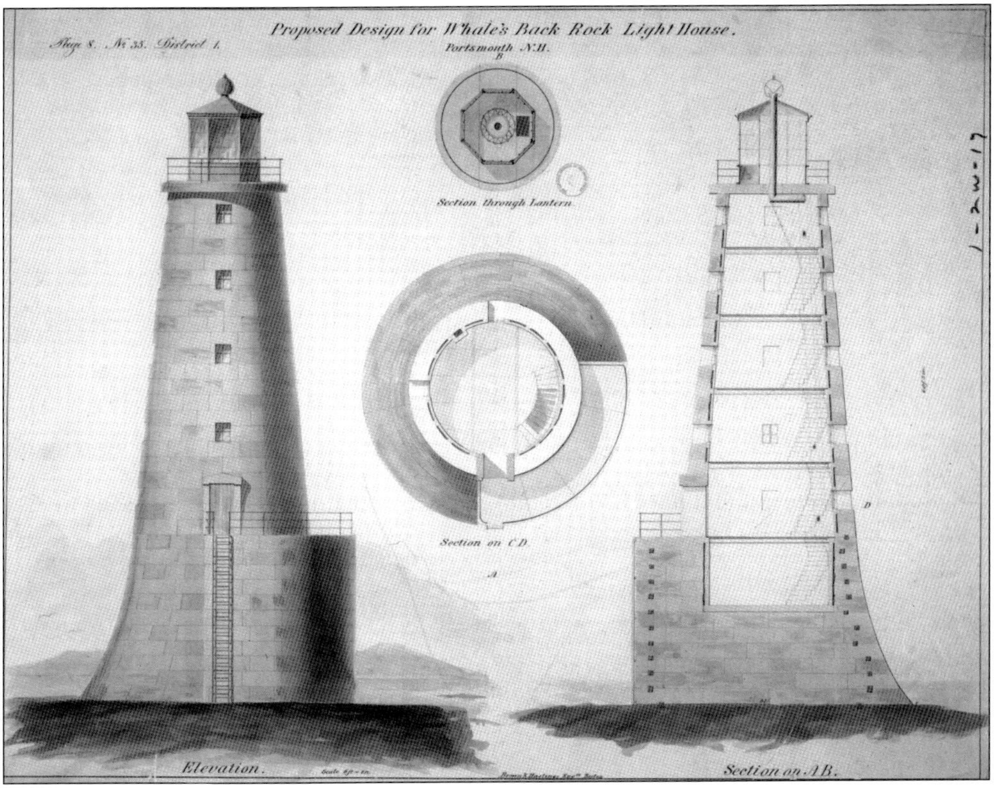

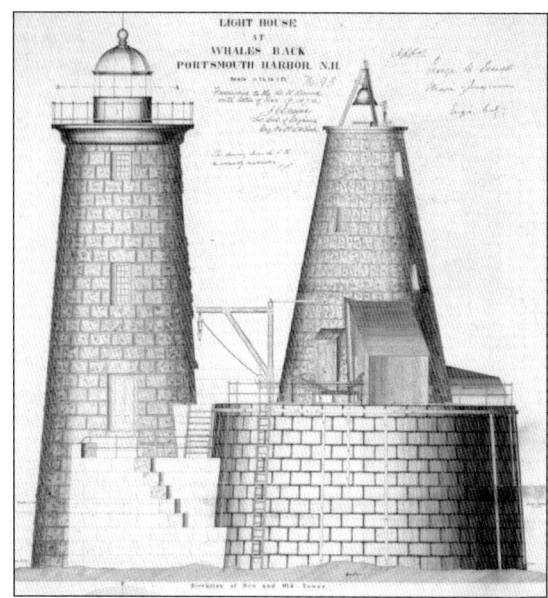

Storms in 1869 caused cracks in the lighthouse, and Congress appropriated $70,000 for rebuilding in July 1870. The new tower, at about 70 feet tall, was constructed of dovetailed granite blocks. The original tower remained standing while the new one was built. In November 1871, keeper William Caswell proclaimed the new tower "perfectly safe" and noted that it did not even tremble in a storm. (National Archives.)

The new tower began operation in 1872. The old lighthouse tower served as a fog signal house for a few years after the new tower was built, but access to the old tower was difficult, and it continued to shake in storms. A more permanent solution was needed. (Author's collection.)

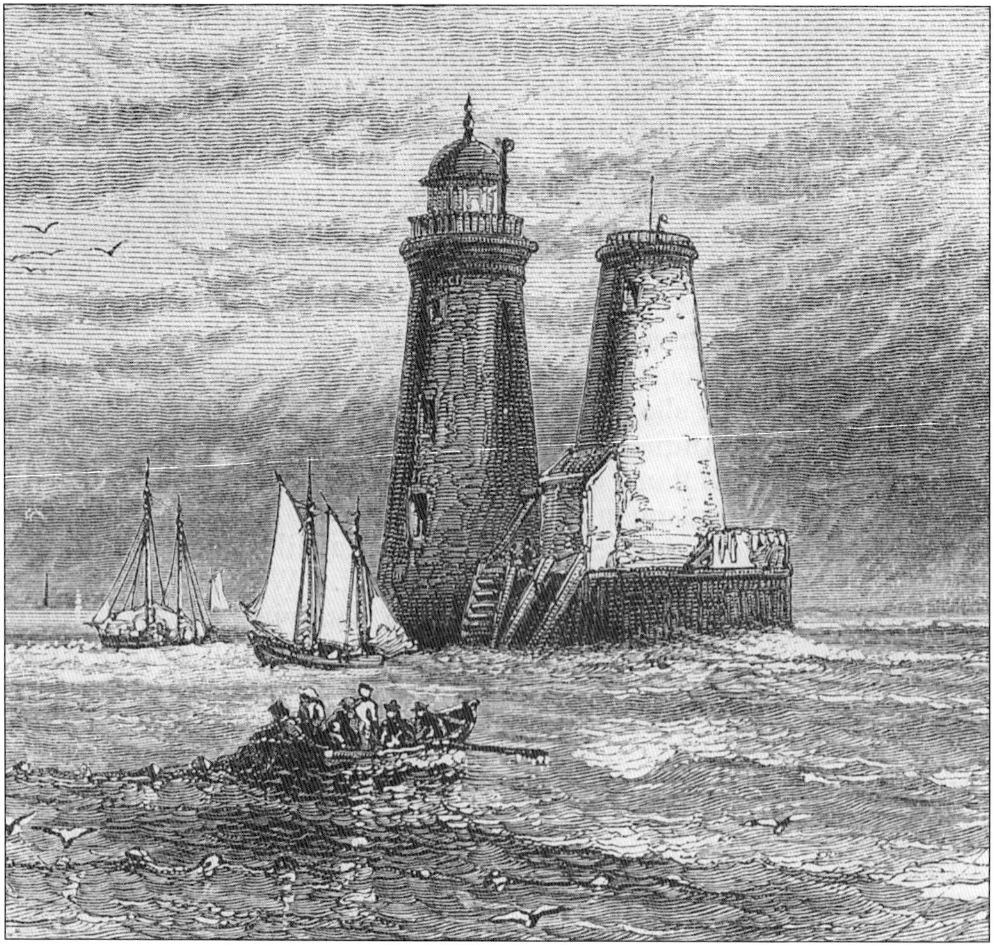

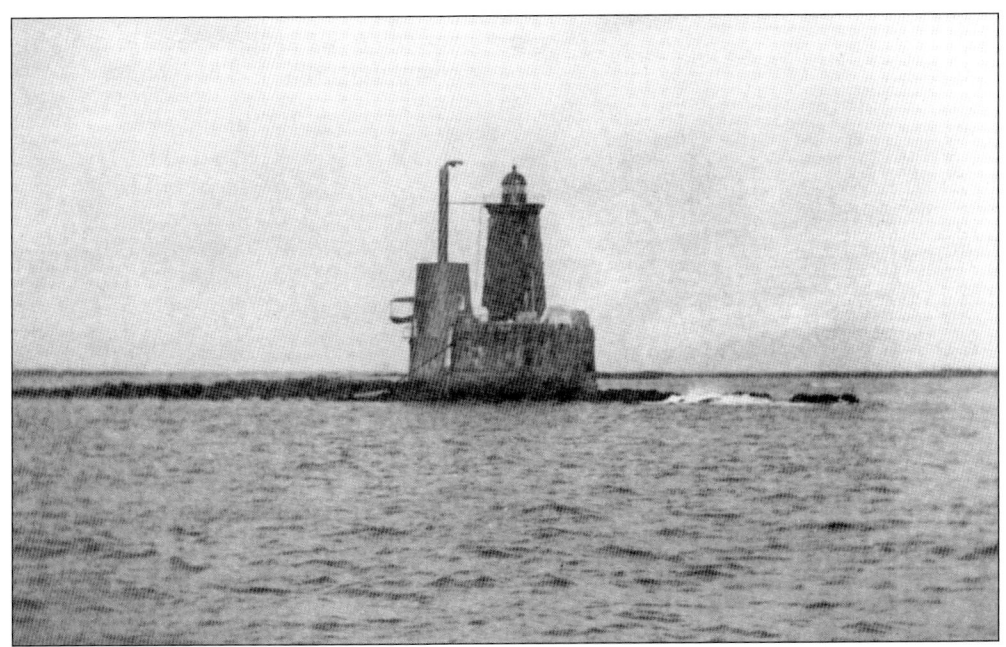

In the summer of 1878, a new cast-iron tower was built just to the north of the 1872 lighthouse to serve as a fog signal house. The cast-iron tower, about half as tall as the lighthouse, was surmounted by a long iron pipe and a third-class fog trumpet that emitted an eight-second blast every 30 seconds. The old lighthouse was removed in 1880. (National Archives.)

The fog signal tower was painted red for some years, and painting it was a precarious proposition for the keepers. In late June 1882, assistant keeper John Lewis fell from the tower as he was painting the apex of the pipe that held the foghorn. A tugboat transported him to shore, but several days later he died from his injuries at his home in Kittery. (US Coast Guard.)

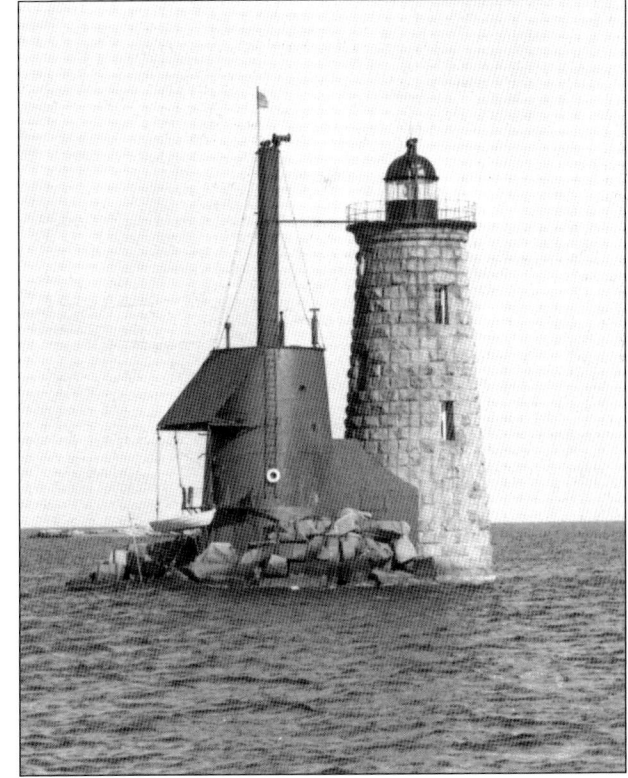

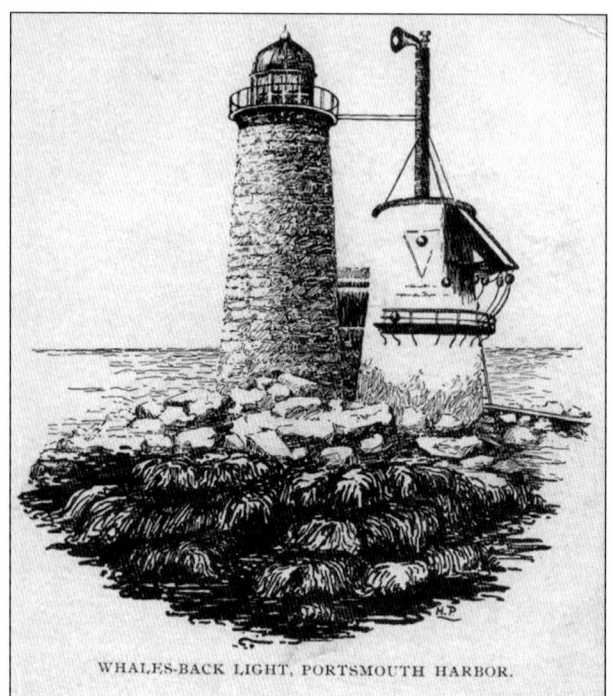

WHALES-BACK LIGHT, PORTSMOUTH HARBOR.

The keepers at Whaleback Lighthouse landed the station's boats on a slip outside the fog signal tower and entered their living quarters in the lighthouse tower by walking through a covered passageway, as shown in this early-1900s drawing. (Author's collection.)

Leander White, shown here with his wife, Elizabeth, was principal keeper of Whaleback Light from 1878 to 1887. According to some sources, a storm in 1886 sent waves smashing through a window of the tower, flooding the living quarters. White displayed a blanket from the tower as a distress signal. Days passed before the seas were calm enough for two Kittery residents to rescue the occupants. (Chuck Petlick.)

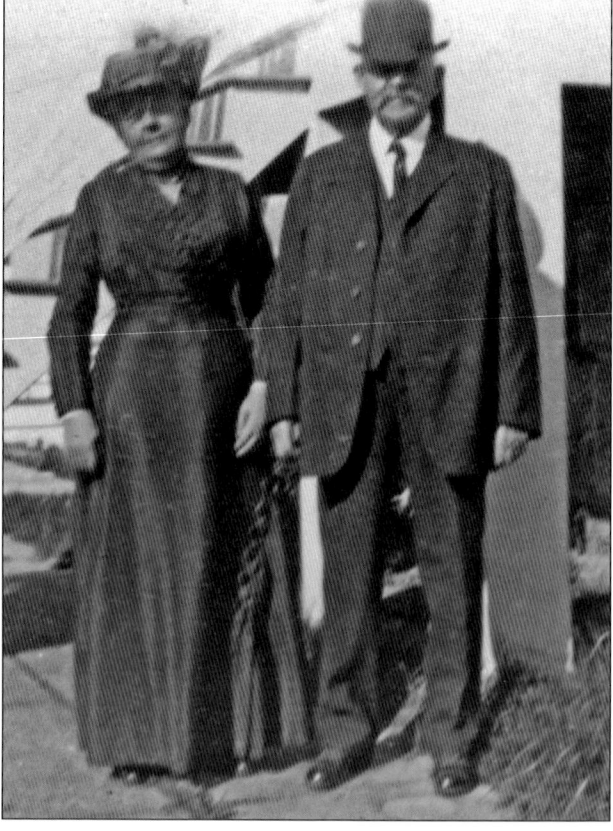

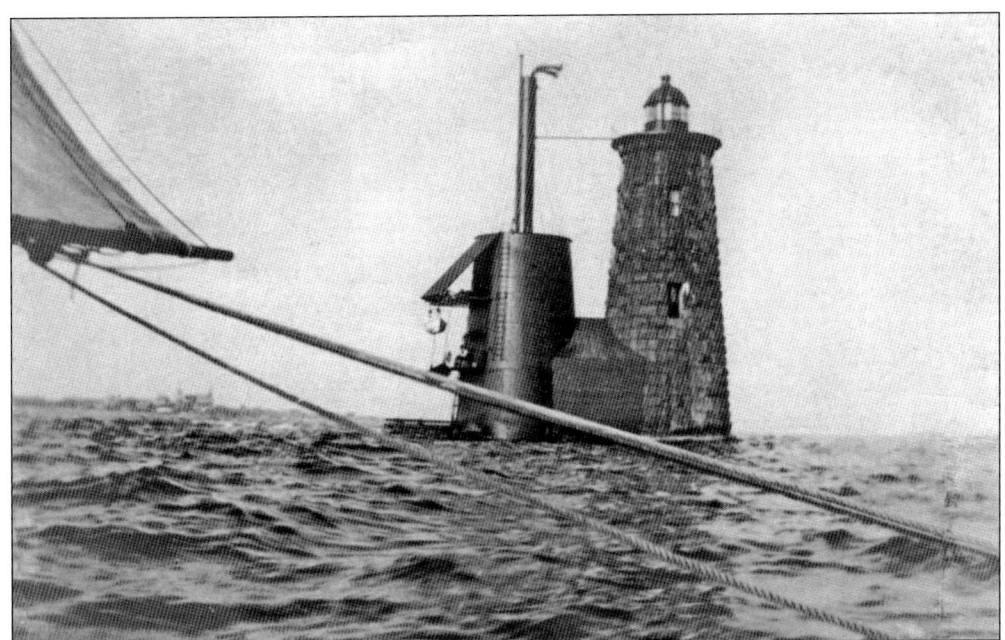

A new 20-foot-high protective bulkhead between the lighthouse and fog signal tower, built of pine timbers and planking, was bolted to both towers and to the ledge itself in the late 1880s. The space between the bulkhead and the towers was filled with masonry from the old lighthouse base. This image is from a real-photo postcard from the early 1900s. (Author's collection.)

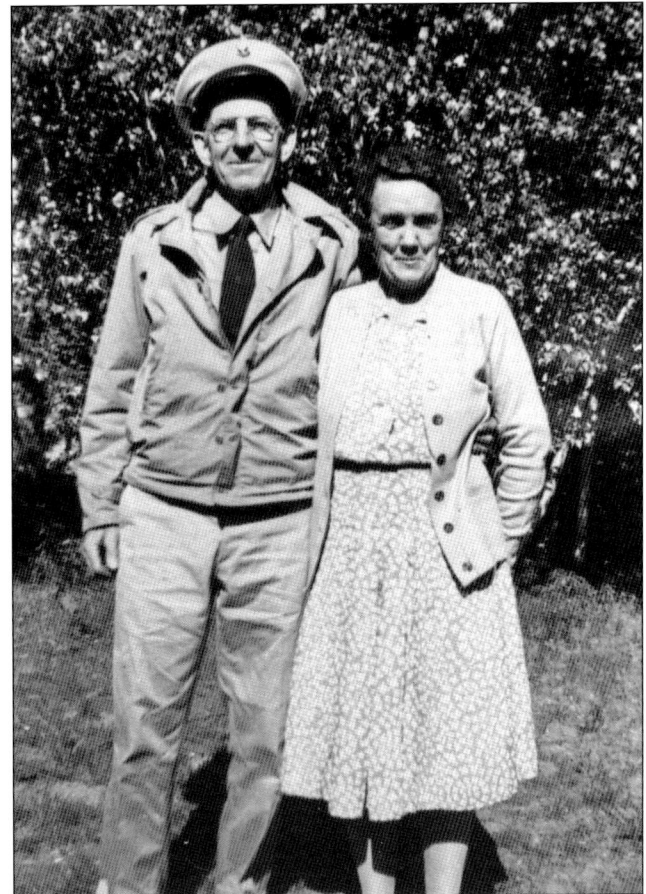

Arnold B. White (pictured here with his wife, Louise), son of former keeper Leander White, became principal keeper in 1921. After the US Coast Guard took over the management of lighthouses in 1939, White joined the Coast Guard. White once explained his general philosophy: "The government tolerates no excuses. You must anticipate trouble and have spare parts on hand at all times." (Chuck Petlick.)

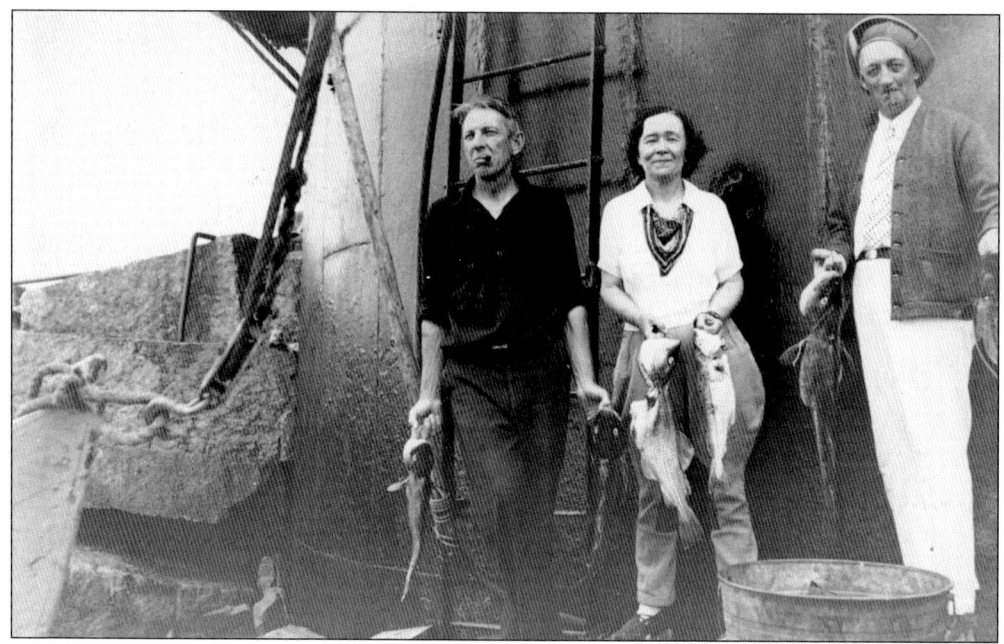

Keeper Arnold White, left, is shown with visitors in this photograph. A 1939 article described the living arrangements in the lighthouse. A cistern in the cellar held drinking water brought from Sebago Lake 2,000 gallons at a time. The next level contained a small kitchen. The principal keeper's quarters were on the floor above the kitchen, and everything was neat and orderly, the furnishings modest. (Chuck Petlick.)

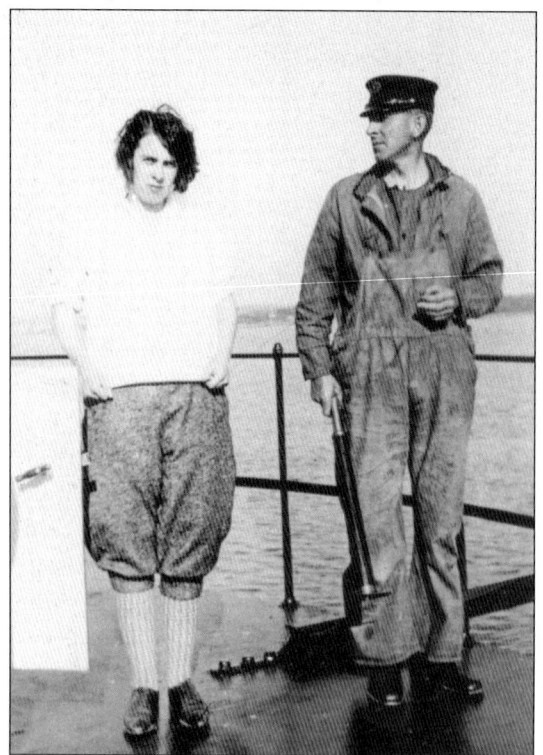

Arnold White is shown here with his daughter Muriel on the gallery near the top of Whaleback Lighthouse. White had a reputation as an excellent cook. His dumplings were described in the *Portsmouth Herald* as "an epicurean's dream." The praise was echoed by White's daughter Marion White Petlick, who said her father usually had some kind of baked treat, such as bread pudding, cooling on a windowsill. (Chuck Petlick.)

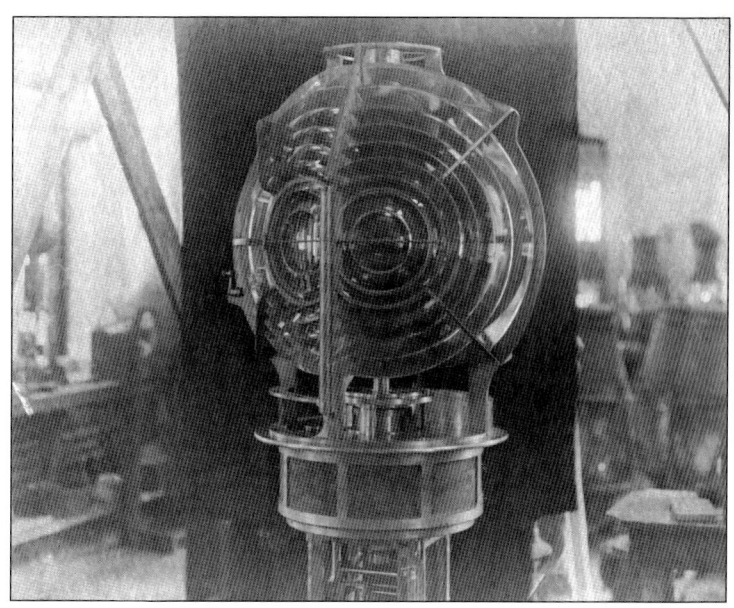

Several different types of optics were used in Whaleback Lighthouse over the years. This rotating fourth-order Fresnel lens was installed in 1898. It was replaced by a rotating aerobeacon when the light was automated in 1963. A modern, solar-powered LED provides the light today. The Fresnel lens is now at the Peabody Essex Museum in Salem, Massachusetts. (National Archives.)

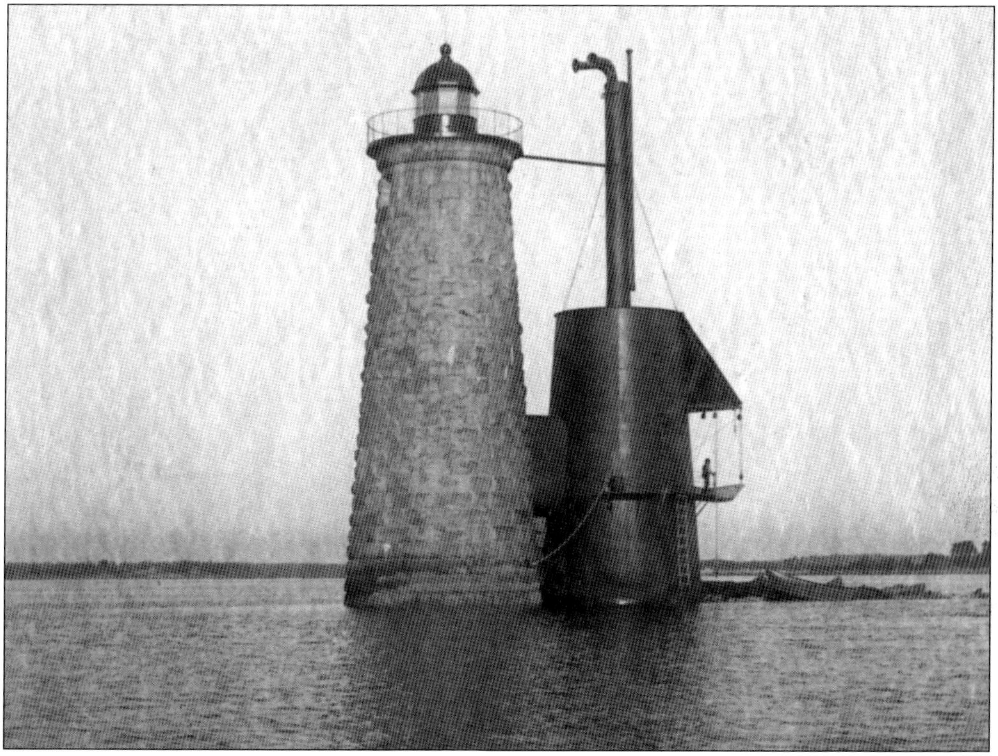

This early-1900s photograph shows a keeper standing on his boat, which is hanging on davits. The keepers carried out many rescues over the years. In July 1911, a powerboat carrying two young men hit a rock and developed a leak. Keeper Walter Amee launched a boat and reached the men, then took them back to the lighthouse for the night. (National Archives.)

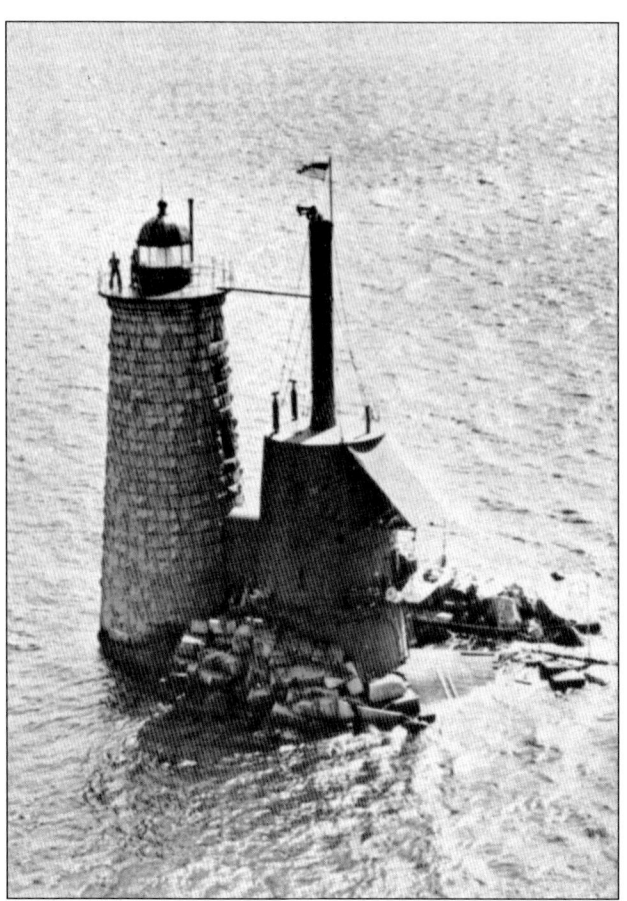

Two Coast Guard keepers are standing on the lantern gallery in this c. 1960 photograph. At that time, when the air-powered fog signal was running, the temperature in the fog signal tower was said to approach 140 degrees and the noise of the engines was deafening. (US Coast Guard.)

A storm in February 1960 did severe damage to the boat slip and caused considerable shifting of the station's protective riprap stones. Whaleback Lighthouse was automated in early 1963, and the Coast Guard keepers were reassigned. The Fresnel lens was replaced by rotating aerobeacons. An emergency generator was installed as a backup to a cable from shore. (Author's collection.)

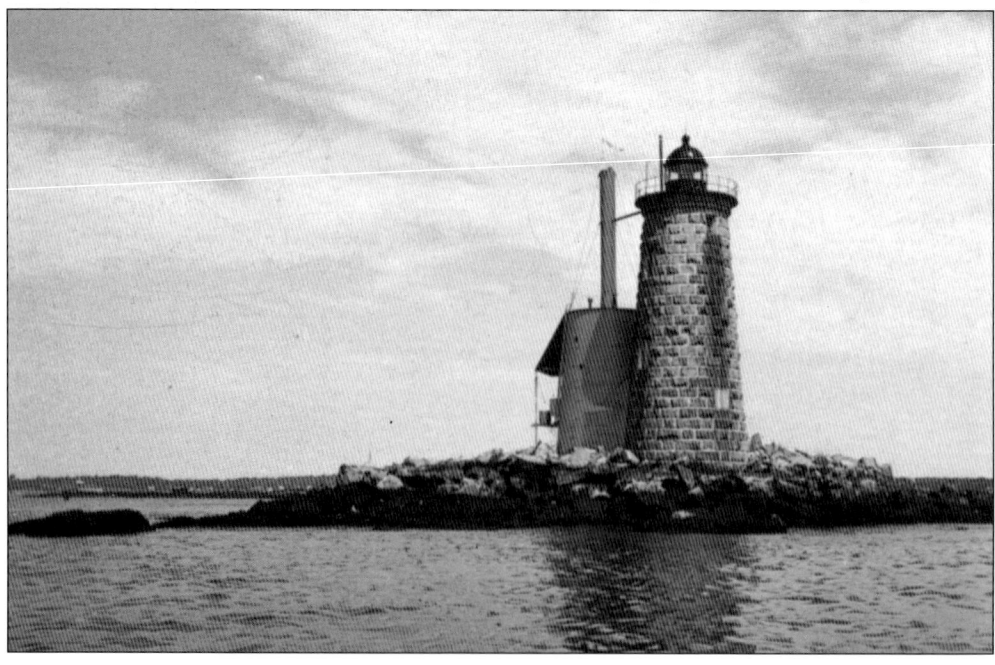

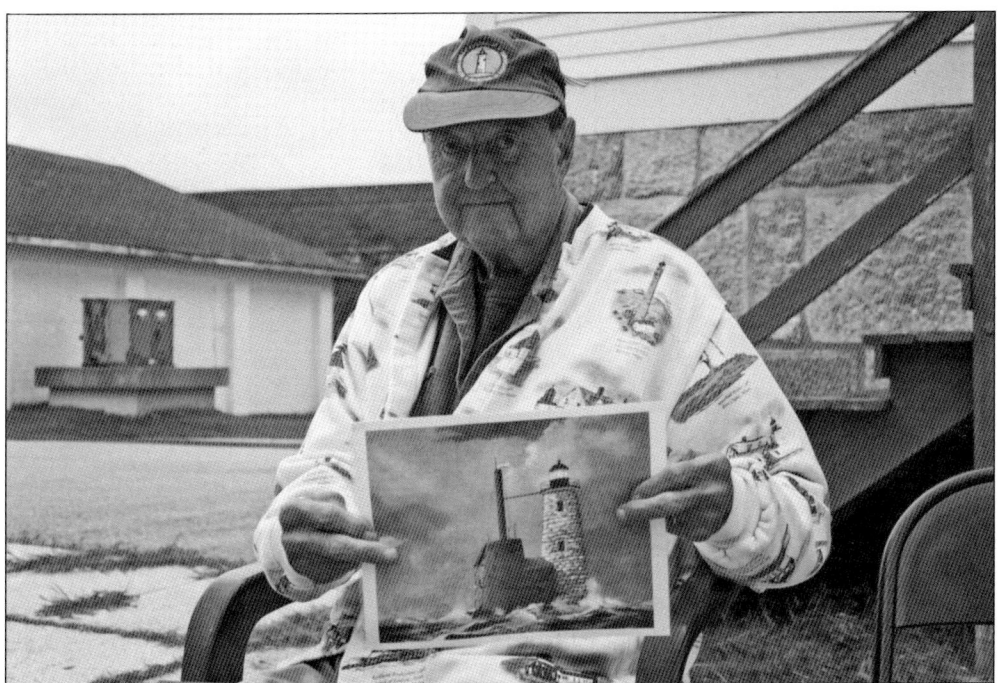

Jim Pope was one of the last Coast Guard keepers at Whaleback Lighthouse. When he arrived at the station at the age of 19 in 1959, the men had 24-day stints on duty followed by six days off. Pope enjoyed fishing around the tower. In the off hours, Pope and the others passed time playing cribbage or watching a television that hung from the ceiling. (Photograph by the author.)

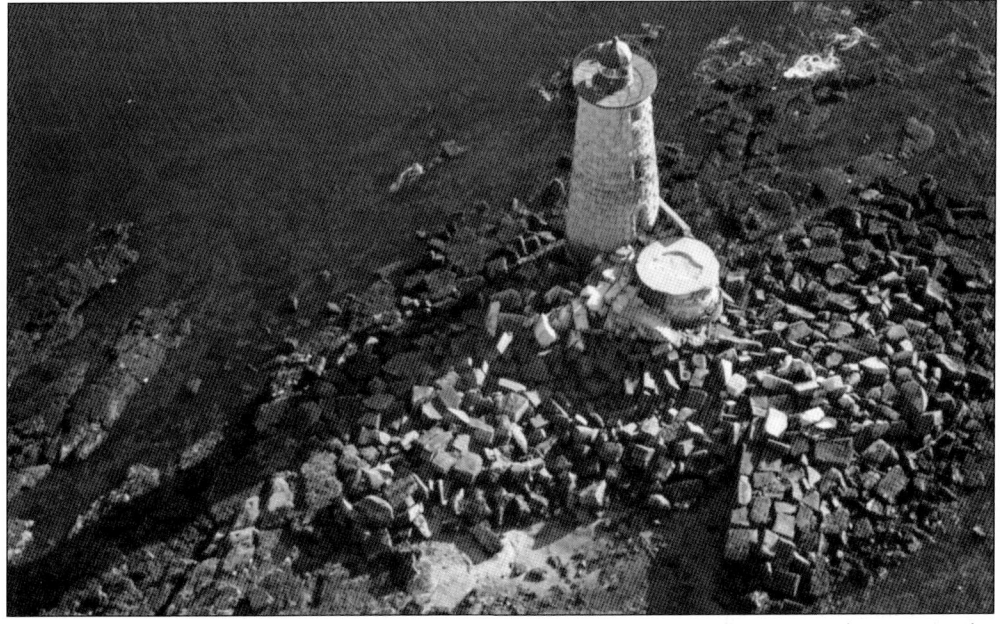

The fog signal tower was dismantled in 1969. In this aerial view taken at low tide in 2012, the base of the old fog signal tower is visible next to the lighthouse. The cast-iron plates that once surrounded the fog signal tower base have been torn away by the seas, showing the exposed stone underneath. (Photograph by the author.)

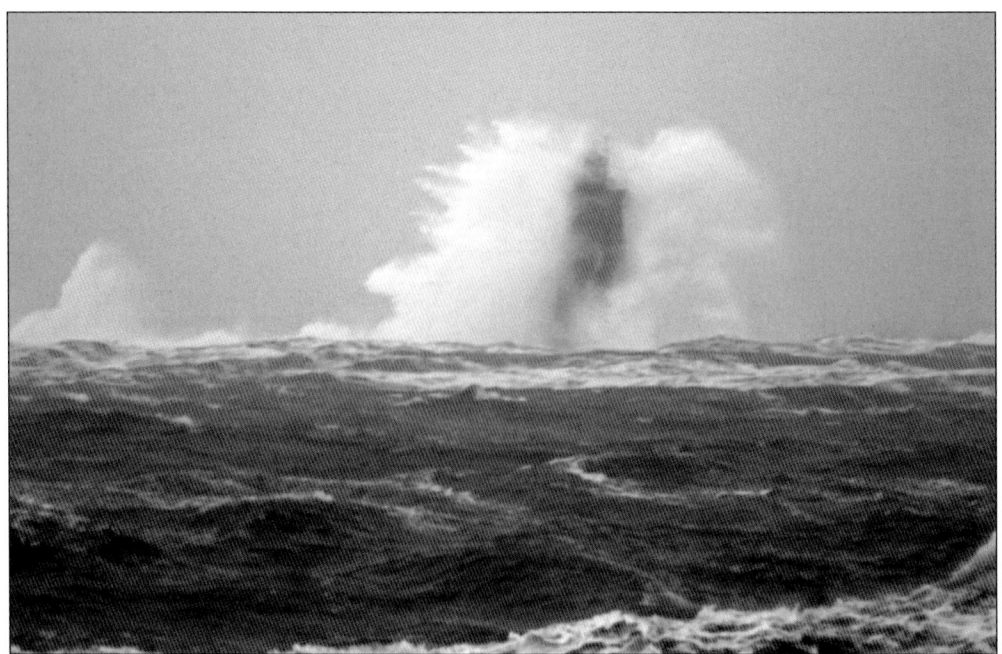

Whaleback Lighthouse continues to take a beating in storms. This view is from the storm of April 16, 2007, which did much damage on the northern New England coast. Former Whaleback keeper Jim Pope jokes that when storms like this struck, you simply brought a bar of soap to the top of the lighthouse so you could enjoy a cold shower. (Photograph by the author.)

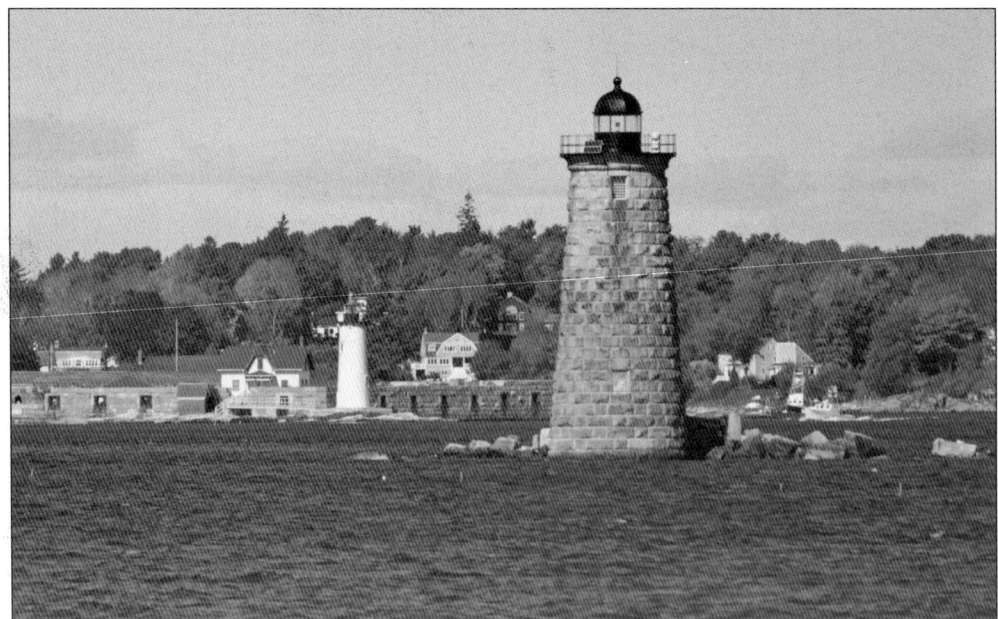

Friends of Portsmouth Harbor Lighthouses, a chapter of the American Lighthouse Foundation, now cares for Whaleback Lighthouse as well as Portsmouth Harbor Lighthouse in New Castle, New Hampshire, shown here in the background. There are plans to establish a docking system at Whaleback Lighthouse that will facilitate public tours and further restoration. (Photograph by the author.)

Three
SADDLEBACK

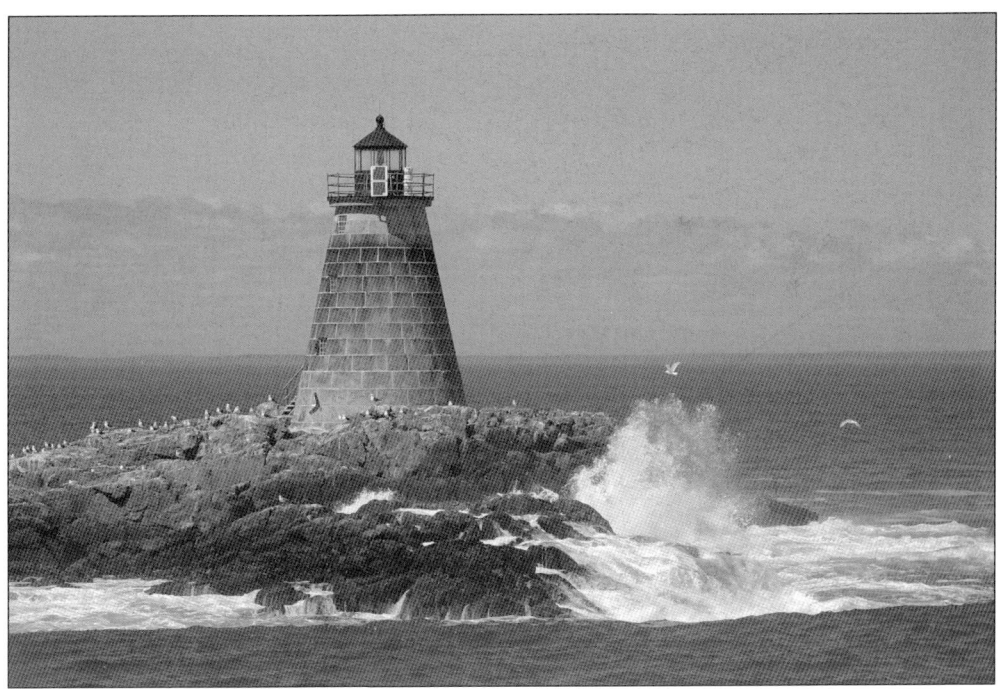

Saddleback Ledge is a small granite outcropping at the southern entrance to Maine's East Penobscot Bay, approximately four miles from the southeastern corner of Vinalhaven to the west and three miles from the southwestern coast of Isle au Haut to the east. The ledge is approximately 17 miles from the nearest point of land on the mainland. (Photograph by the author.)

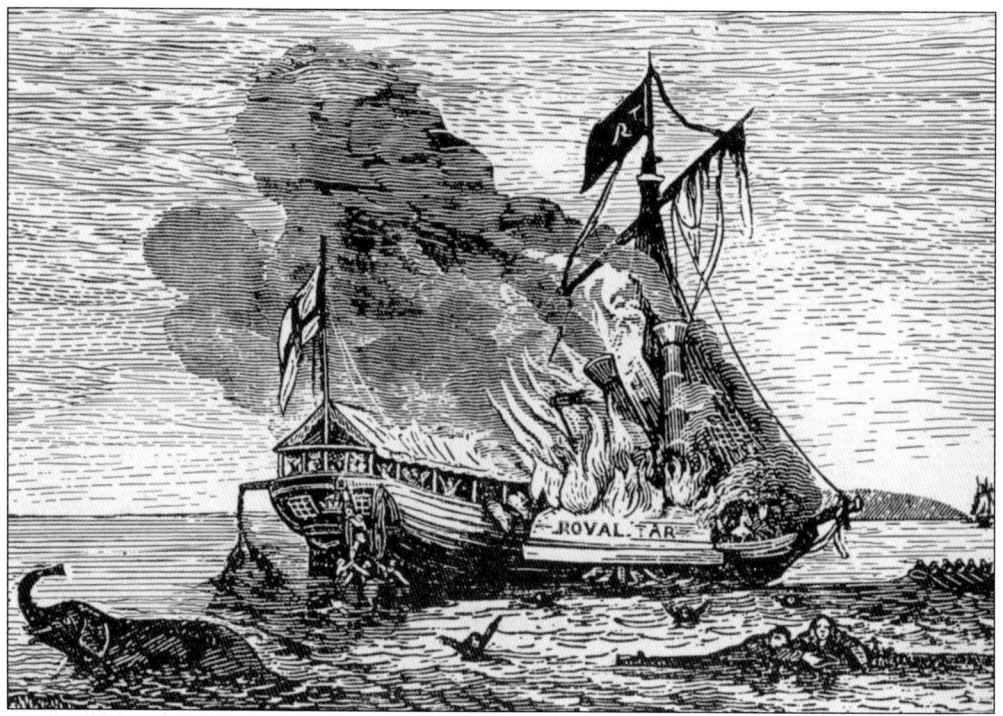

In 1836, the ship *Royal Tar*, carrying circus performers and animals, caught fire and sank near the ledge. Of the 93 people on board, 32 died. Partly in response to the tragedy, Congress appropriated $5,000 for a lighthouse on Saddleback Ledge in March of the following year. (Dolly Bicknell.)

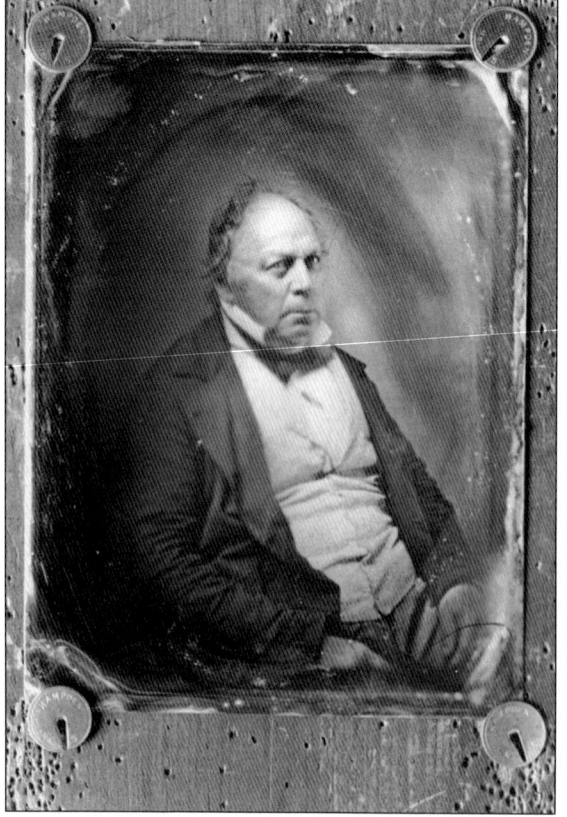

Noted architect and engineer Alexander Parris (1780–1852) designed the tower. Parris is best remembered for designing Boston's Quincy Market, the executive mansion of the Commonwealth of Virginia, and various buildings at the Portsmouth Naval Shipyard. Saddleback Ledge Lighthouse is one of six Maine lighthouses or keepers' dwellings attributed to Parris. (Parker Collection, Thomas Crane Public Library.)

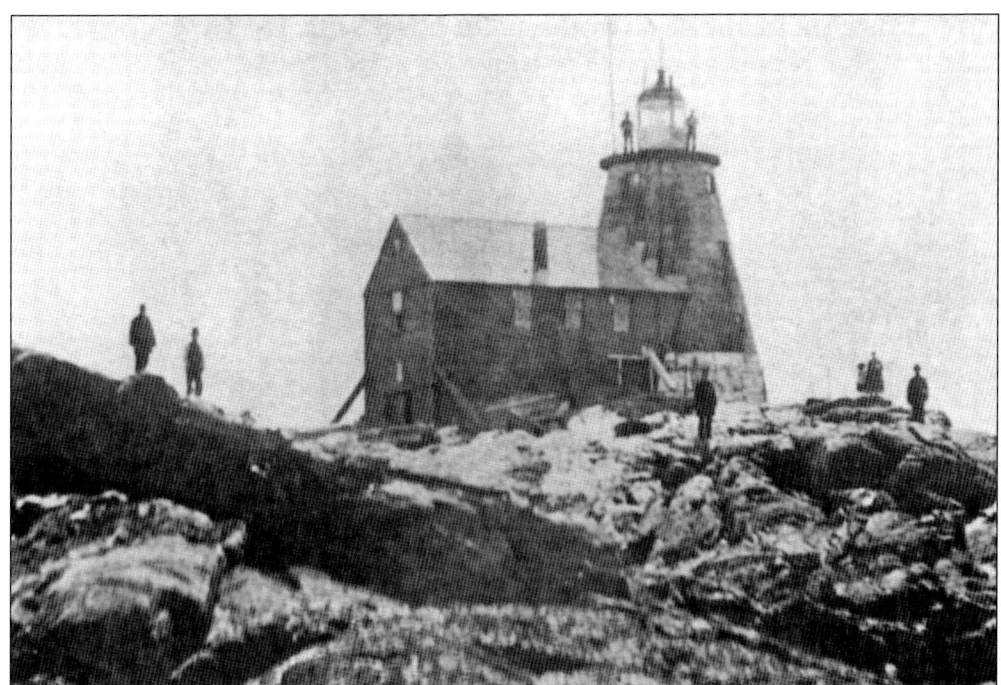

The station went into service in 1839; the conical granite tower is 43 feet tall. The attached wooden building shown in this 1859 photograph was not added until some years after the lighthouse was built. In his 1843 report to Congress, the engineer I.W.P. Lewis praises Alexander Parris's work: "It is the most economical and durable structure that came under my observation during the survey." (National Archives.)

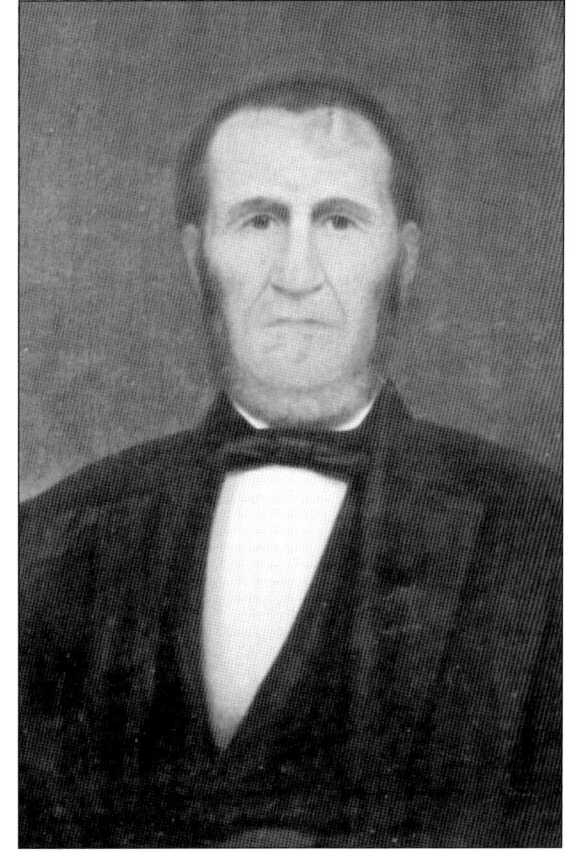

The first keeper was Watson Y. Hopkins, a Maine native. Hopkins moved into the lighthouse with his wife and six children, and another child was born a short time later. In a letter included in the 1843 report, Hopkins writes: "I am obliged to bring my water from shore, a distance of seven miles." Hopkins remained keeper for a decade. (Margo Burns.)

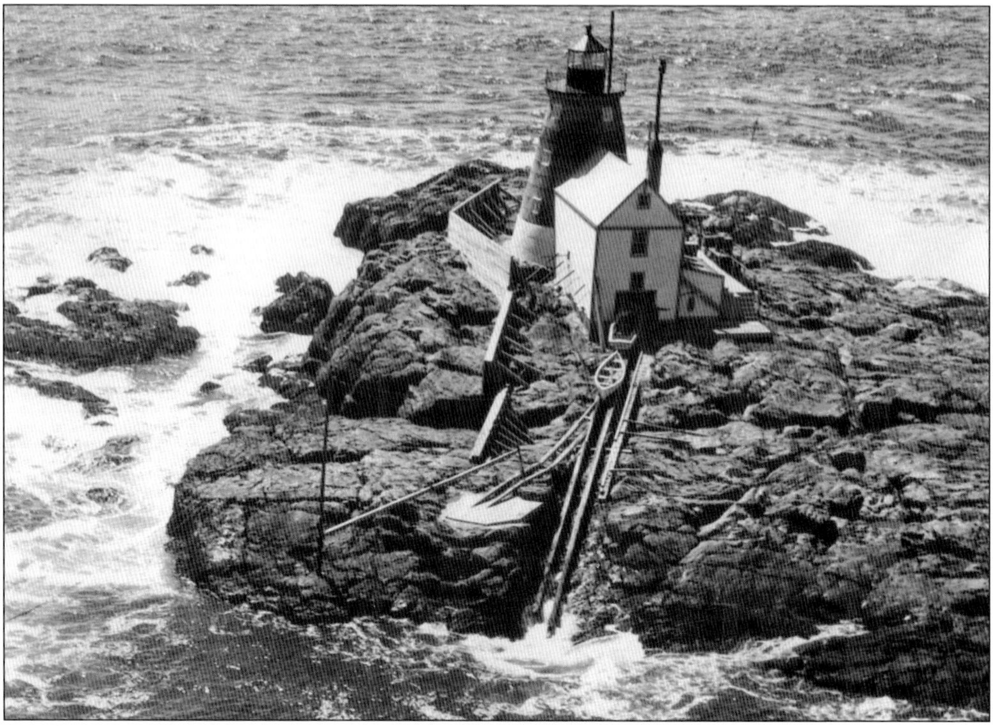

The local lighthouse superintendent wrote in 1850: "I consider it a dangerous place to live in, in its present condition. The lantern is very rusty; consequently a large number of panes of glass are cracked and broken. Immediate attention should be paid to this establishment, as it is an important light-house." An attached wooden building was added before 1868, somewhat improving the cramped living conditions. (US Coast Guard.)

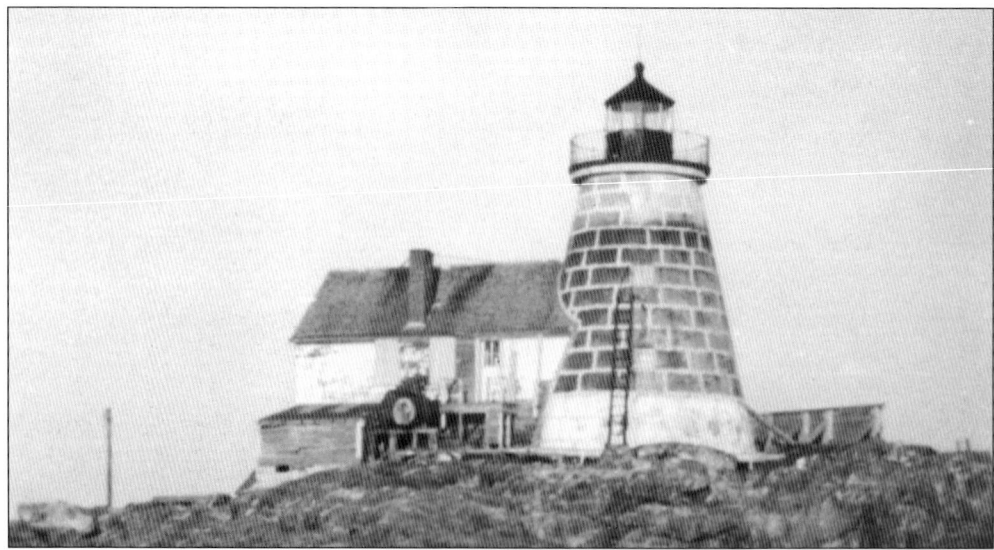

A story repeated in several late-1800s publications claims that a keeper once went to get supplies from the mainland, leaving his 15-year-old son alone at the ledge. The seas grew stormy, and it was three weeks before the keeper was able to return to the ledge. His son was exhausted, but he had managed to keep the light burning every night. (US Coast Guard.)

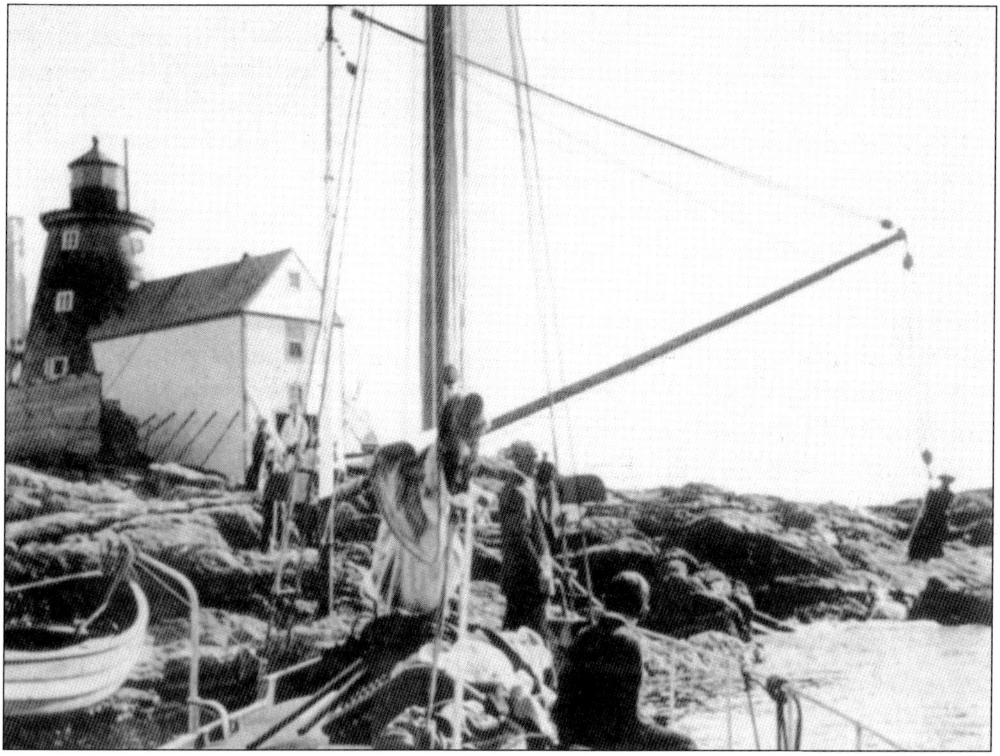

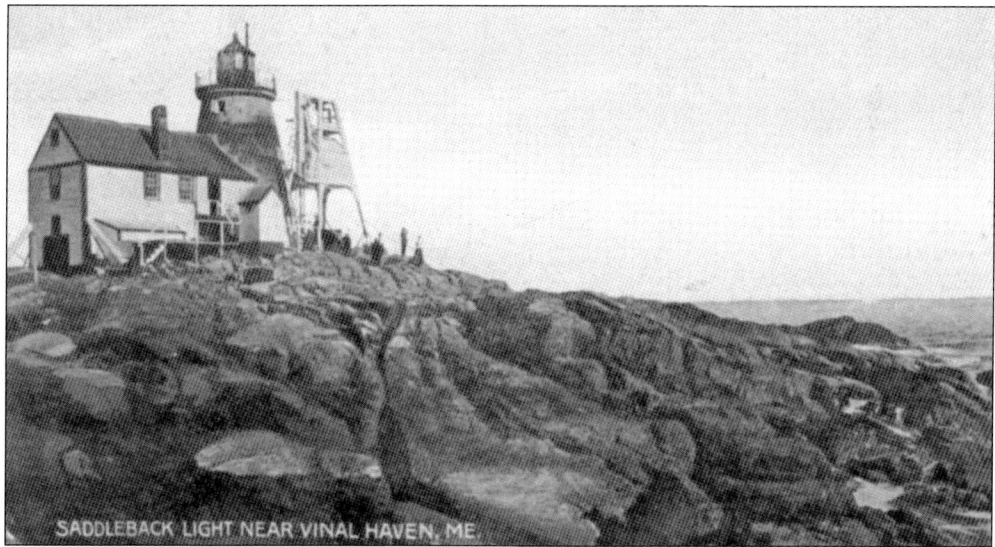

It was extremely difficult to land a boat at the ledge, especially when the seas were rough. In 1885, an iron derrick with a swinging arm was added. The arm held a bosun's chair on a hoist. This method was used for many years. A woman can be seen being hoisted on the right side of this photograph. (Vinalhaven Historical Society.)

A fog bell tower stands near the lighthouse in this postcard view from the early 1900s. A 1,000-pound bronze bell served as the fog signal at Saddleback beginning in 1887. In times of poor visibility, the keepers wound a mechanism that powered a hammer that would strike the bell at precise intervals. A storm in March 1947 washed the tower into the ocean. (Author's collection.)

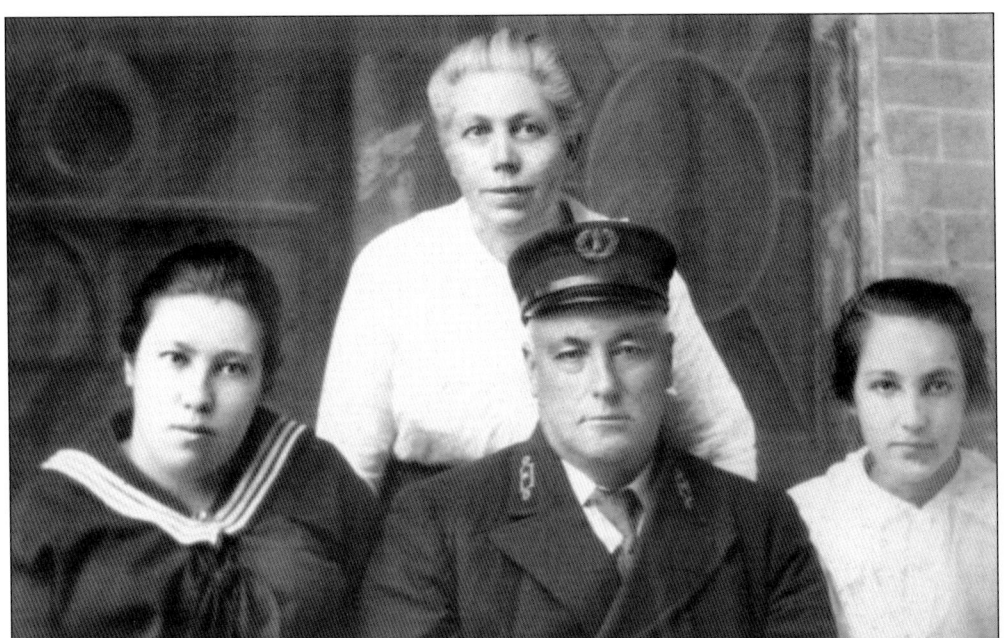

Pictured here is Leonard Bosworth Dudley, who was stationed at Saddleback Ledge in the early 1920s, with his wife and daughters. Saddleback was eventually made a "stag" (males only) station, but the families often visited in good weather. Dudley's daughter June later said that she was always relieved to be in her father's strong arms after the hair-raising ride in the bosun's chair. (Maine Lighthouse Museum.)

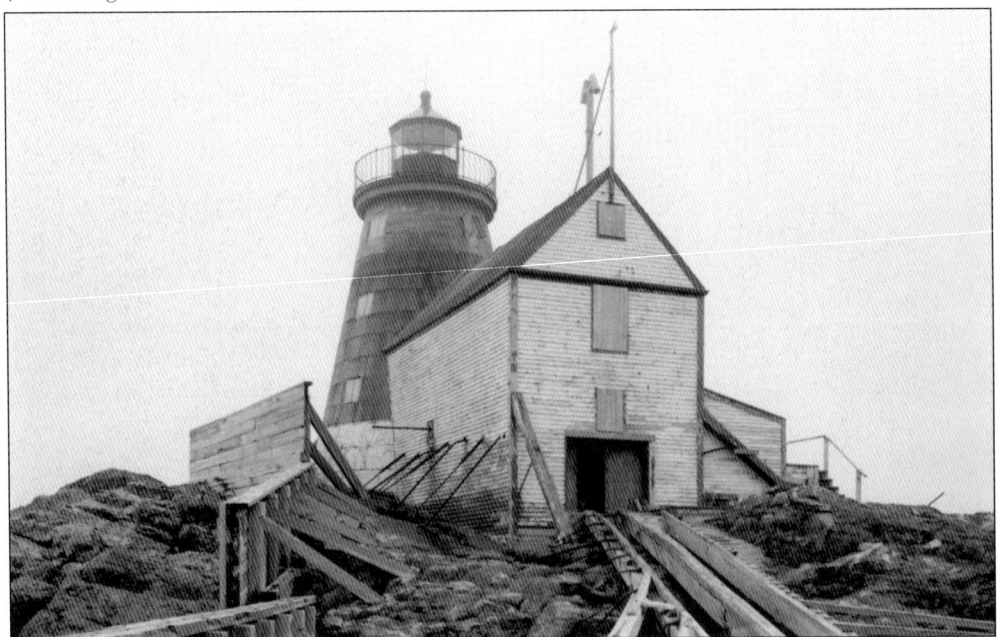

Keeper W.W. Wells was interviewed by Robert Thayer Sterling for his 1935 book *Lighthouses of Maine and the Men Who Keep Them*. "Winter we all hate the most," he said, "beginning when the summer guests have gone. This means we will have to bank up the old station, get some good reading matter and snuggle down for a long period of isolation." (Library of Congress.)

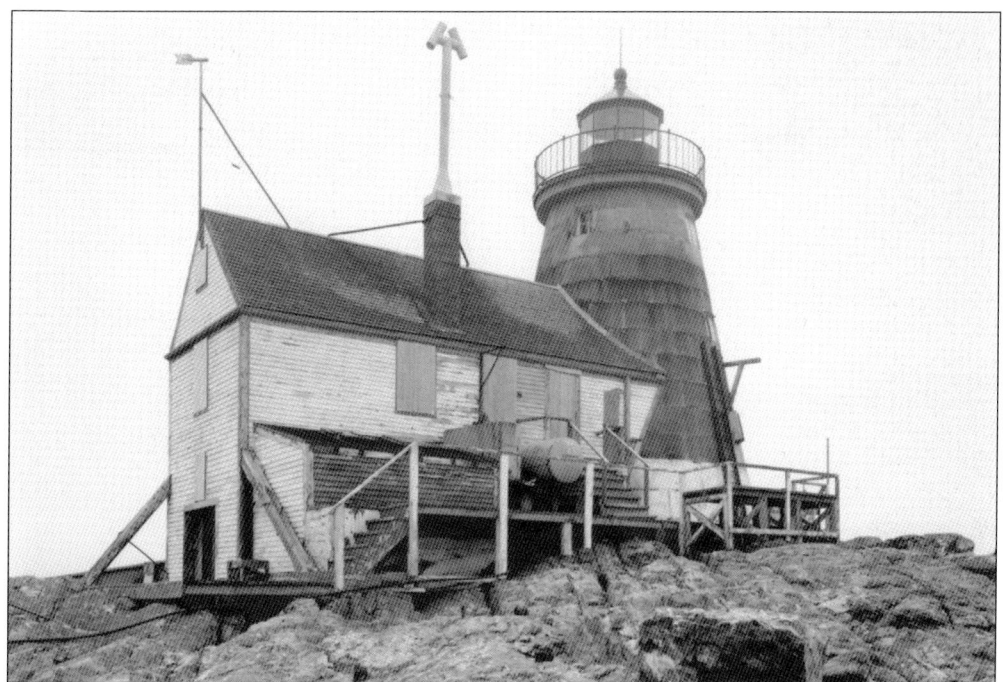

A ferocious storm in March 1947 almost washed away the attached wooden building. The same storm sent the hand-wound fog bell into the ocean, never to be seen again. The light was automated and de-staffed in late 1954, and the attached building was subsequently torn down. (Library of Congress.)

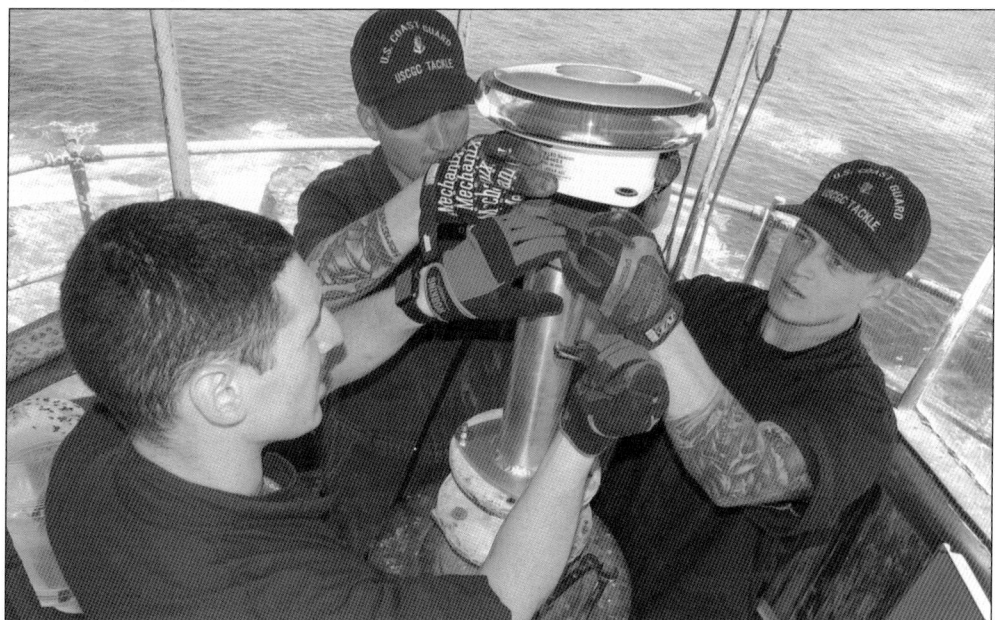

Crew members from the US Coast Guard Cutter *Tackle* are shown here on June 8, 2017, installing the new VLB-44 optic in the lantern room at Saddleback Ledge Lighthouse. This optic uses LEDs and operates on solar power; it is very efficient and low-maintenance compared to conventional lamps. (Photograph by Bob Trapani Jr.)

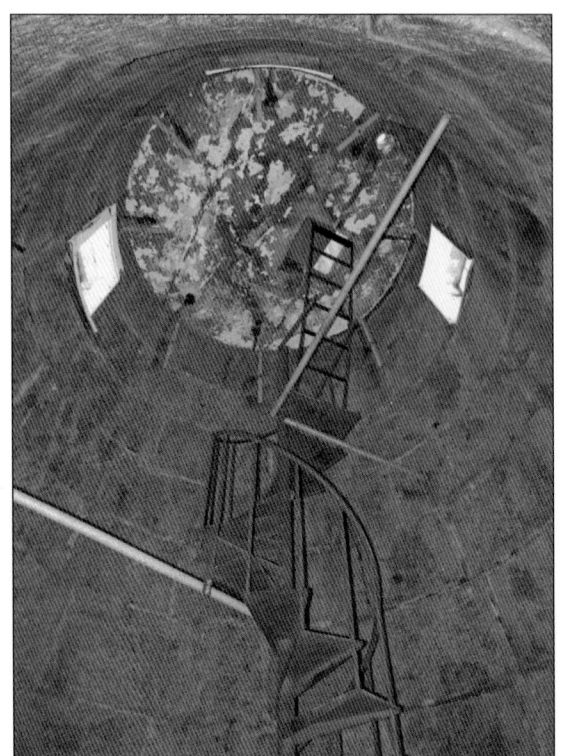

In 1987, the Coast Guard replaced Saddleback's original stairs with a modern metal stairway. Bob Trapani Jr., lighthouse preservationist and historian, said after visiting Saddleback, "As I looked around, I could only imagine the utter bleakness of this location during the winter—not to mention the harrowing experiences that must have been encountered by keepers during serious storms when waves swept across the entire ledge." (Photograph by Bob Trapani Jr.)

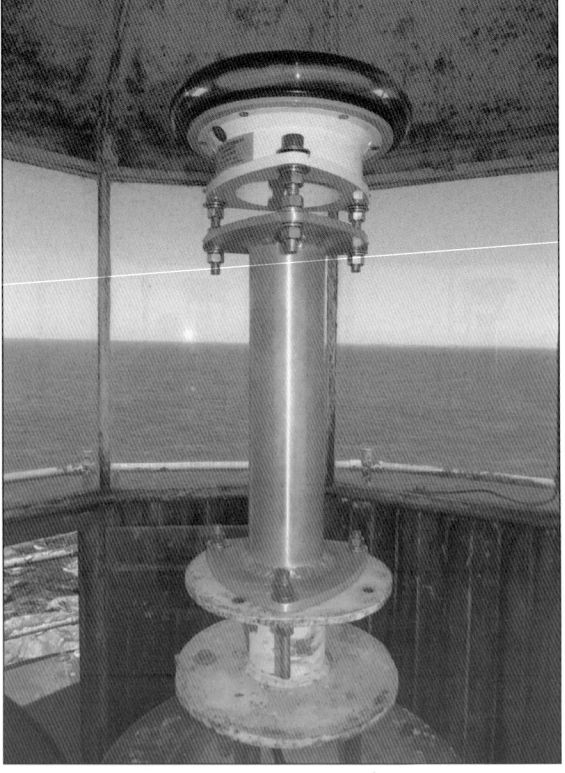

The characteristic of the light at Saddleback, produced by the VLB-44 optic, is now a white flash every six seconds. The fog signal now operates using the MRASS (mariner radio activated sound signal) system, meaning mariners can activate it with a VHF radio as needed; it produces a single blast every 10 seconds. (Photograph by Bob Trapani Jr.)

Four
Minot's Ledge

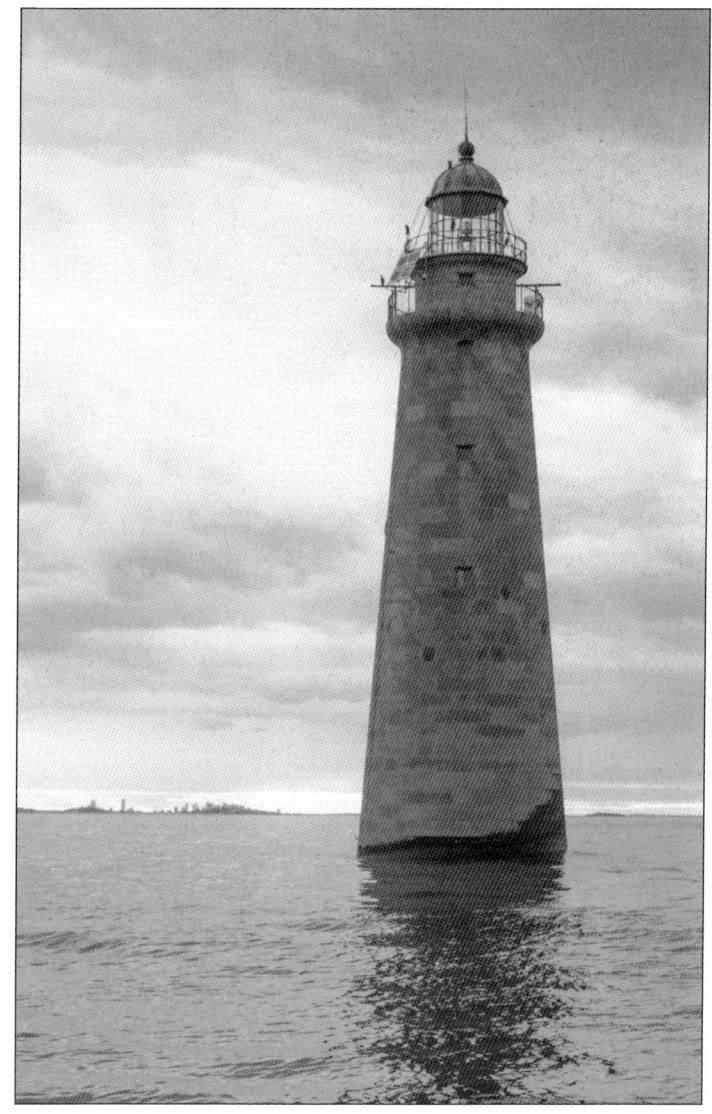

Minot's Ledge—about a mile offshore near the towns of Cohasset and Scituate, Massachusetts—is part of the treacherous Cohasset Rocks. Minot's Ledge was named for George Minot, a merchant who owned T Wharf in Boston in the mid-1700s. The granite lighthouse that stands on the ledge today is regarded as one of the most important achievements of lighthouse construction in the United States. (Photograph by the author.)

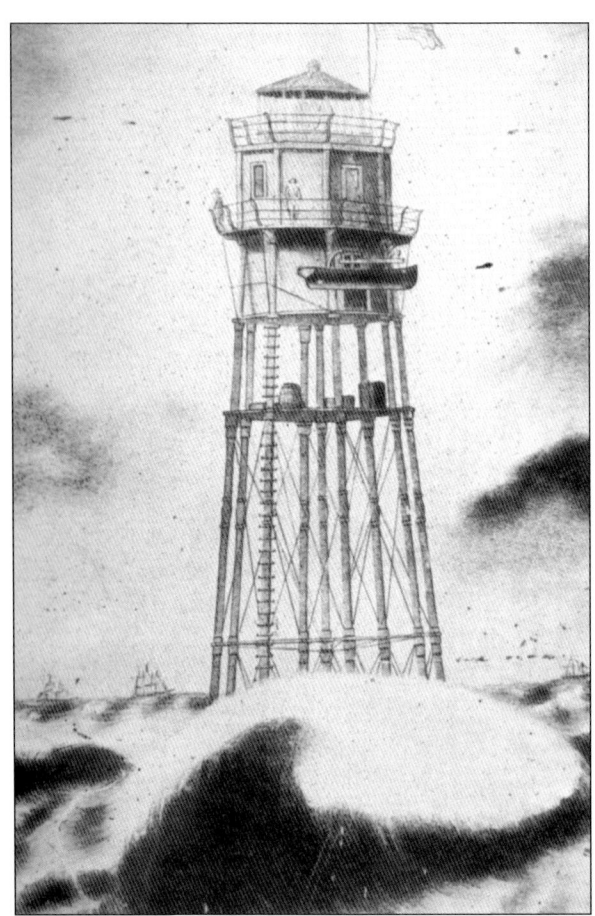

There were many shipwrecks near the Cohasset Rocks, and in 1843, the civil engineer I.W.P. Lewis wrote that a lighthouse was required more urgently on Minot's Ledge than any other location in New England. The architect Alexander Parris recommended a granite tower similar to England's Eddystone Light. Congress appropriated $20,000 for a lighthouse in 1847. An additional $19,500 would eventually be needed. (National Archives.)

Capt. William H. Swift of the Corps of Topographical Engineers designed an iron pile lighthouse—a 70-foot-tall, spidery structure with piles drilled into the rock—at Minot's Ledge on the theory that waves would pass harmlessly through the structure. The lighthouse went into service on January 1, 1850—the first lighthouse in the United States to be subjected to the full fury of the ocean. (Dolly Bicknell.)

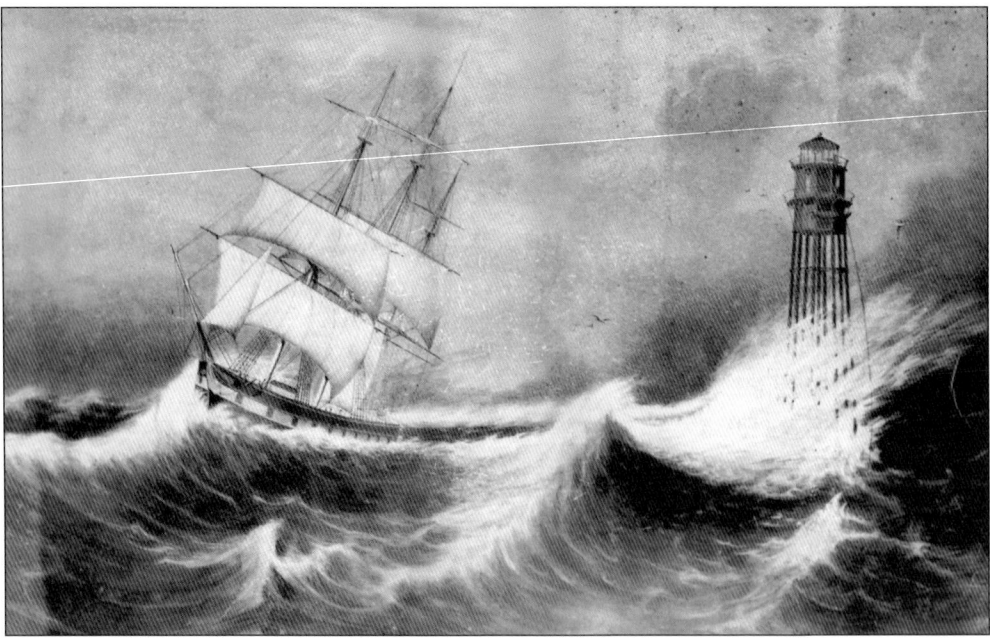

The first principal keeper was Isaac Dunham. During a storm in early April 1850, Dunham wrote in his log: "I hope God will in mercy still the raging sea—or we must perish. . . . God only knows what the end will be." Dunham resigned on October 1 after 10 months as keeper. His two assistants also resigned. (Dolly Bicknell.)

Notice to Mariners.
FOG BELL ON MINOT'S ROCK.

CUSTOM HOUSE, BOSTON,
Collector's Office, Oct. 26, 1850.

NOTICE IS HEREBY GIVEN,

That a *Fog Bell*, of the weight of about 640 lbs. has been placed upon the *Light-House on Minot's Rock*, which will hereafter be rung by the Keeper during fogs and snow storms, or other thick weather.

Those interested will govern themselves accordingly.

P. GREELY, JR., COLLECTOR.

A 640-pound fog bell installed at a cost of about $200 in late October 1850 was to be sounded in times of "fog and snow storms, or other thick weather." Along with making sure the light was shining from sunset to sunrise, the most important duty of the keepers was to make sure the fog bell was operating in times of reduced visibility. (Dolly Bicknell.)

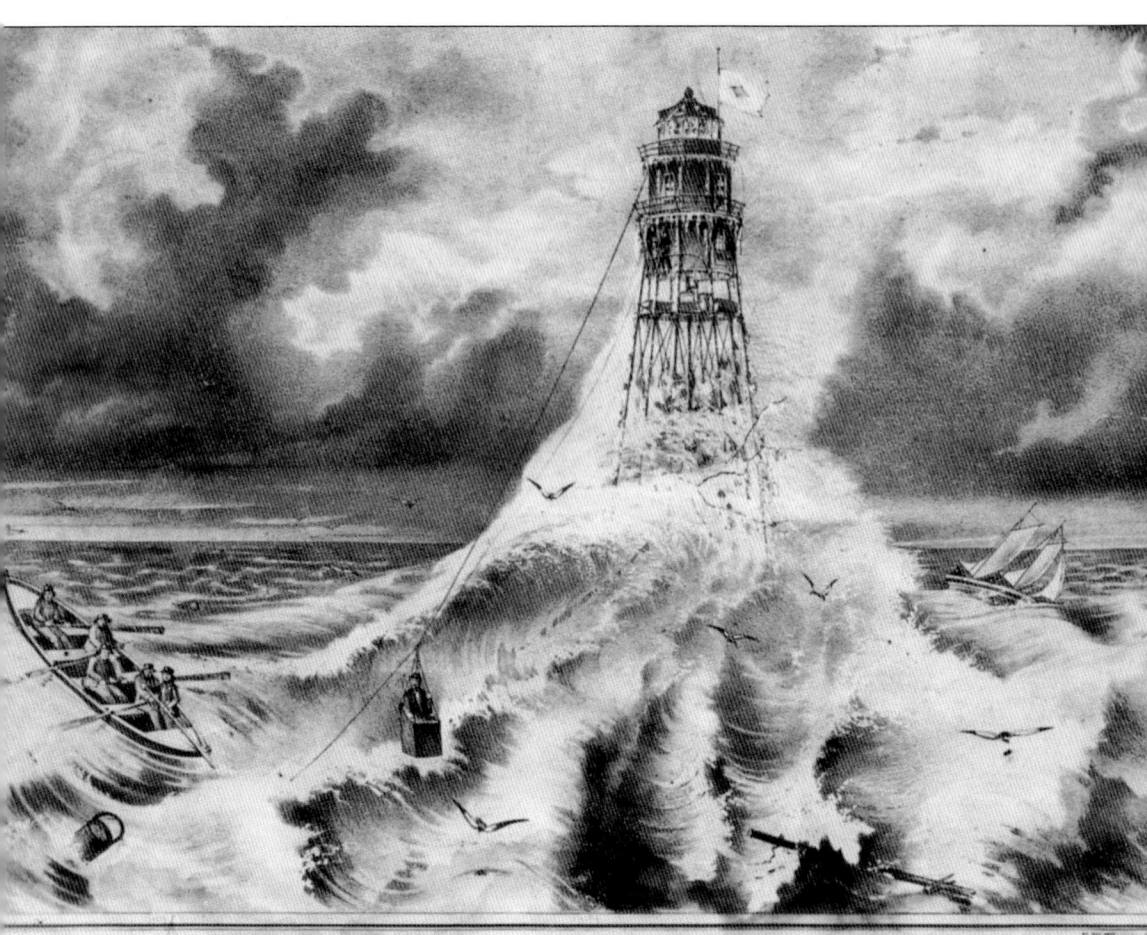

THE IRON LIGHT HOUSE ON MINOTS ROCK, MASSACHUSETTS BAY.

The second keeper was John W. Bennett, a veteran of 25 years at sea and a former first lieutenant in the British navy. During a particularly bad storm, Bennett wrote in a letter: "Our situation is perilous. If anything happens before day dawns on us again, we have no hope of escape. But I shall, if it be God's will, die in the performance of my duty." Bennett installed a thick rope hawser extending from the tower to a rock about 200 feet away. A basket was suspended from the rope with the idea that the keepers could use it as an escape route in emergencies. A visitor in late 1850 wrote in the *Boston Journal* that the lighthouse swayed two feet in each direction in a storm, which made it "quiver and jerk in such a manner as to make it seem impossible for the legs to sustain the thirty tons weight which rested upon them." This illustration is said to be based on a drawing by John Bennett. (Dolly Bicknell.)

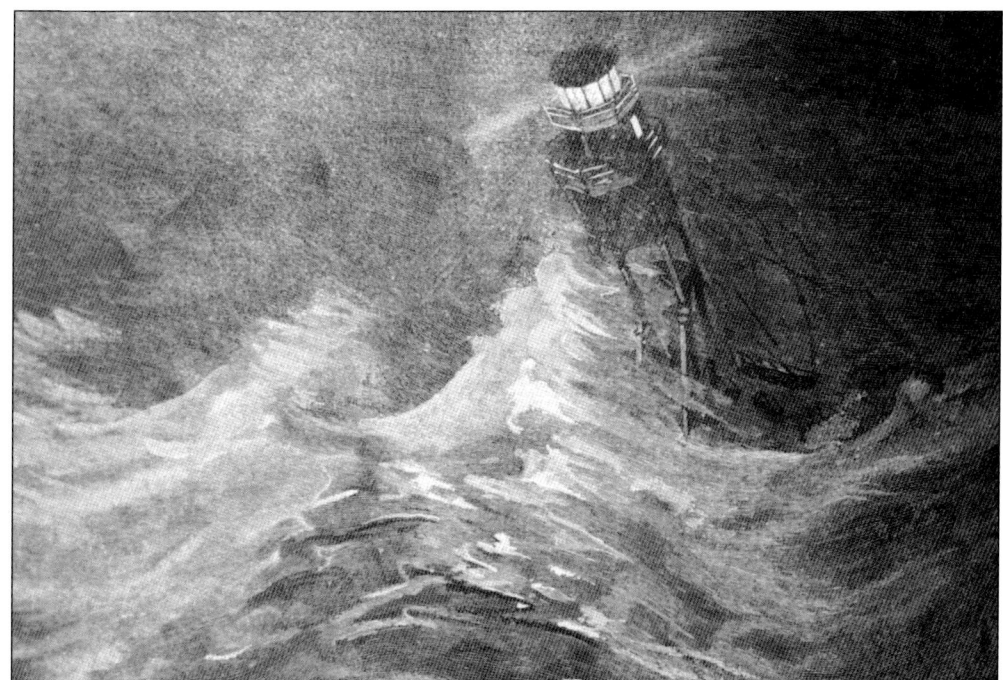

A storm on April 9, 1851, washed away the keepers' boat. Bennett went to Boston to procure a new boat on April 11 and was unable to return to the lighthouse for the following few days because of rough seas. Two assistant keepers, 20-year-old Joseph Wilson and Joseph Antoine, a 25-year native of Portugal, were on duty. (Dolly Bicknell.)

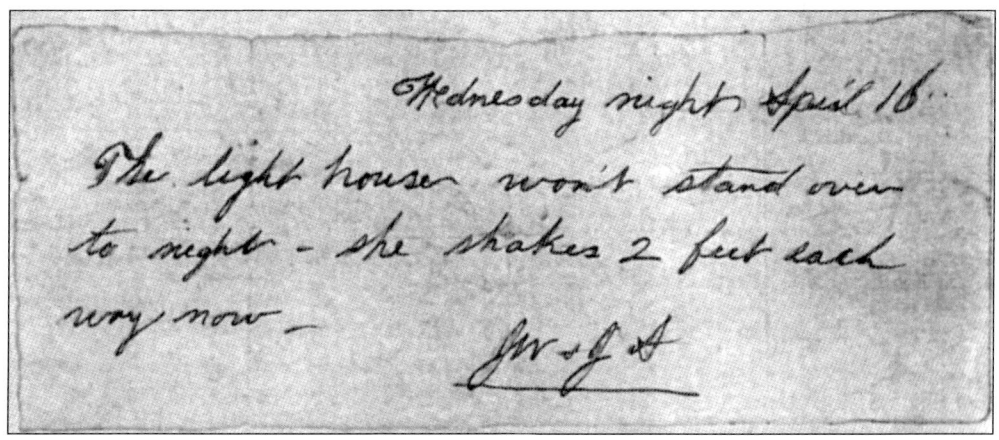

Increasing winds and rain arrived in the area late in the day on Monday, April 14. As the seas grew more turbulent, Antoine and Wilson dropped a note in a bottle into the waves. A Gloucester fisherman found the note the following day. It read: "The light house won't stand over to night—she shakes 2 feet each way now. JW + JA." (Dolly Bicknell.)

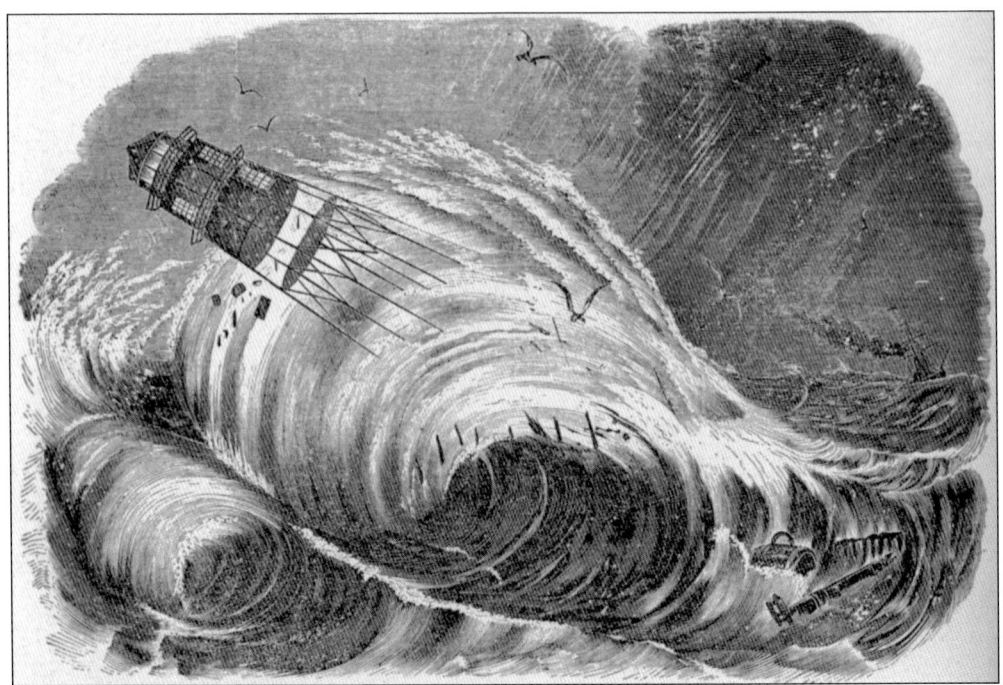

The lighthouse fell sometime in the early hours of April 17. Bennett went to the shore around 5:00 a.m. He saw fragments of the lighthouse lantern and keepers' quarters washing ashore, along with bedding and some of his own clothing. Two miles of beach were eventually littered with furniture and fragments of the wooden parts of the lighthouse. (Dolly Bicknell.)

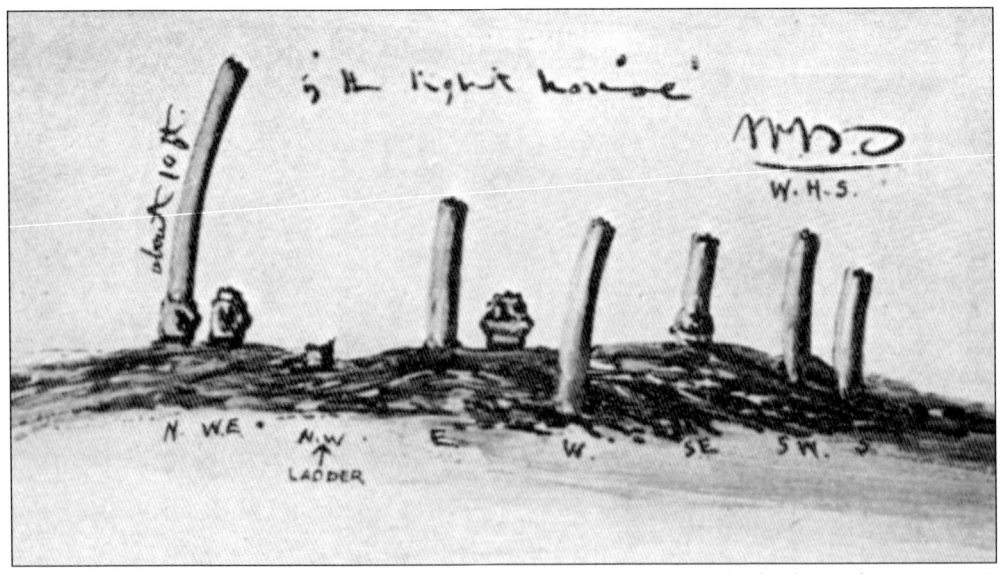

Capt. William Swift, the lighthouse's designer, signed this sketch of the broken piles at Minot's Ledge. Swift had a long and successful career after the Minot's disaster. From 1846 to 1877, he was the chairman of the board of the Hannibal & St. Joseph Railroad, and he was also a director of the St. Louis, Iron Mountain & Southern Railroad. (Dolly Bicknell.)

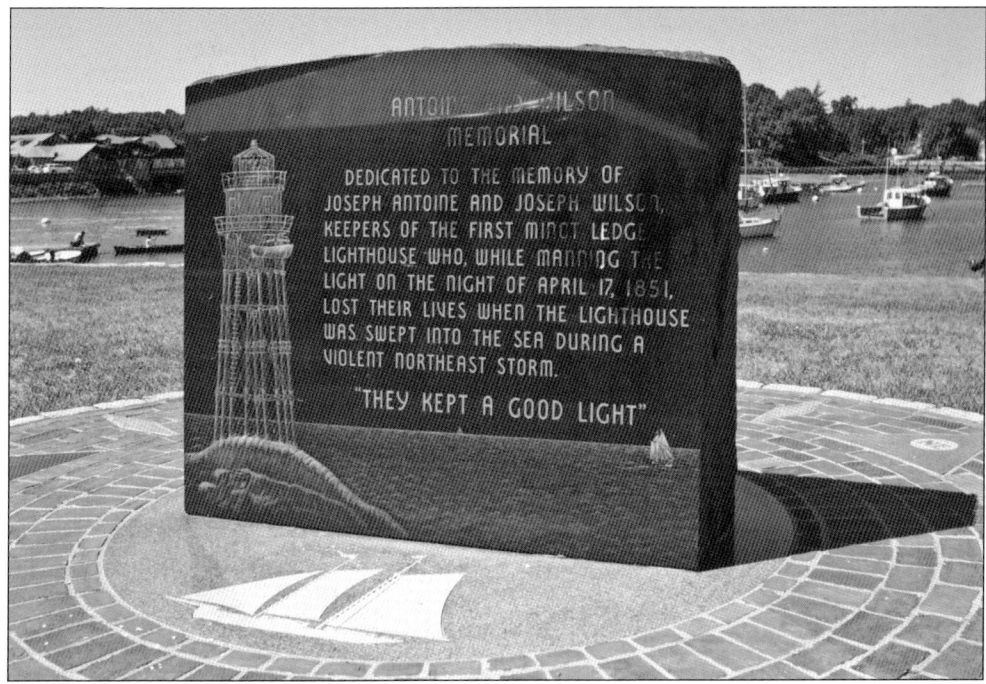

The great storm of April 16–17, 1851, is remembered as the Minot's Light Gale. No monument was erected to the two young keepers who died until, in 1997, a group of local residents began a campaign to erect a granite memorial to Joseph Antoine and Joseph Wilson. The memorial was finished and dedicated in 2000 on Government Island in Cohasset. (Photograph by the author.)

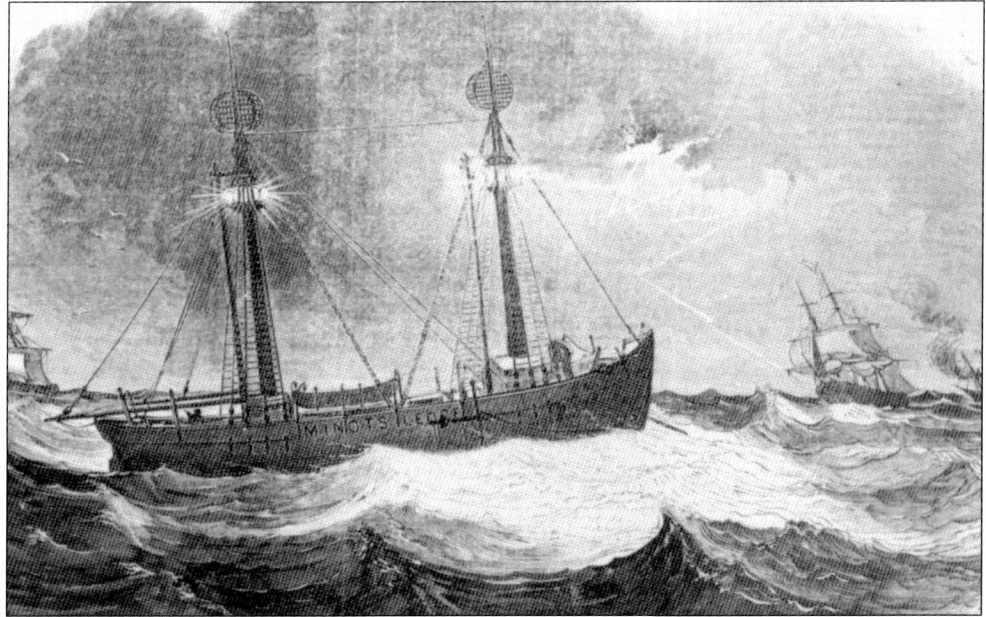

Soon after the disaster, a small lightship was anchored in position at the ledge. John Bennett was put in charge of the vessel. A new lightship, built for about $27,000 at Somerset, Massachusetts, served at the station from 1854 to 1860. This 1854 illustration of the lightship at Minot's Ledge is from *Gleason's Pictorial*. (Author's collection.)

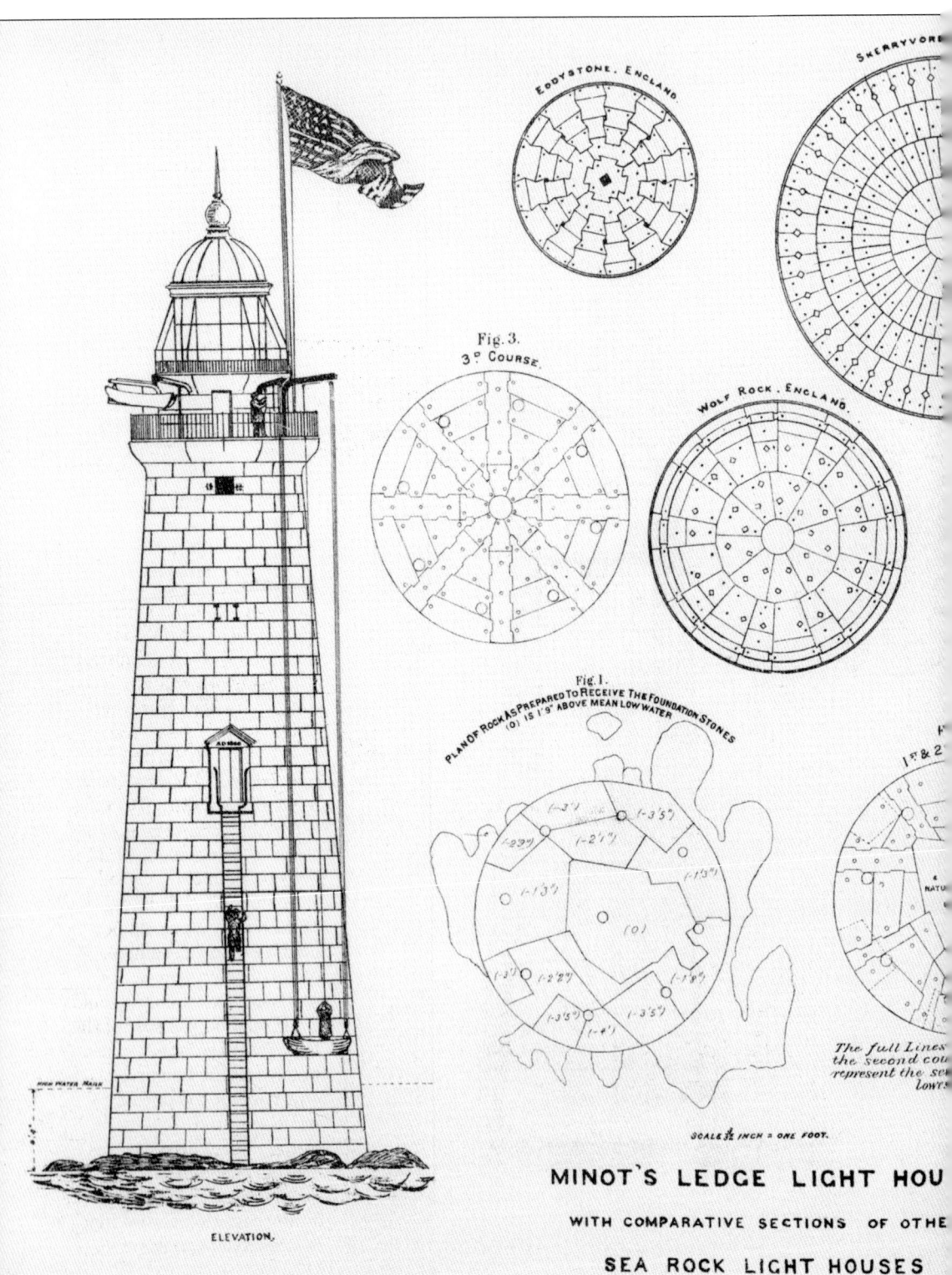

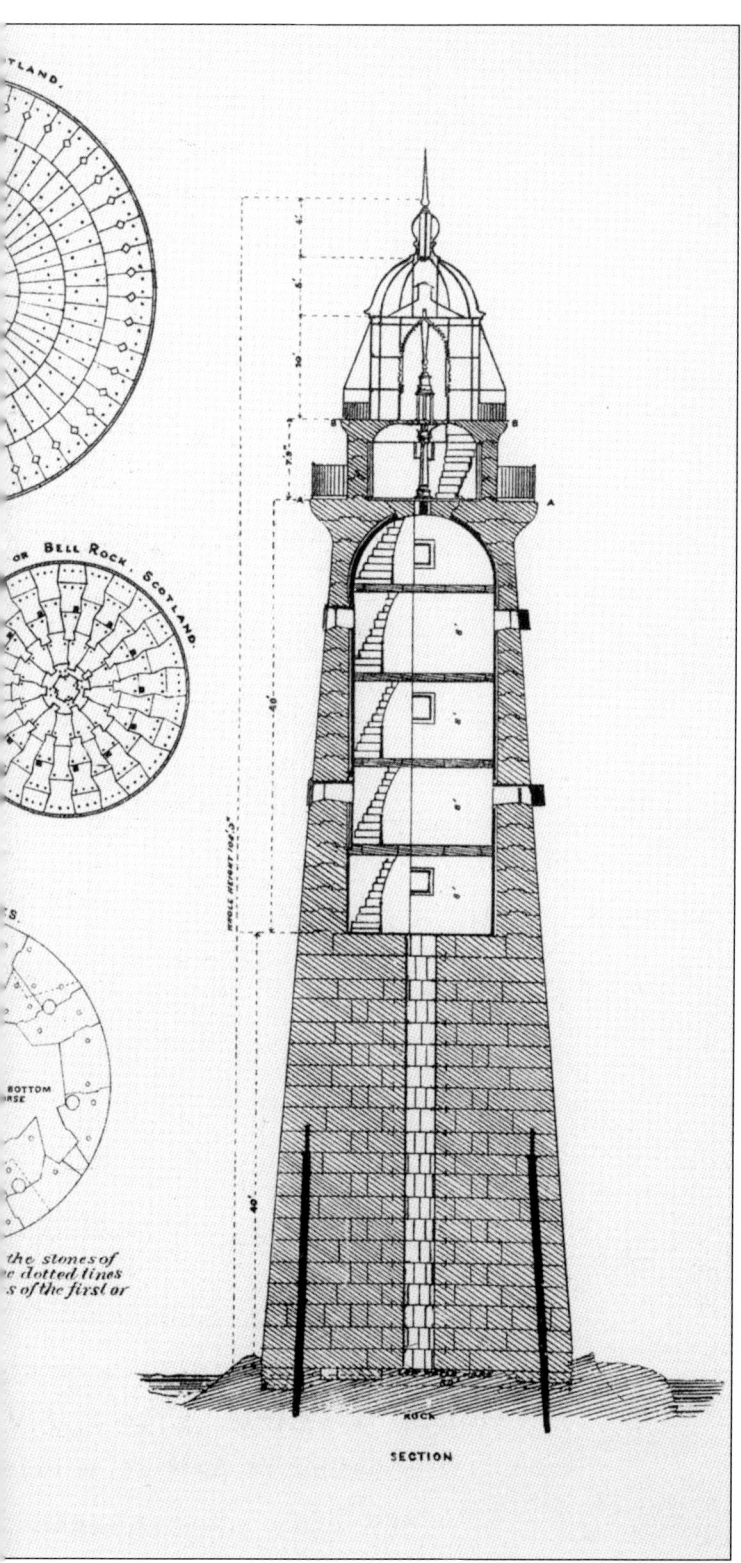

In August 1852, Congress appropriated $80,000 for a new lighthouse "of granite, iron, or a combination of both." Like the great wave-swept lighthouses in the British Isles, the second lighthouse at Minot's Ledge was constructed of interlocking, dovetailed granite blocks. Lt. Barton S. Alexander later described the challenge of building the lighthouse: "We could not land, even in the summer season, at times for weeks together; and when we could effect a landing, a part of the ledge was at all times under water, and the remainder only bare for the one or two hours at low water of spring tides. The space was contracted, and the sea broke with such violence during easterly weather that no cofferdam was possible. How were we to begin?" (Library of Congress.)

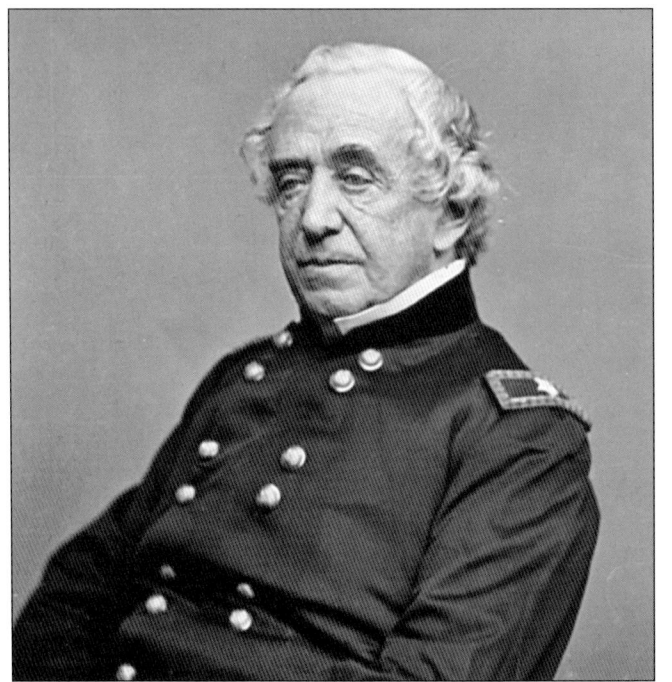

Gen. Joseph Gilbert Totten, chief engineer of the US Army and a member of the new US Lighthouse Board, designed the second Minot's Ledge Lighthouse. Totten was one of only three cadets to graduate from the US Military Academy at West Point as part of the class of 1805 and was the tenth graduate in the academy's history. (National Archives.)

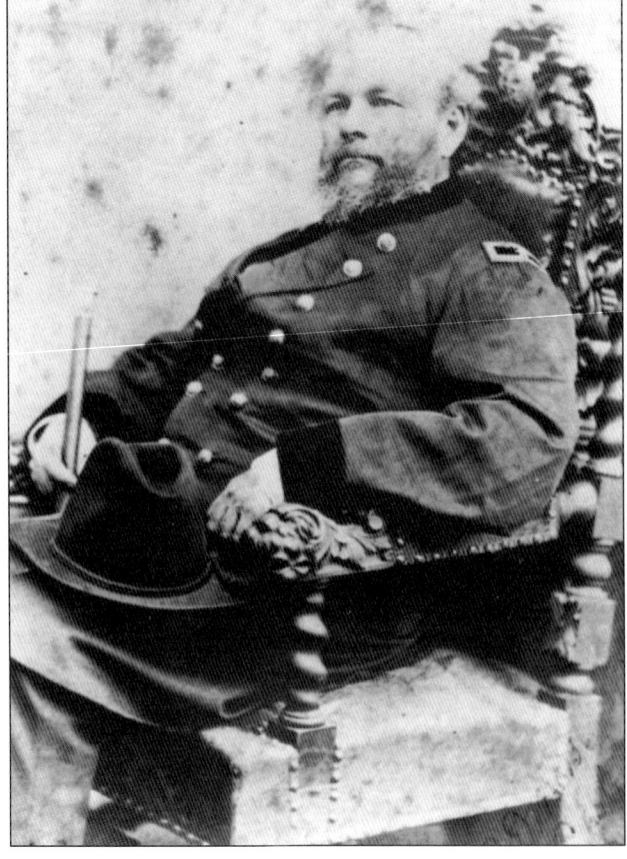

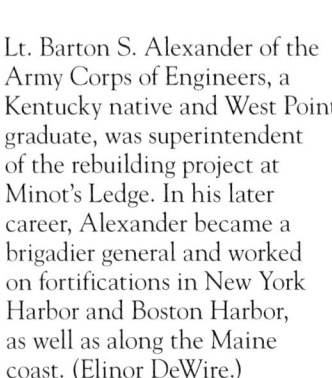

Lt. Barton S. Alexander of the Army Corps of Engineers, a Kentucky native and West Point graduate, was superintendent of the rebuilding project at Minot's Ledge. In his later career, Alexander became a brigadier general and worked on fortifications in New York Harbor and Boston Harbor, as well as along the Maine coast. (Elinor DeWire.)

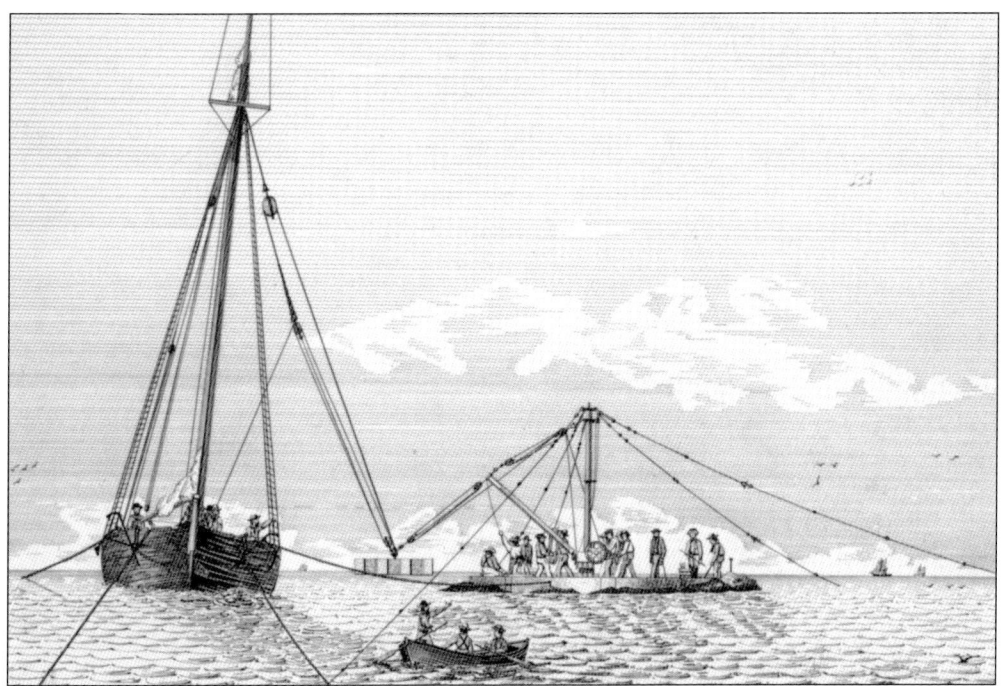

A scaffold was erected at the ledge in June 1856. The scaffold consisted of nine wrought-iron shafts inserted into the holes left by the original lighthouse and rising to a height of 20 feet above low water, with the upper portion bound together by a wrought-iron frame. The scaffold was destroyed when a ship collided with it during a January 1857 storm. (National Archives.)

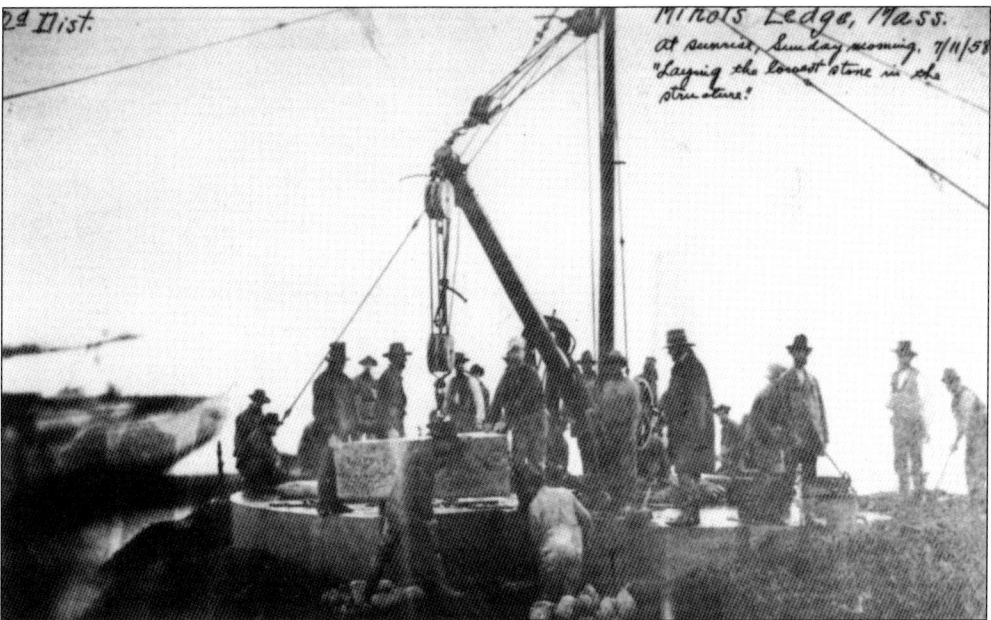

One of the problems posed by the project was how to make the lowest granite blocks adhere to the underwater ledge. Experiments produced a solution—the blocks were surrounded with a layer of thin muslin, which protected the mortar from the dissolving action of the ocean water. The lowest stone of the tower was laid on July 11, 1858. (National Archives.)

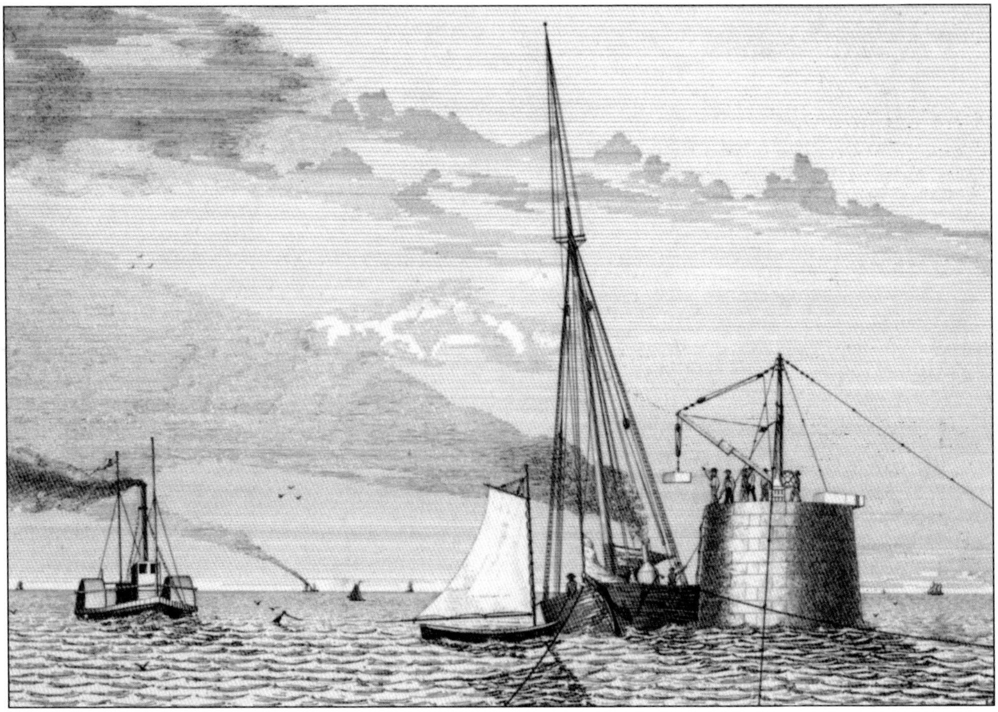

Eight posts were inserted into the outer holes left by the former lighthouse and extended through the first ten courses in the tower, with the space around the posts filled with portland cement. A prize was offered for the best plan for a derrick to be used for raising the stones at the site, and John Newell Cook of Cohasset submitted the winning design. (US Coast Guard.)

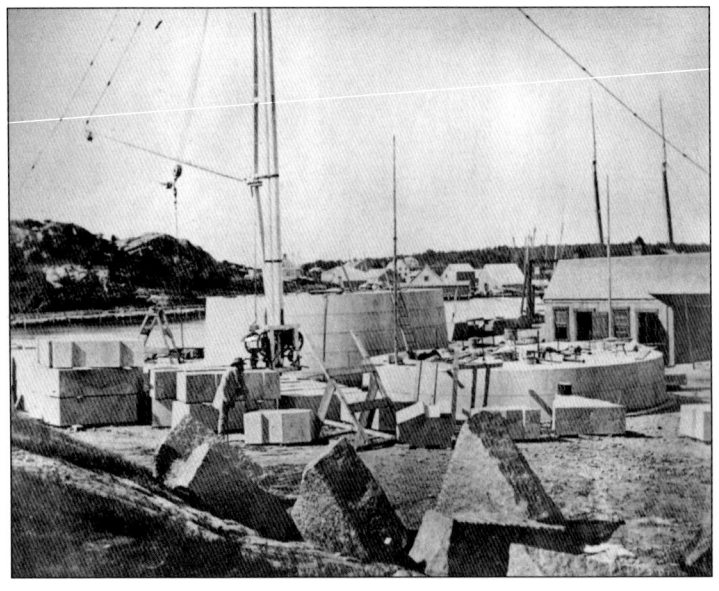

Granite from the Granite Railway Company's quarry in Quincy, Massachusetts, was chosen because it was considered "finest of grain, toughest and clearest of sap." In all, 1,079 blocks of granite were used. The painstaking assembling of the granite took place at Government Island in Cohasset, which is attached to the mainland. Lt. Barton S. Alexander is visible in this photograph. (US Coast Guard.)

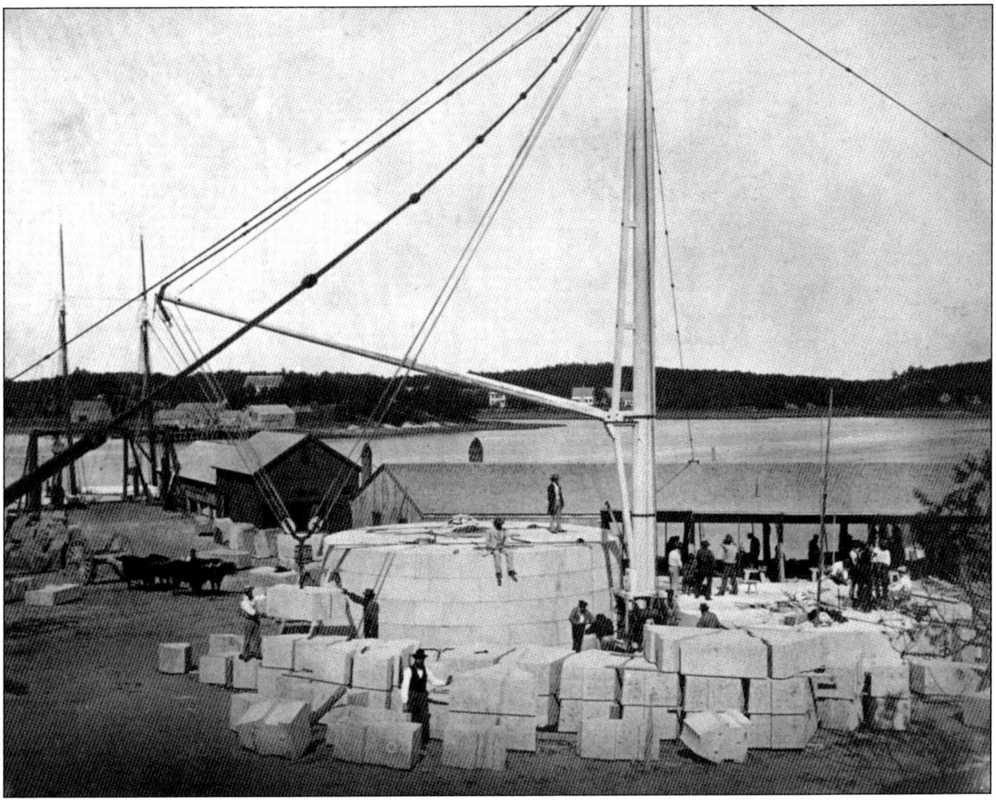

A team of oxen moved the blocks from Government Island to a vessel that took them to Minot's Ledge. A 1915 article in the *Boston Evening Transcript* states: "The Quincy granite cutters declared that such chiseling never had left the hands of man before; and truly there was need of workmanship of supreme excellence." (US Coast Guard.)

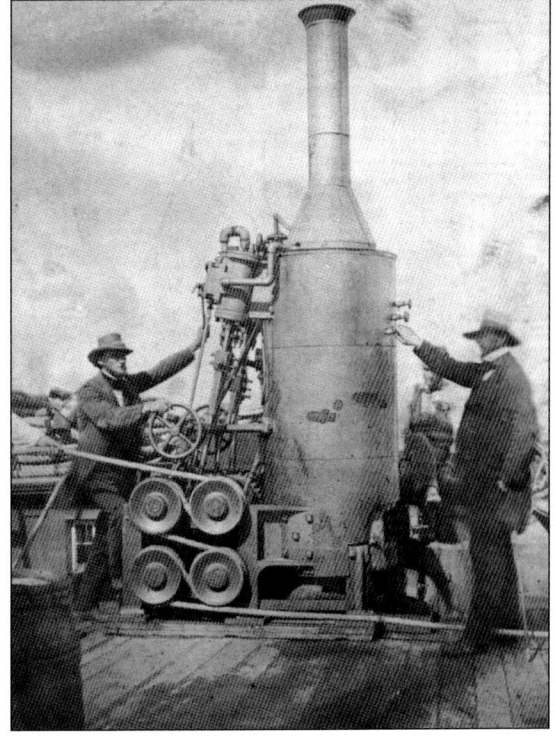

Lt. Barton S. Alexander described the use of a derrick: "All the lower courses of stone in the tower were laid from an iron mast, which was set up in the centre hole of the former lighthouse." Power for the derrick was provided by a large steam engine called a donkey engine, shown here. (National Archives.)

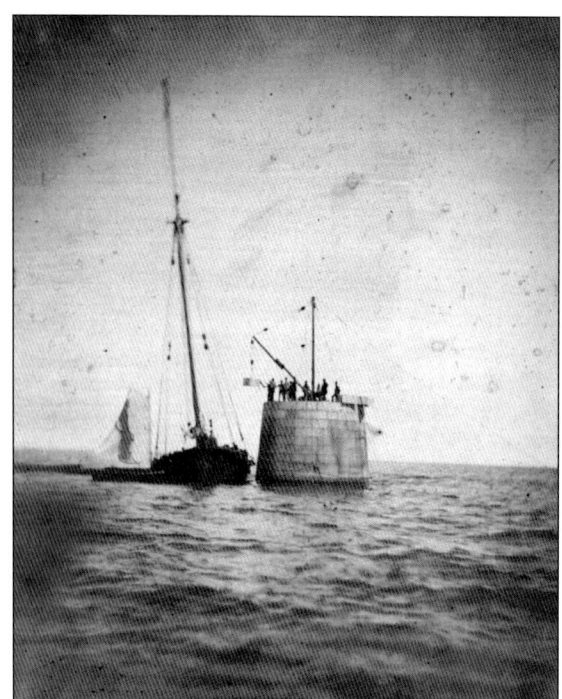

Not a single man was seriously injured in the course of construction. When a wave hit, the men learned to hold on tightly until the danger passed. While the crews were working on the ledge, there was always a boat nearby waiting to pick up anyone who was washed from the site. A Cohasset diver, Michael Neptune Brennock, was hired to act as a lifeguard. (National Archives.)

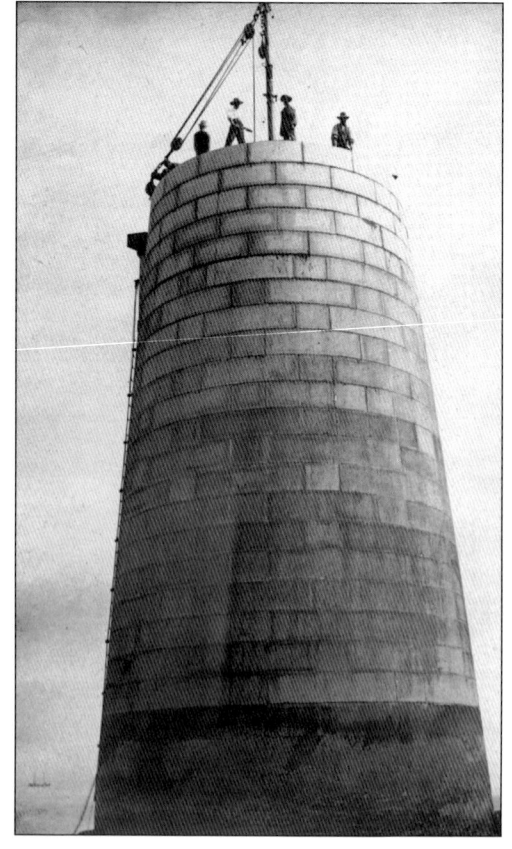

A local man named Noyes worked on both the first and second lighthouses at Minot's Ledge. After a minor altercation on the job, Noyes disappeared to parts unknown. He resurfaced during the Civil War as a Confederate naval officer aboard the *Alabama*. Noyes was recognized by Cohasset men aboard the clipper *Golden Fleece*, which had been captured by the *Alabama*. (National Archives.)

On October 2, 1858, an official dedication was held. The great orator Edward Everett, one of the speakers, said, "In the course of that tremendous night, the lighthouse on Minot's Ledge disappeared . . . and with it the two brave men who, in that awful hour, stood bravely at their posts. We have come now, sir, to repair the desolation of that hour." (Library of Congress.)

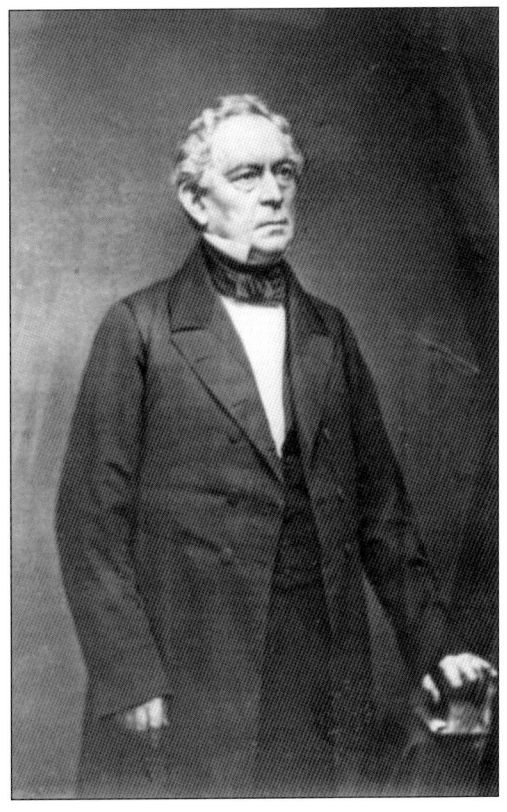

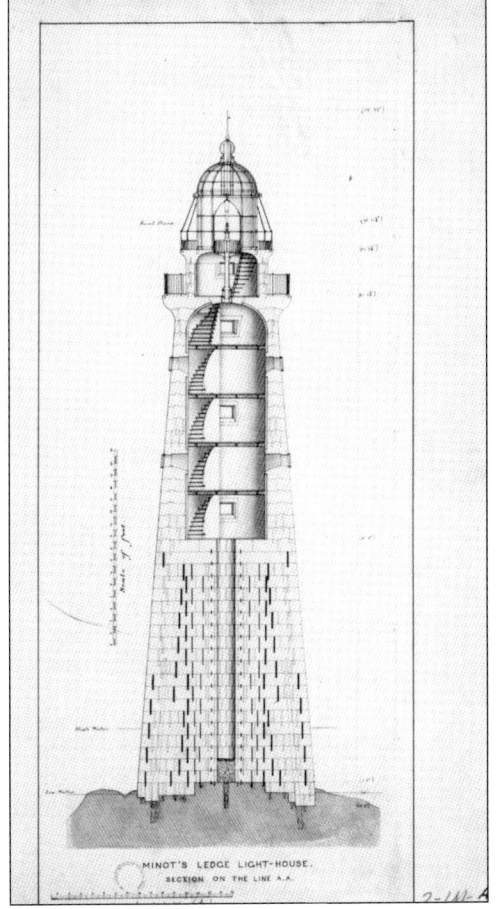

The first 40 feet of the tower consist of solid granite topped by a storeroom for coal, wood, and other supplies. The galley (kitchen) was located above the supply room. The levels above that contained living space for a principal keeper and an assistant keeper. Below the lantern was a watch room and space for the machinery that rotated the lens. (National Archives.)

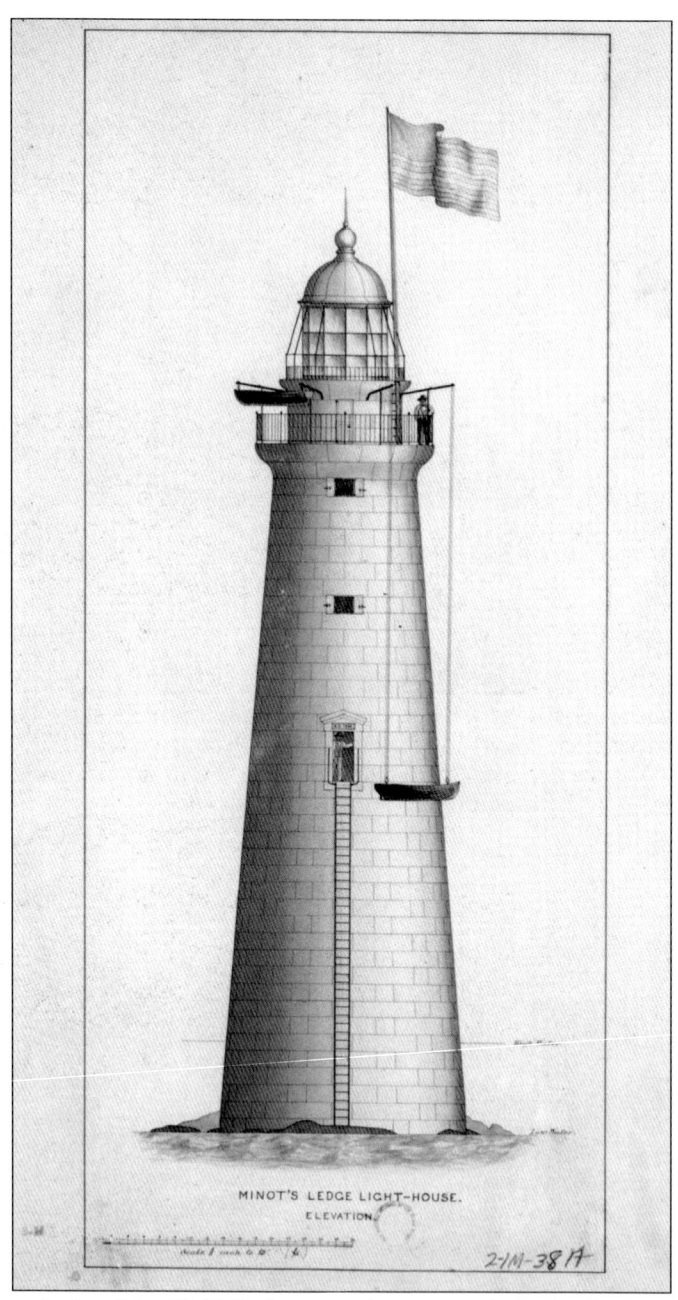

MINOT'S LEDGE LIGHT-HOUSE.
ELEVATION.

The last stone was laid on June 29, 1860, five years (minus one day) after Lt. Barton S. Alexander and his workmen first landed at the ledge. The lantern and a second-order Fresnel lens were put into place, and the lighthouse was first illuminated on November 15, 1860. The height of the focal plane—the center of the lens—is listed as 85 feet above mean high water. The power of the light shown by the lightship that had served in the interim was described by the *Boston Post* as "farthing candles" compared to the brilliance of the new light. The final cost of about $330,000—including two keepers' houses onshore—made it one of the most expensive lighthouses in the United States. The tower has stood through countless storms and hurricanes, a testament to its designer and builders. (National Archives.)

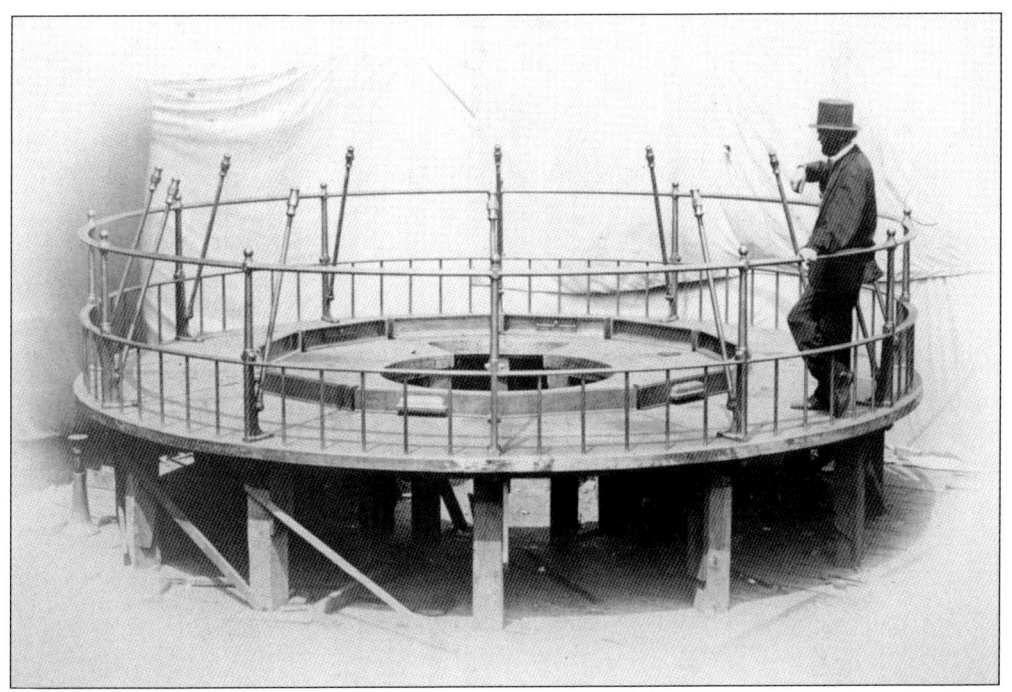

A few years after the tower was built, it was found that the granite deck at the lantern level had cracked. A new bronze deck, consisting of 12 sections weighing a total of 17,000 pounds, was constructed in 1866 at the Portland, Maine, facility of Ira Winn. Winn had built the lanterns and stairs for a number of lighthouses, mostly in Maine. (National Archives.)

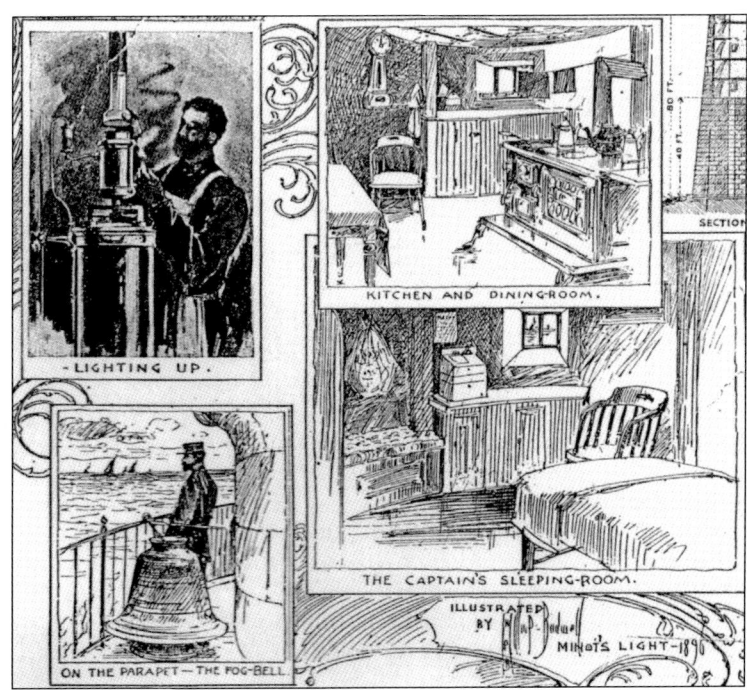

An illustrated 1890 newspaper article showed the living quarters in the lighthouse. Generally, three male keepers were assigned to the lighthouse, and there were usually two there at any given time. In the early 1900s, the keepers each spent 20 days at the lighthouse followed by 10 days onshore. It was reported that one keeper had to resign because he could no longer stand round walls. (Author's collection.)

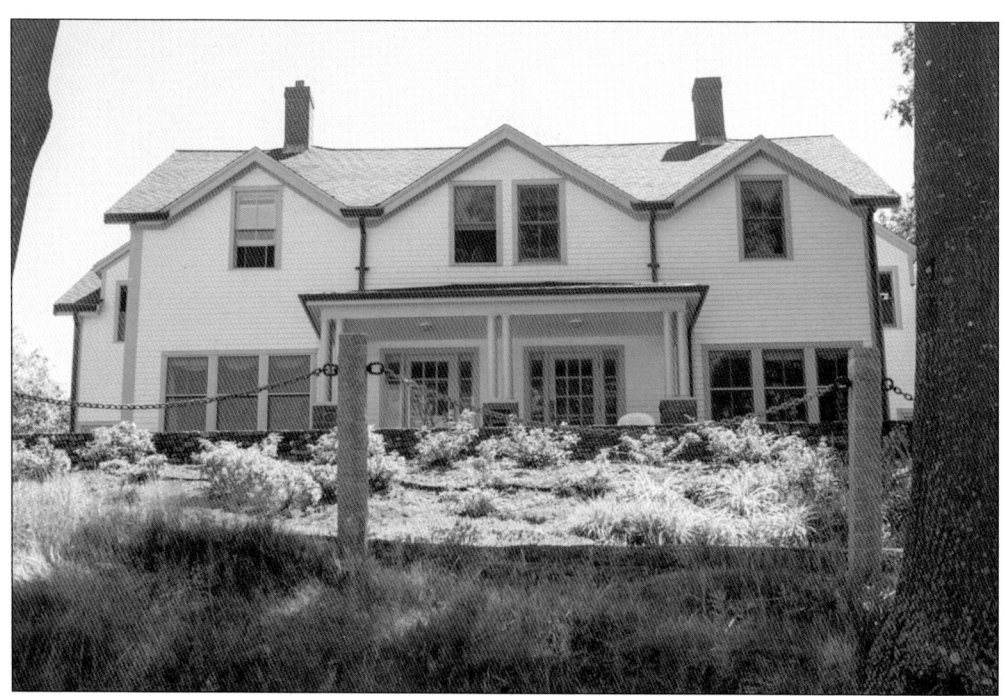

When they were on shore leave, the keepers lived with their families onshore in two duplex houses at Government Island in Cohasset. One of the houses has been razed, but in 1992–1993, the remaining keeper's house at Government Island was restored by the nonprofit Cohasset Lightkeepers Corporation. The house contains two upstairs apartments and a downstairs hall for community use. (Photograph by the author.)

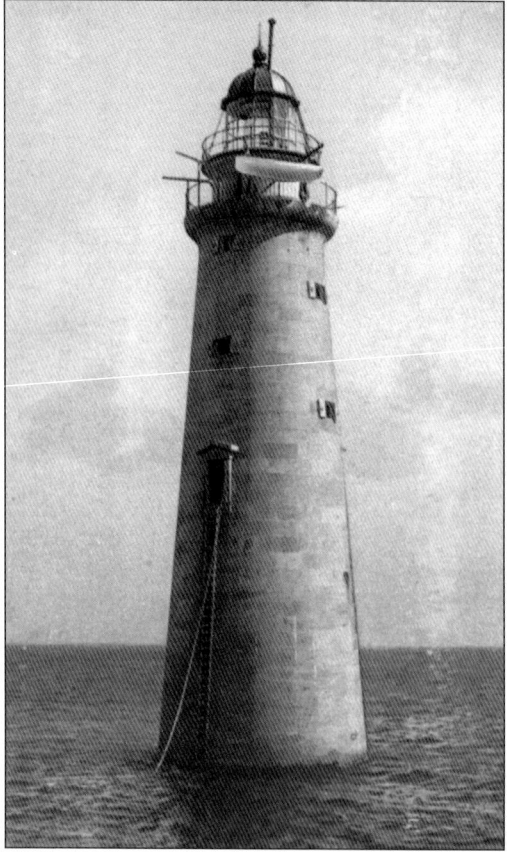

On May 1, 1894, a new 12-panel rotating second-order Fresnel lens was installed, displaying a distinctive 1-4-3 flash. Someone decided that 1-4-3 stood for "I love you," and the Minot's Ledge Light was soon popularly referred to as the "I Love You Light," an appellation that has inspired numerous songs and poems. (National Archives.)

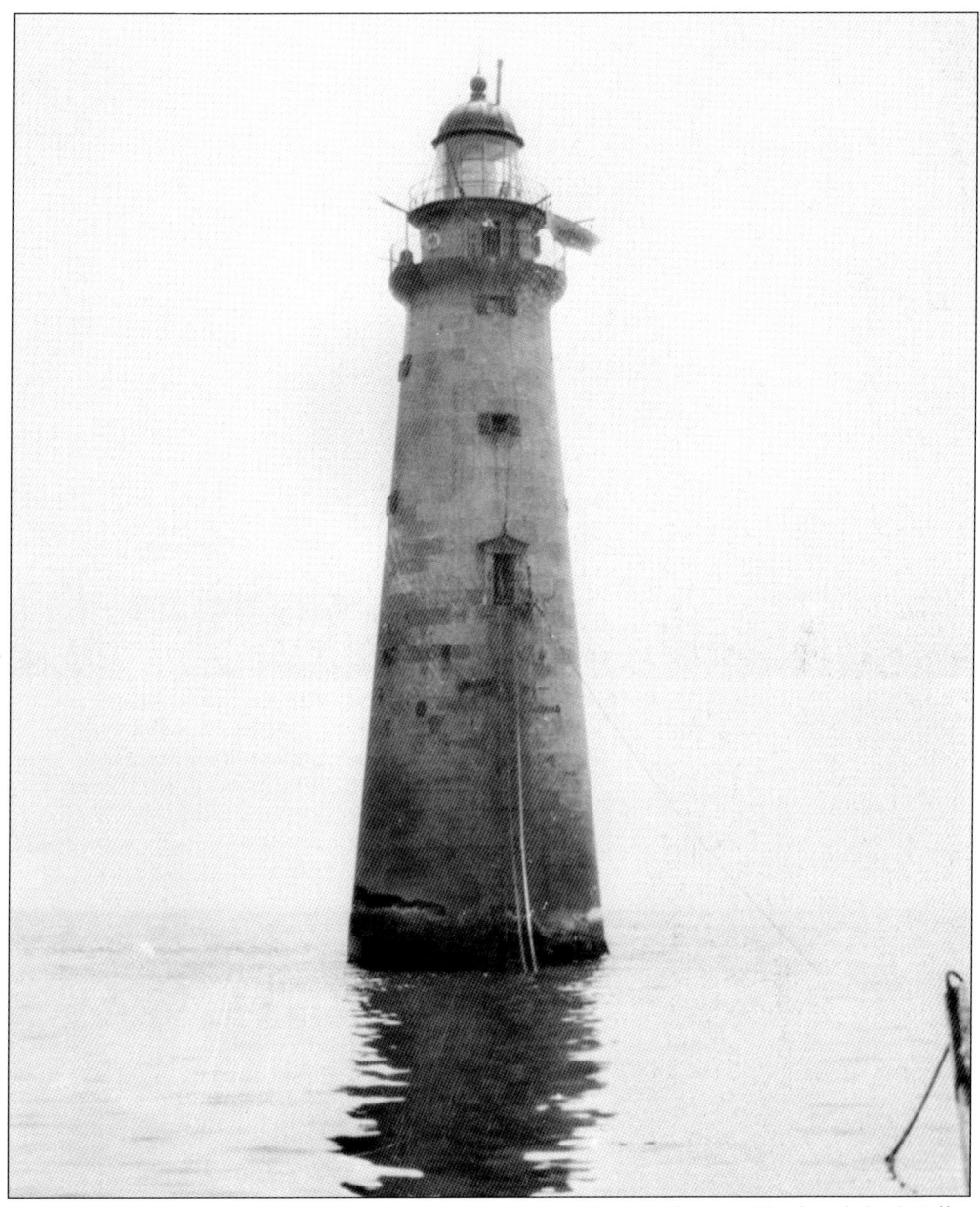

Helen Keller wrote of passing Minot's Ledge in 1901. Although she was blind and deaf, Keller often described things as if she could see them. She wrote: "The colors warmed and deepened as we watched the beautiful, gold-tinted clouds peacefully take possession of the sky. . . . The ocean awoke, ships and boats of every description sprang from the waves as if by magic; and as we sighted Minot's Ledge Light, a great six-masted schooner with snowy sails passed us like a beautiful winged spirit, bound for some unknown haven beyond the bar. How delightful it was to see Minot's Ledge in the morning light. There one expects to see the ocean lashed into fury by the splendid resistance of the rocks; but as we passed the 'light' seemed to rise out of the tranquil water, like Venus from her morning bath. It seemed so near, I thought I could touch it; but I am rather glad I did not; for perhaps the lovely illusion would have been destroyed had I examined it more closely." (National Archives.)

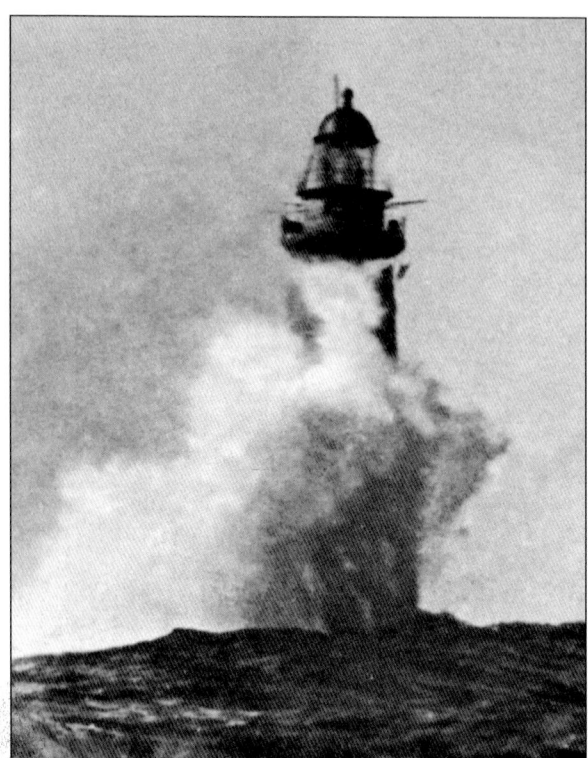

A young Cohasset man named George F. Newton Jr. took this photograph on Thanksgiving Day in 1915. Just after the photograph was taken, Newton's boat was swamped by a wave and lost its anchor. Keeper Octavius Reamy signalled for help from the local lifesaving station, and a lifesaving boat soon arrived to rescue the photographer and a friend. (Dolly Bicknell.)

Edward Rowe Snow told the story behind this 1935 photograph: "The craft which was rowed out to the vicinity of the light was owned by Joseph Lee Jr., and manned by Sea Scouts. . . . They arrived in the vicinity of the Light at half tide. Since the boat was at times almost perpendicular, Larry McDavitt had a hard task keeping the tower in range on his camera." (Dolly Bicknell.)

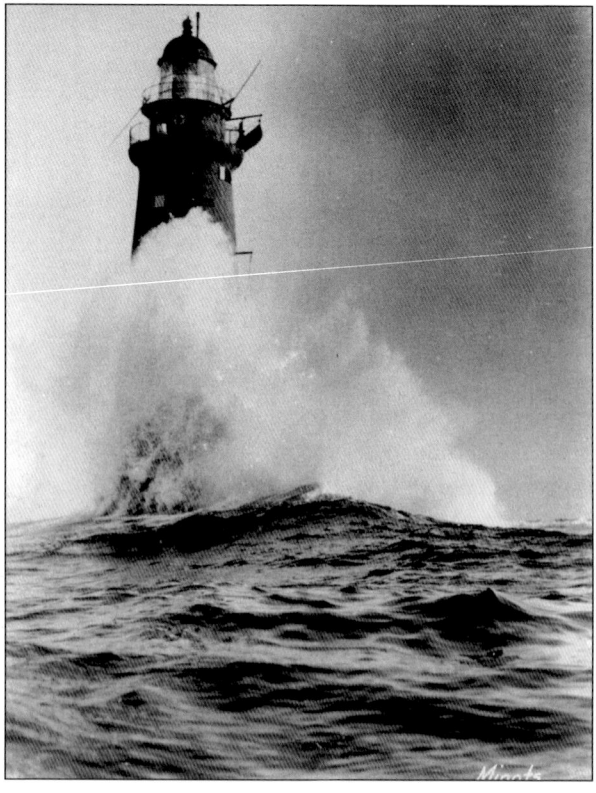

When the poet Henry Wadsworth Longfellow visited Minot's Ledge Light in 1871, he was hoisted on a chair to the doorway in the tower. That method of entry was thereafter known as "Longfellow's chair." In this 1932 photograph, Anna-Myrle Snow, wife of the historian Edward Rowe Snow, is being hoisted up to the entryway—but there is no chair to be seen. (Dolly Bicknell.)

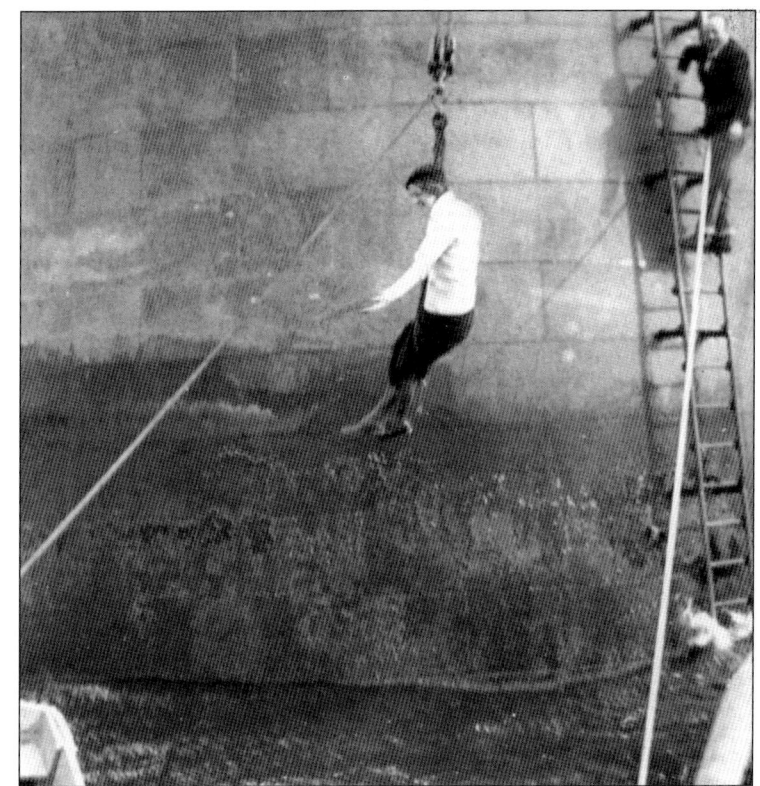

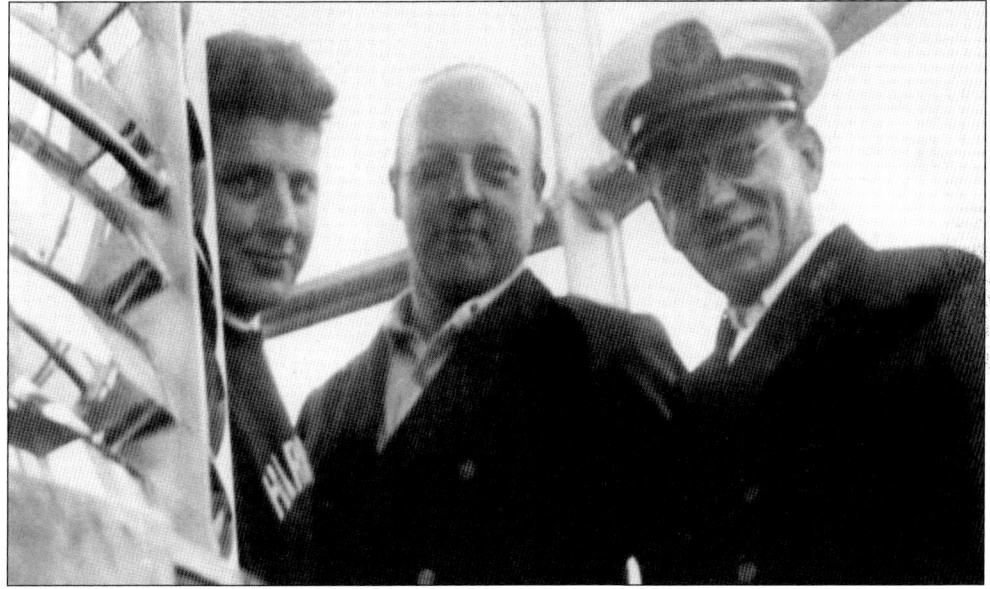

This photograph was taken in the lantern room at Minot's Ledge Light on April 17, 1936. From left to right are historian Edward Rowe Snow, First Assistant Keeper Otis Walsh, and Principal Keeper Per Tornberg. Tornberg—a native of Sweden who was educated in Germany—was principal keeper from 1924 until 1936. (Dolly Bicknell.)

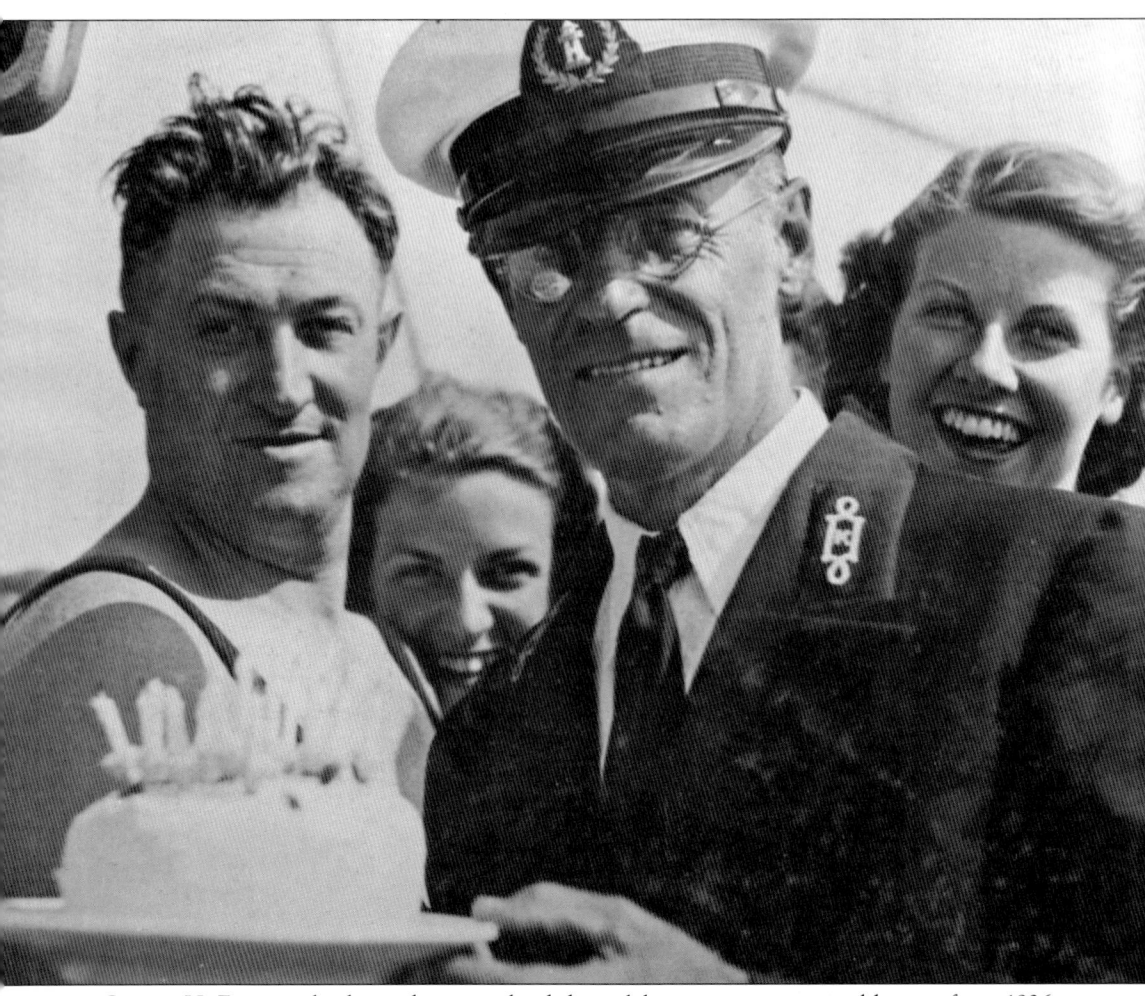

George H. Fitzpatrick, shown here at a birthday celebration, was principal keeper from 1936 to 1941. Fitzpatrick and the assistant keepers shared the living quarters with a pet canary named Dick. The bird's singing "gave an air of cheerfulness in the atmosphere of isolation," wrote historian Edward Rowe Snow. By 1940, Fitzpatrick and two assistants were spending 20 days in the tower followed by 10 days off. His wife and their 15-year-old daughter lived onshore. A severe storm in January 1941 sent spray cascading over the lighthouse, leaving a thick cake of ice that sealed the entrance door. Two assistant keepers were trapped inside. The men had plenty of provisions on hand and were in telephone contact with the mainland, so they were in no particular danger while they waited for the ice to melt. A transfer of keepers was made a couple of days later, when Fitzpatrick was hoisted from a boat using a boatswain's chair and entered through a window. Assistant keeper Patrick Brides left the lighthouse the same way. (Dolly Bicknell.)

This 1930s photograph shows popular historian/author Edward Rowe Snow diving from the doorway of Minot's Ledge Lighthouse, which was located about 55 feet above the water. According to a newspaper account, Snow's dive took place at low tide, and he landed in water just a little more than seven feet deep. He repeated the dive on other occasions, including his 60th birthday in 1962. (Dolly Bicknell.)

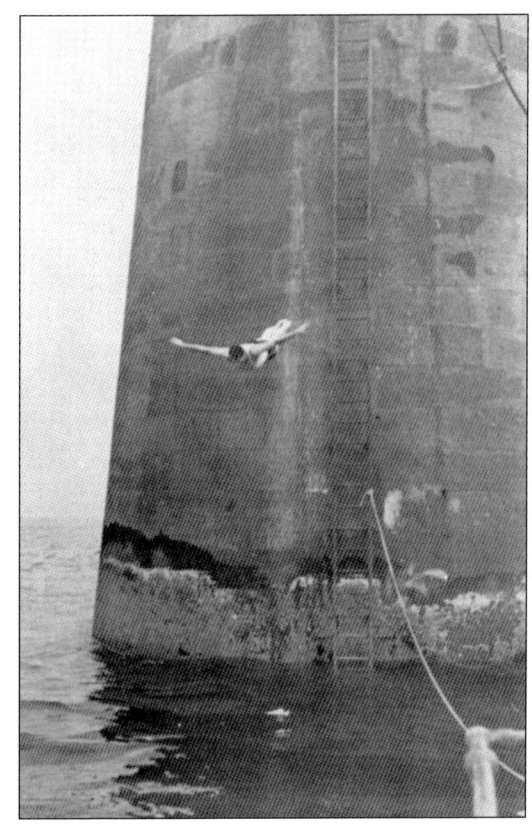

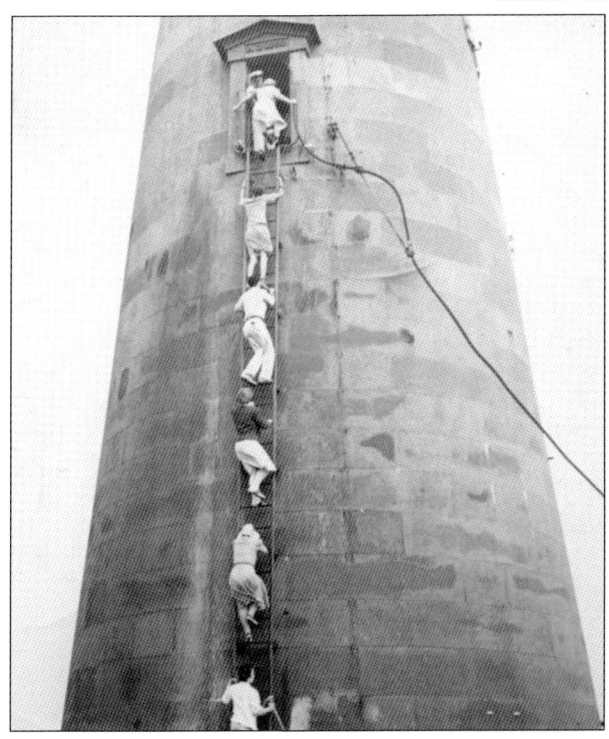

Edward Rowe Snow sometimes brought tour groups to Minot's Ledge, such as on this occasion in 1941, when he brought a group of 100 people to the lighthouse. The Coast Guard was considering automation of the light by the mid-1940s. A report called the station "one of the most undesirable . . . assignments that can be given a man." (Dolly Bicknell.)

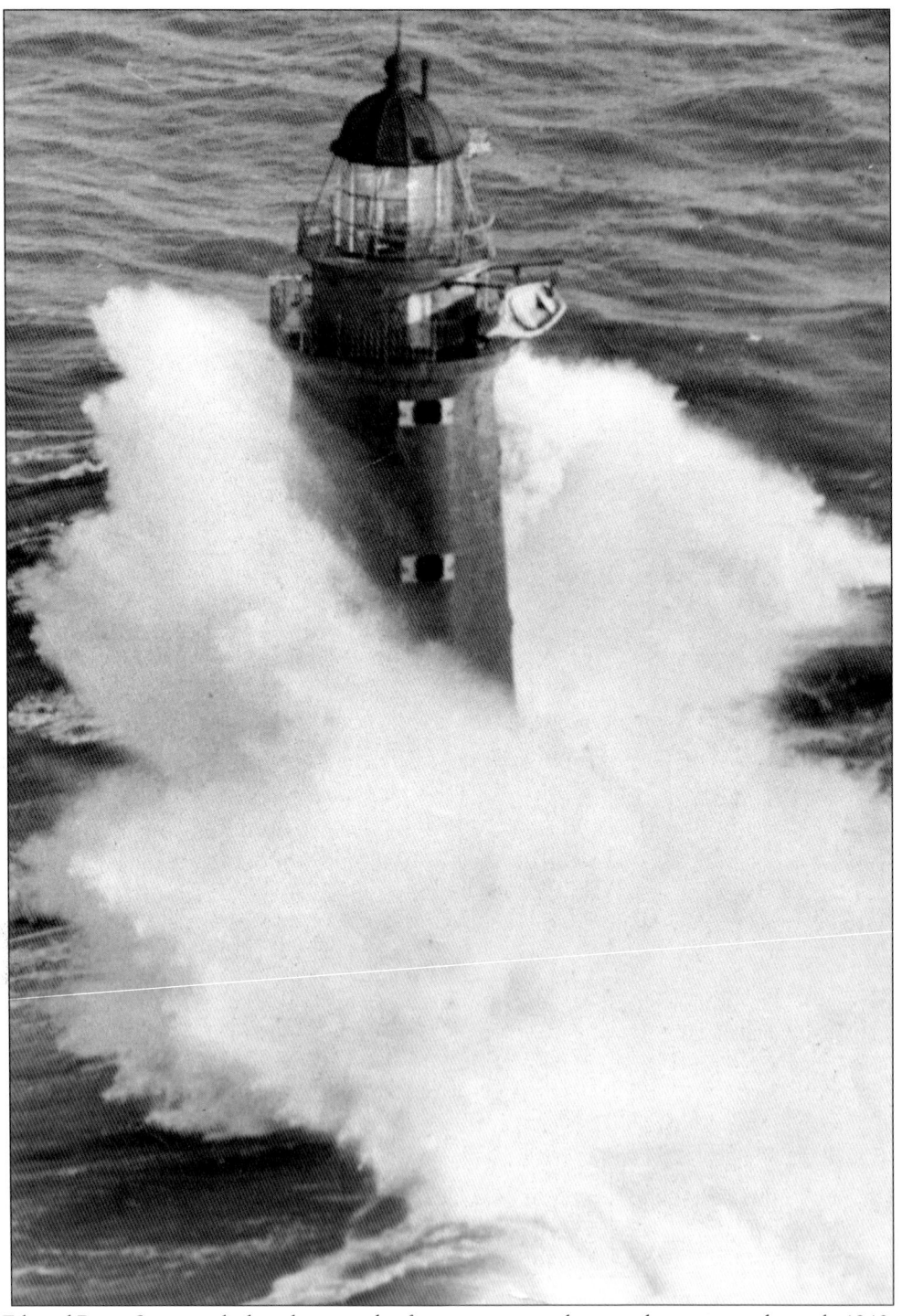
Edward Rowe Snow took this photograph of a gigantic wave hitting the tower in the early 1940s. In 1947, the light was automated and converted to electric operation and the keepers were removed. The fog signal was discontinued at the same time. The new electric apparatus produced a 4,500-candlepower light. (Dolly Bicknell.)

A renovation of the tower was carried out from 1987 through 1989. The lantern was lifted off by helicopter and subsequently cleaned, and about 40 of the damaged upper granite blocks were removed and replaced. The Gayle Electric Company of New Jersey, under contract with the Coast Guard, performed the work. (US Coast Guard.)

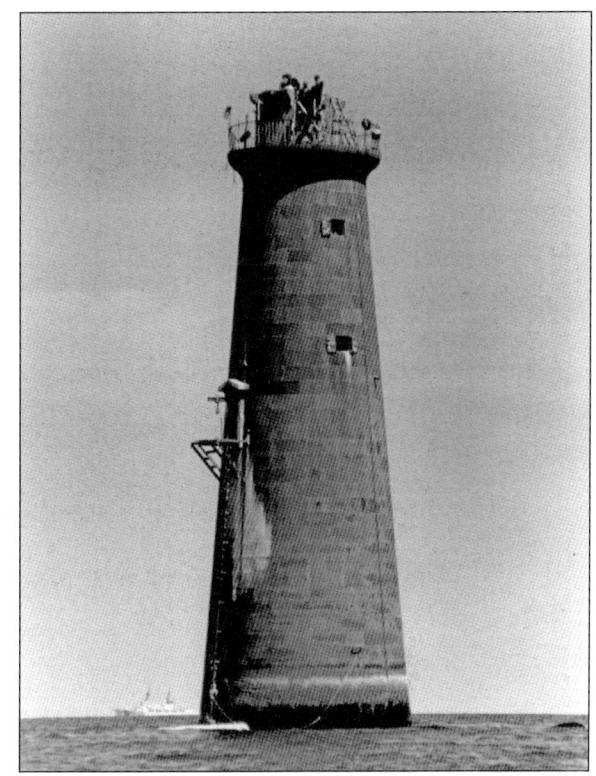

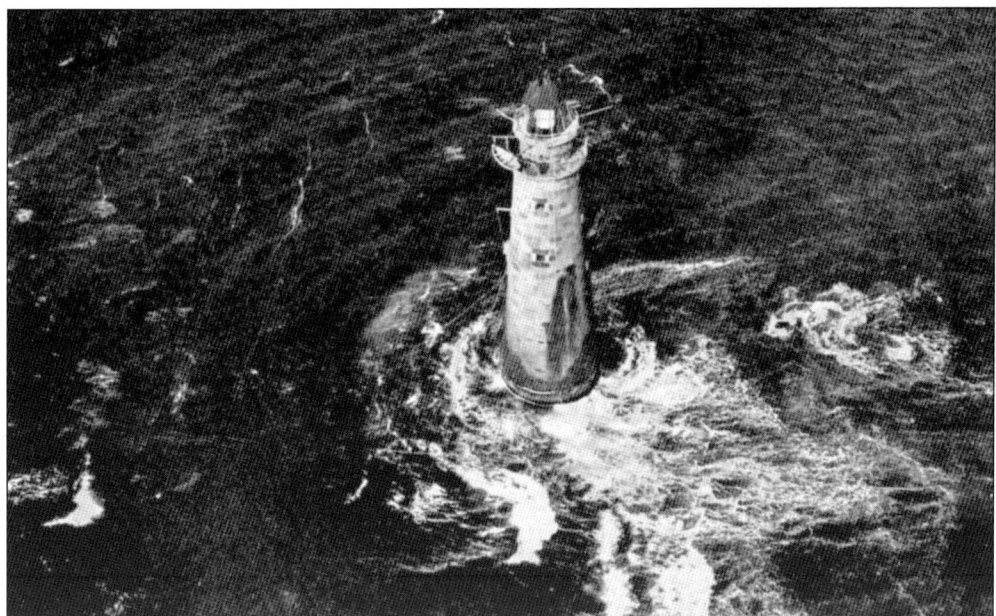

Under the National Historic Lighthouse Preservation Act of 2000, the lighthouse was made available for transfer to a suitable new owner. No applications were submitted by nonprofit organizations or government entities, so in June 2014, the property was put up for sale to the public via online auction. The high bidder—at $222,000—was Bobby Sager, a well-known philanthropist. (US Coast Guard.)

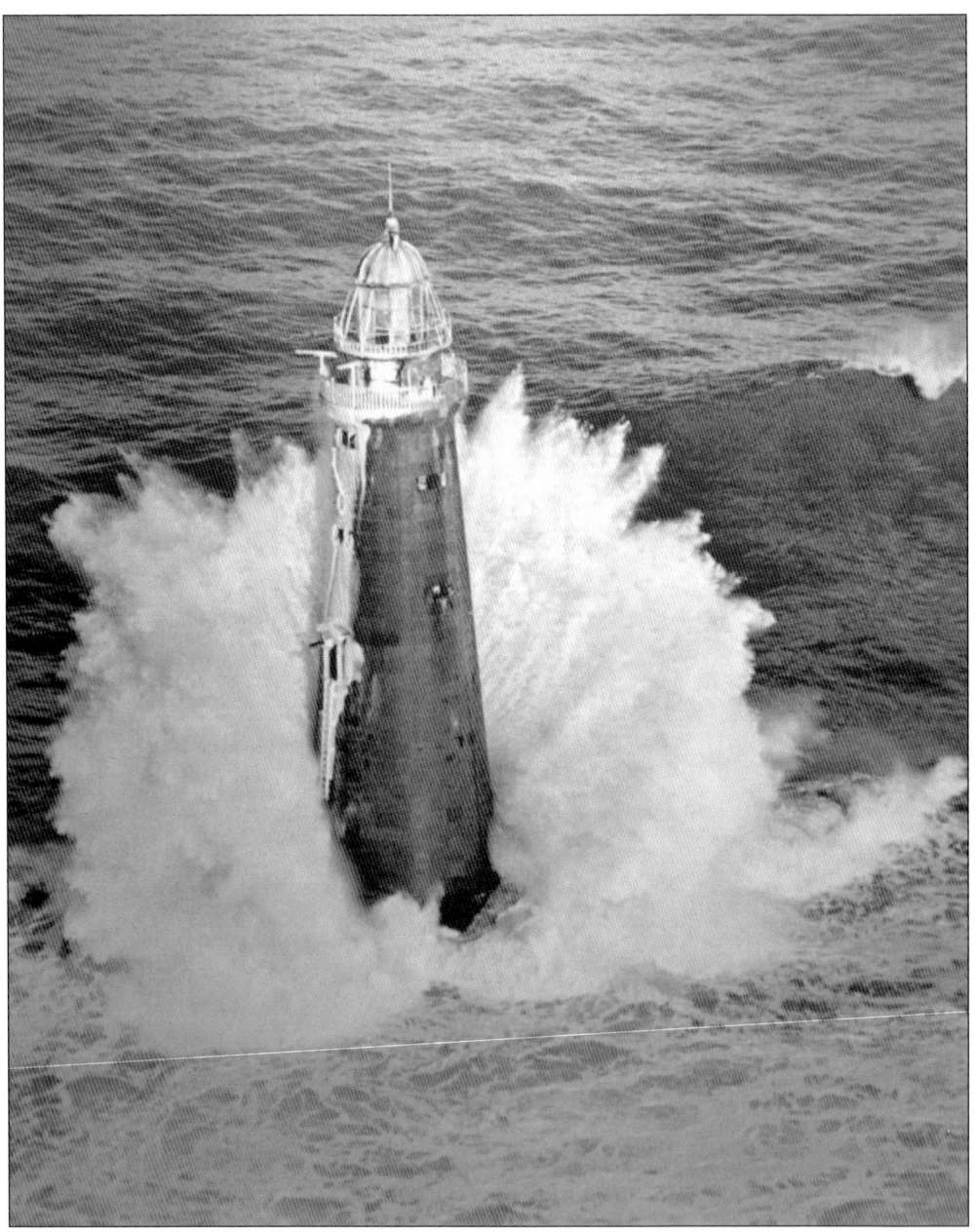

The blizzard of February 7–8, 1978, was one of the worst storms in recorded New England history, leaving 54 people dead and 10,000 homeless or evacuated. Whole communities were flooded in freezing waters, and commuters were trapped in snow-covered cars. Keepers had to be rescued by helicopter from at least two remote Maine lighthouses. On February 8, Kevin Cole, chief photographer at the Boston Herald American, boarded a small plane at Hyannis on Cape Cod. "It was this little, tiny plane," he said later. "We took off. The whole coastline was gone, houses in the water, houses floating, waves crashing inside them. About two miles out, I saw Minot's Light." Just as the pilot turned to head back to the airport, Cole saw a huge wave. "That's when I got that shot," he said, "and that's the same time I threw up." (Photograph by Kevin Cole; Creative Commons license.)

Five
Halfway Rock

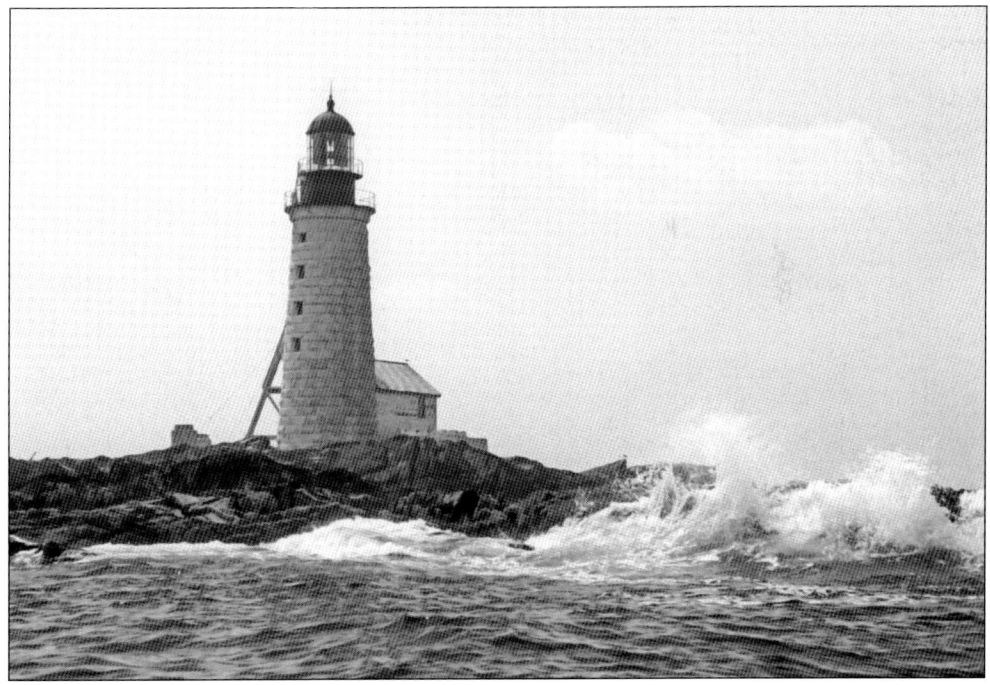

Halfway Rock is in Maine's Casco Bay, about ten miles east of the entrance to Portland Harbor. The ledge stretches for about a quarter mile to the southwest and to the north from the lighthouse location, most of it lurking just under the surface. It is approximately halfway between Cape Elizabeth, to the west-southwest, and Cape Small in Phippsburg, to the east-northeast. (Photograph by the author.)

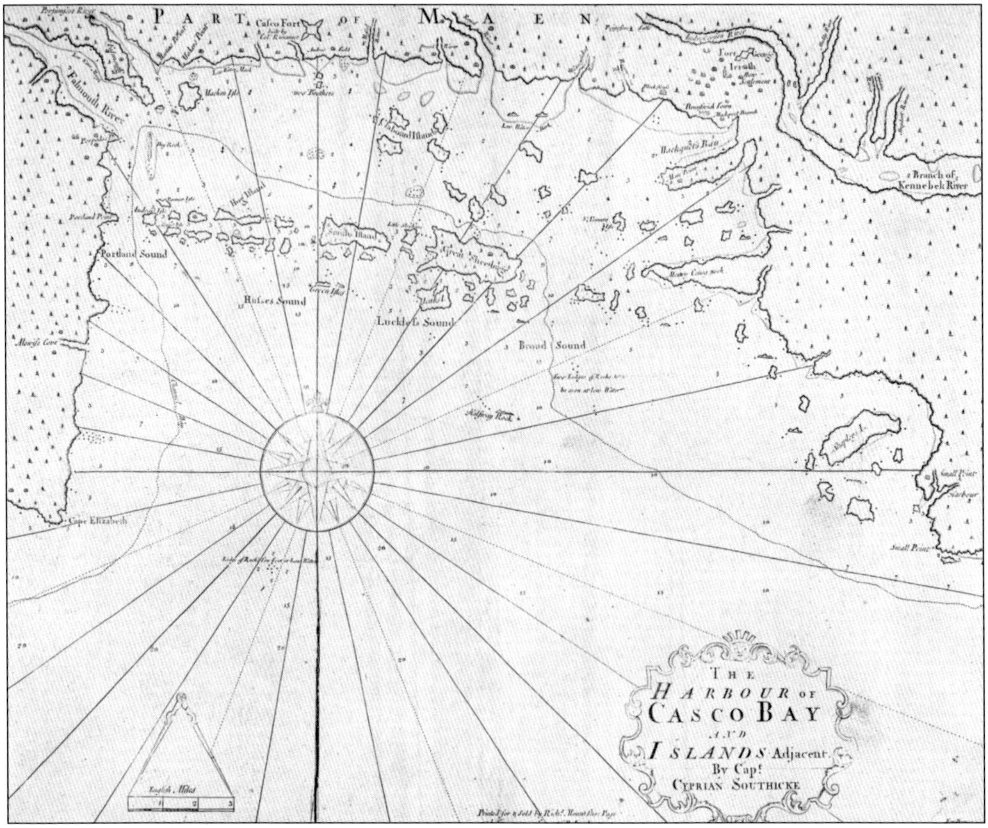

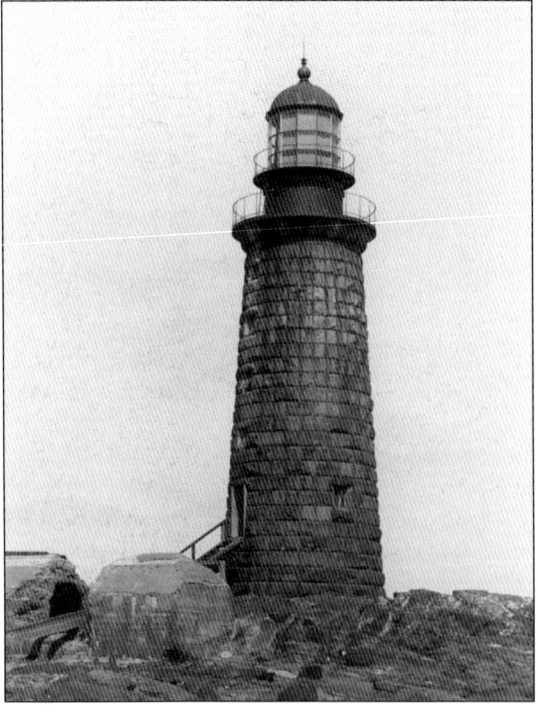

Published in 1720, this is the earliest known chart of Casco Bay. Agitation for an aid to navigation in the vicinity began as early as 1837, when Capt. Joseph Smith recommended the construction of a stone monument because of the dangers the ledge presented in foggy weather. It was not until March 1869 that Congress appropriated $50,000 for the construction of a lighthouse. (Boston Rare Maps, Southampton, Massachusetts.)

Storms in September and October 1869 slowed construction, but the foundation was finished by the end of the year. The work crew had to be dismissed when funds ran out, but an additional $10,000 was appropriated, and the 76-foot granite tower was completed in summer 1871. The granite was quarried at Chebeague Island, and the blocks were prepared at Fort Scammel in Portland Harbor. (National Archives.)

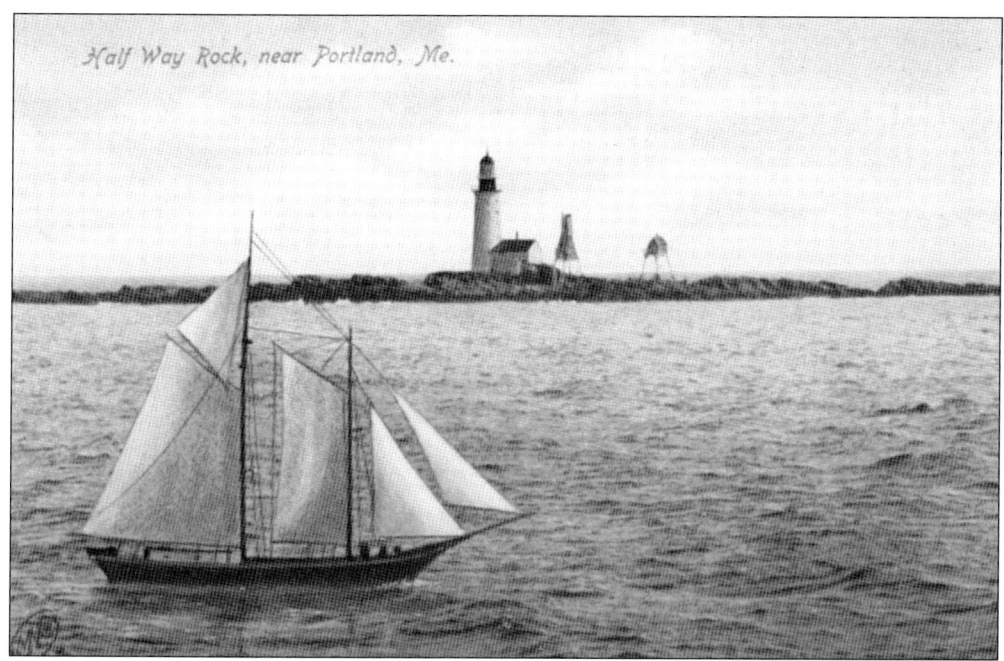

The keepers lived in rooms inside the tower on the barren two-acre island. The first keeper was John T. Sterling. His daughter later recalled how she would anxiously walk to the shore of Peaks Island in Portland, where the family lived, to watch for her father's arrival after days or weeks at the light station. (Author's collection.)

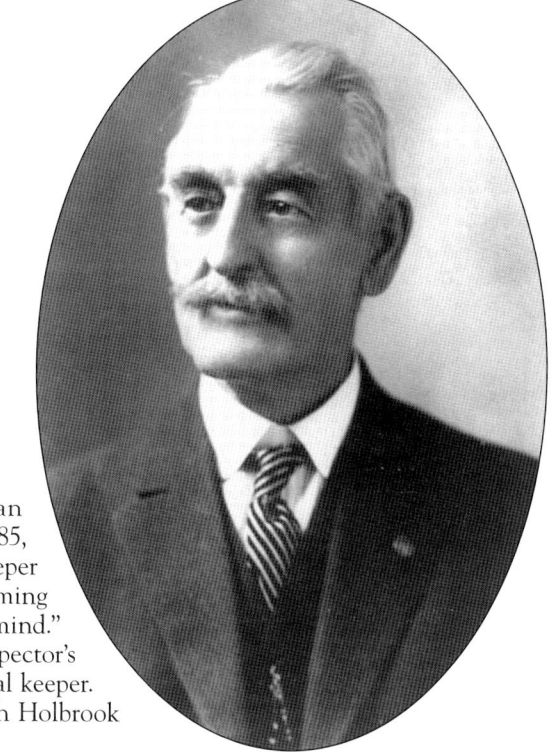

William Holbrook, shown here, was an assistant keeper from 1881 to 1885. In 1885, Holbrook expressed a fear that assistant keeper George Toothaker might attack him, claiming that Toothaker was "at times out of his mind." Toothaker soon resigned at the district inspector's urging, and Holbrook became the principal keeper. (South Portland Historical Society, Judith Holbrook Kelley collection.)

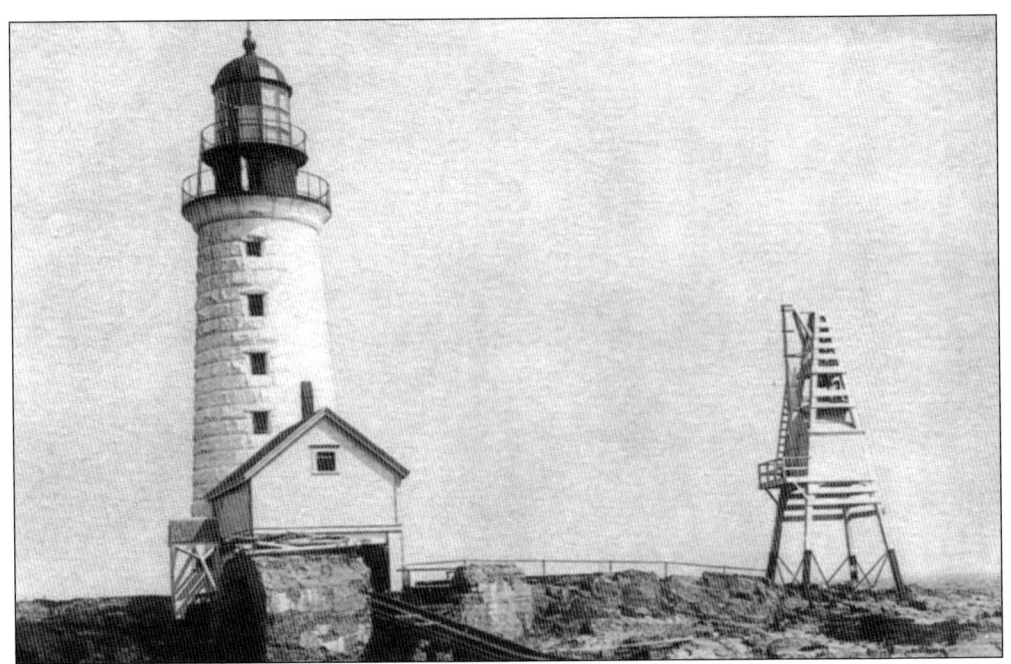

The station got its first fog signal when a 43-foot, pyramidal, skeleton-type bell tower was bolted to the rock near the lighthouse in 1887, with a 1,000-pound fog bell and striking machinery. Soon after its construction, the bell tower survived a fierce December storm that buried Halfway Rock under eight feet of water. (Author's collection.)

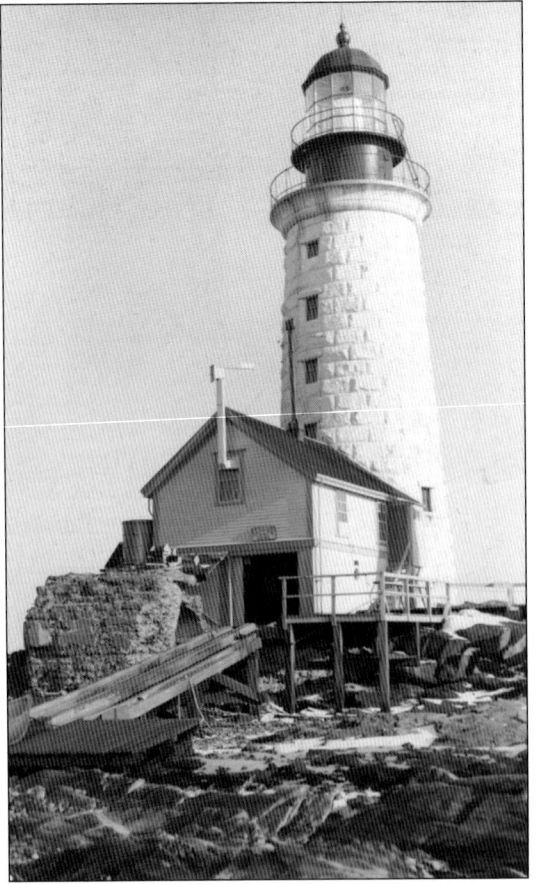

In 1888, a new boathouse—with an 18-by-24-foot foundation—was built and attached to the tower. Its upper story contained two additional rooms of living space for the keepers. This improved living conditions, but the tower was always the safest place in a storm. (US Coast Guard.)

Arthur Strout, who came from a famous lightkeeping family mainly identified with Portland Head Light, was an assistant keeper from 1929 to 1934. He was promoted to principal keeper and was the last civilian in that position. When the Coast Guard took over management of the station in 1939, Strout joined that branch of the service and remained in charge until 1945. (Photograph by Herb Giles; author's collection.)

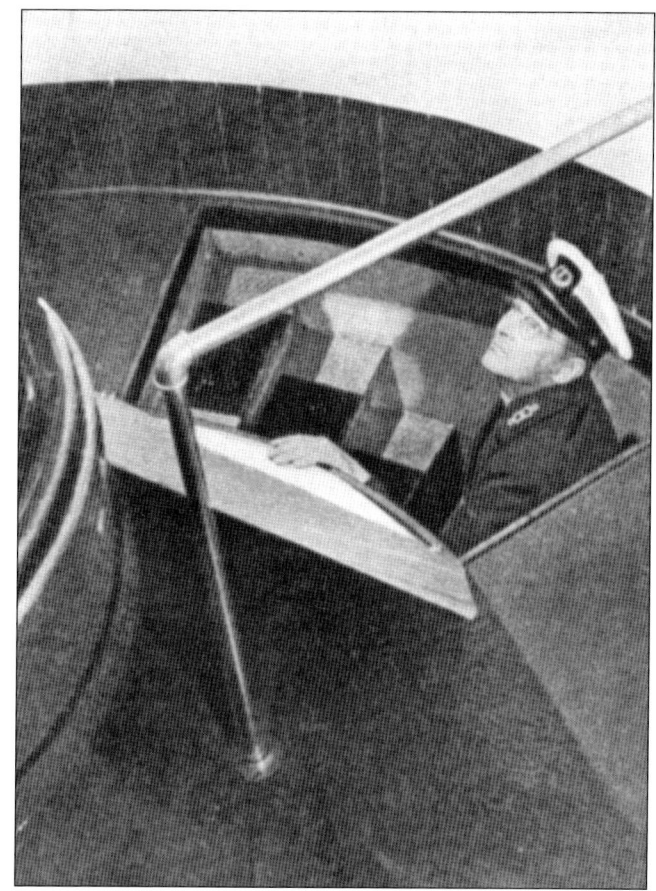

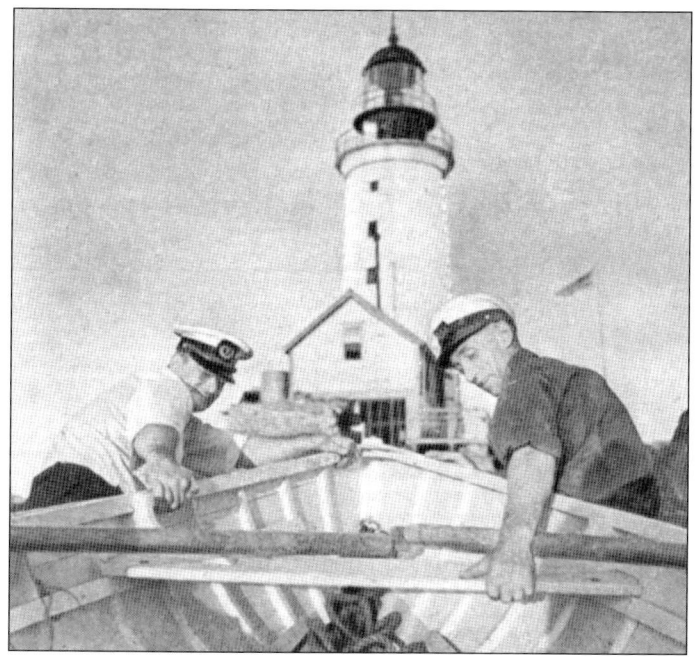

Here, keeper Arthur Strout (left) and his assistant Hoyt Cheney haul their boat up the ramp. Reaching the mainland for supplies required an 11-mile row to Portland, often made difficult or impossible by rough seas or ice. In February 1934, the keepers reported that ice an inch thick extended all the way past Halfway Rock. (Photograph by Herb Giles; author's collection.)

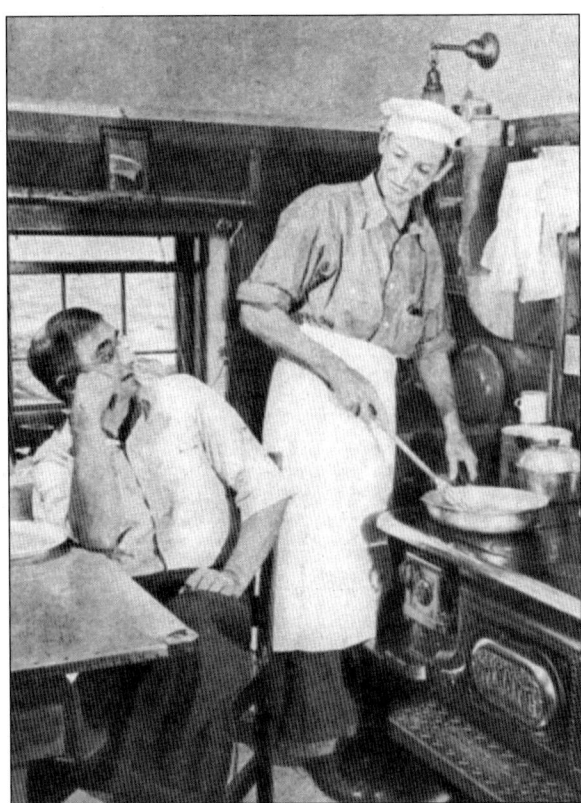

Here, assistant keeper Hoyt Cheney cooks as keeper Arthur Strout waits for his meal. During a 1936 storm, Strout was ashore and telephone communication was down, so Strout went to the home of a ham radio operator. With the young man's help, he was able to contact the assistant keeper. The assistant was fine, but the boat slip was damaged. (Photograph by Herb Giles; author's collection.)

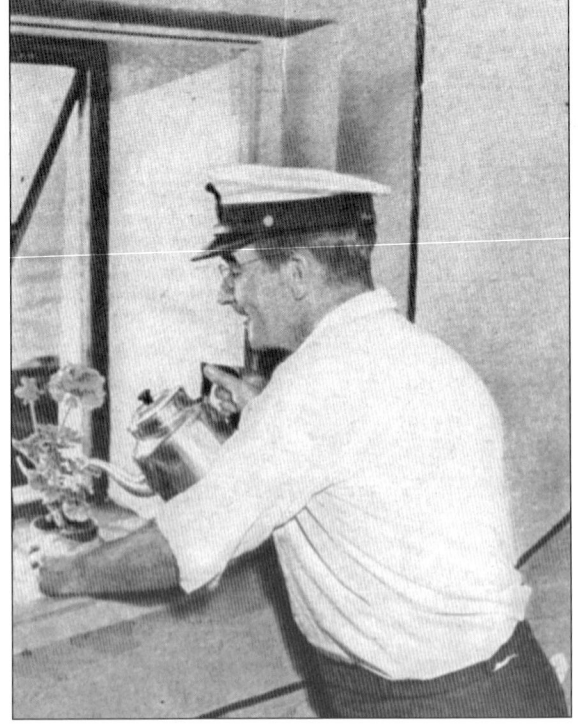

Keeper Arthur Strout is shown watering a geranium on a lighthouse windowsill. During restoration, lighthouse owner Ford Reiche found an empty whiskey bottle put inside a wall and signed by Strout and an assistant. Reiche theorized that the bottle may have been a sign of protest over the 1939 change from the civilian US Lighthouse Service to the US Coast Guard. (Photograph by Herb Giles; author's collection.)

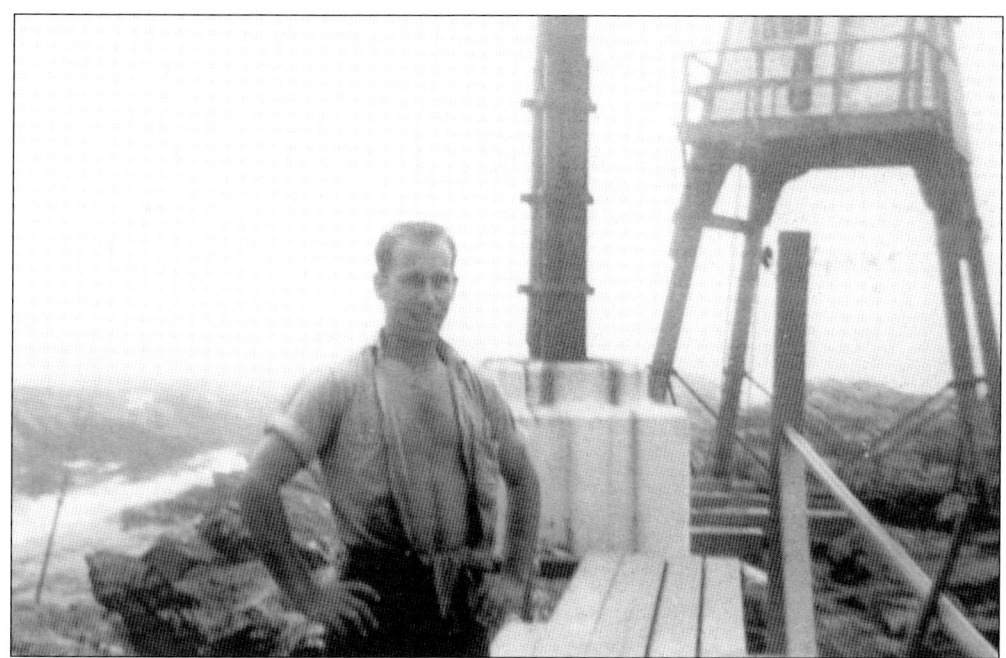

Ken Rouleau of Derry, New Hampshire, was barely out of his teens when he arrived at the station in 1960 as a Coast Guard keeper. For a young Coast Guardsman, the isolated station was not ideal duty. "We didn't have any fun—I didn't, anyway," he said in a 2002 interview. "There was not much social life. You took care of yourself." (Ken Rouleau.)

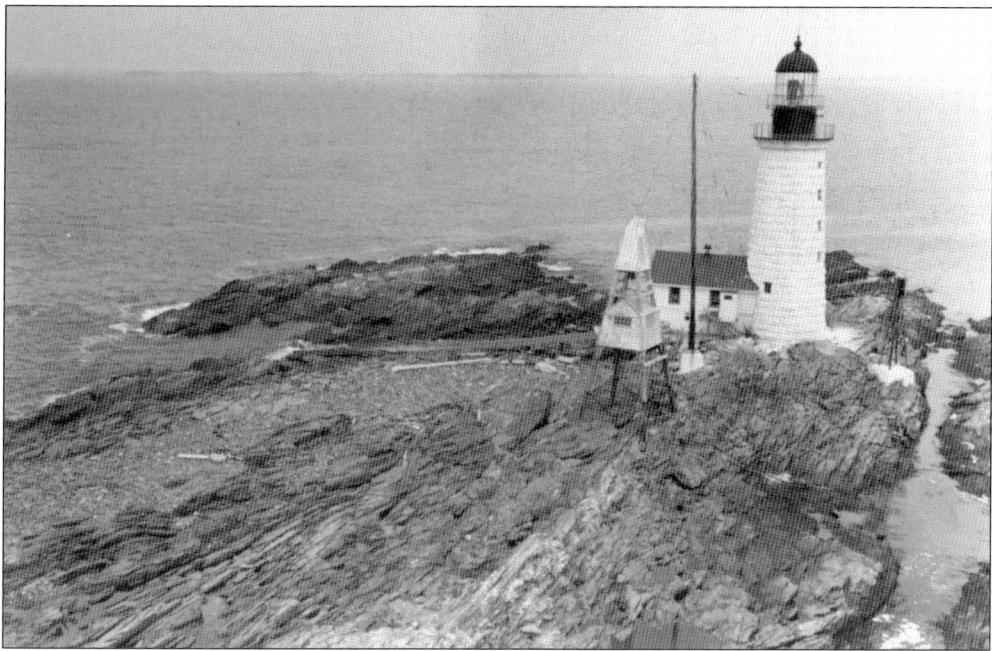

The fog bell tower was still standing when Rouleau arrived in 1960, but there was a modern fog signal that is visible to the right of the lighthouse in this photograph. "The foghorn would drive you completely bonkers when it would be foggy for seven or eight days at a time," said former keeper Ken Rouleau. (US Coast Guard Historian's Office.)

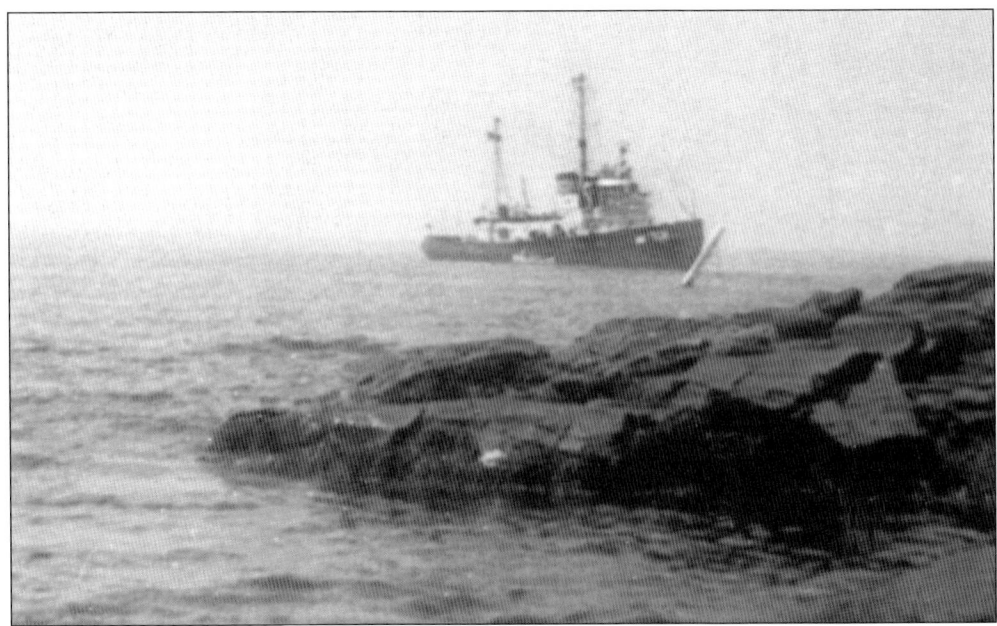

The Coast Guard sent a large tender, like the one shown here, to pick up the men or take them to the station, but it was necessary to transfer to a small peapod boat to land at Halfway Rock. It took skill to land the boat on the ramp in heavy seas. (Ken Rouleau.)

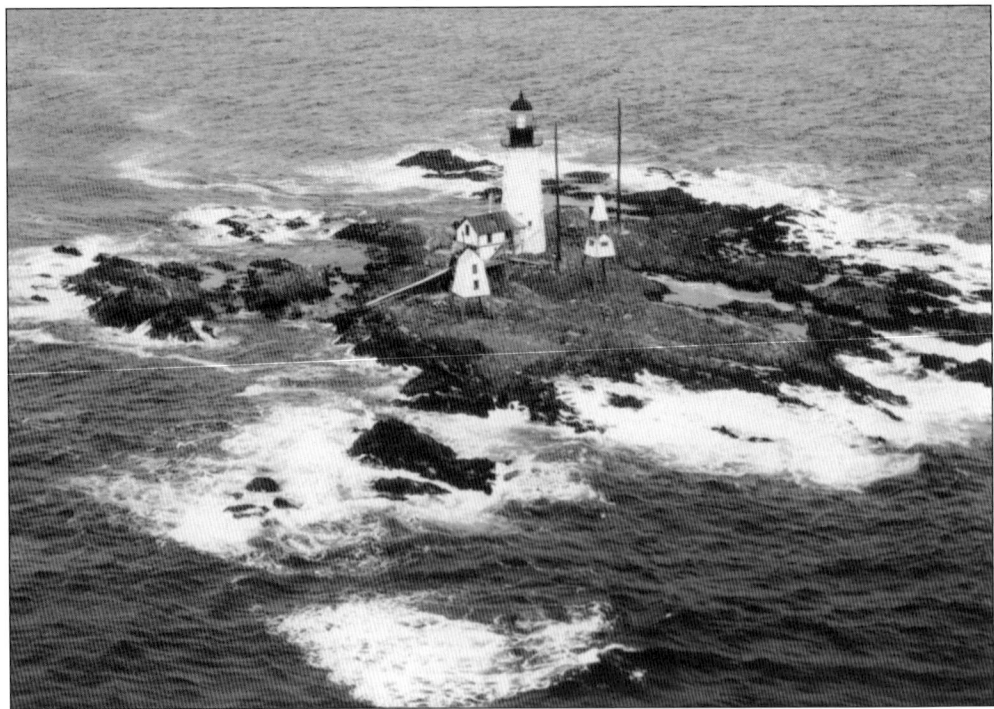

One time, a keeper was returning with a television that had just been repaired. The boat flipped as he tried to land on the ramp (visible to the left of the lighthouse in this photo), and Ken Rouleau got a sinking feeling as he thought, "No TV for another three weeks!" Launching the peapod down the ramp was just as hazardous. (US Coast Guard.)

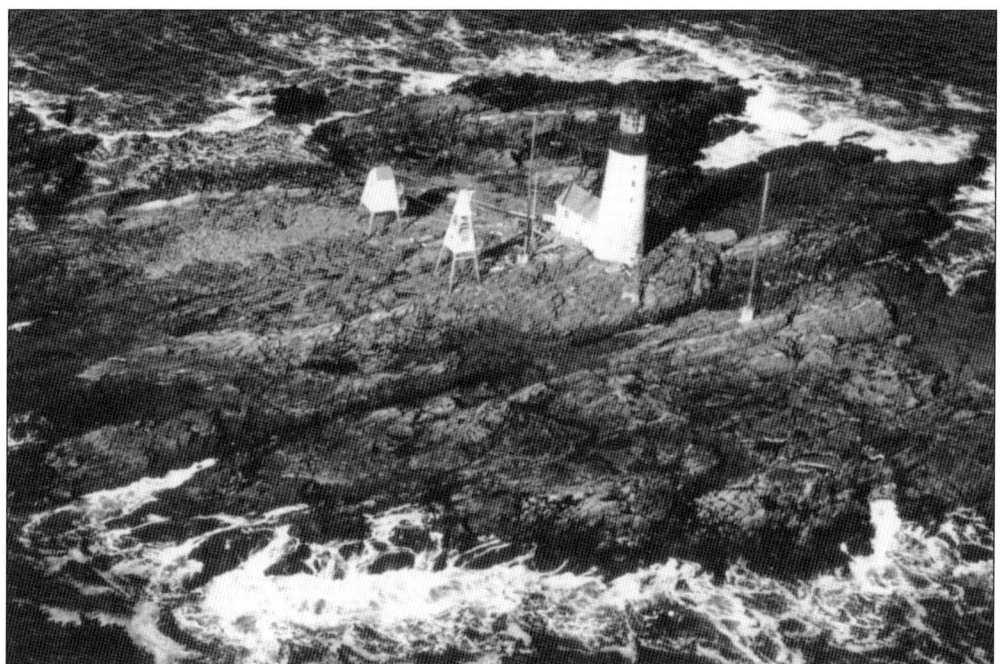

Storms frequently did great damage at the exposed location. One gale in December 1945 bent two 60-foot steel radio towers to the ground. On February 18, 1972, a severe winter storm washed away a fuel tank for the generator, leaving the crew without power or heat for some time. This photograph was taken in 1956. (US Coast Guard Historian's Office.)

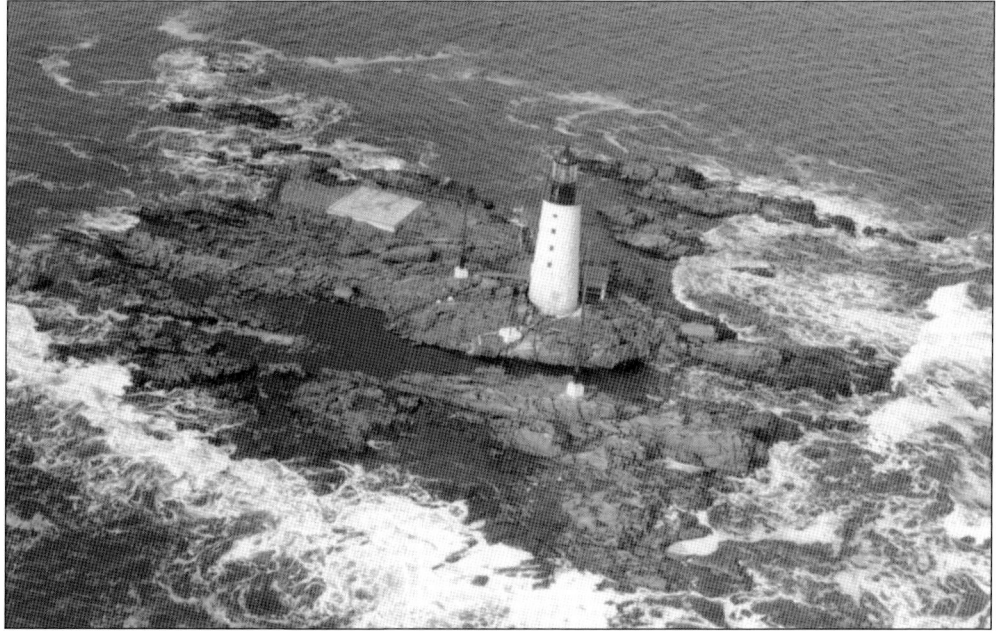

This view is from 1966. By this time, the fog bell tower and oil house had been removed and a helicopter pad had been added. During a spell of murky weather in July 1972, the foghorn blasted for 10 seconds every minute for about two weeks. "You just learn to live with it, and think about something else," said one of the crew. (US Coast Guard Historian's Office.)

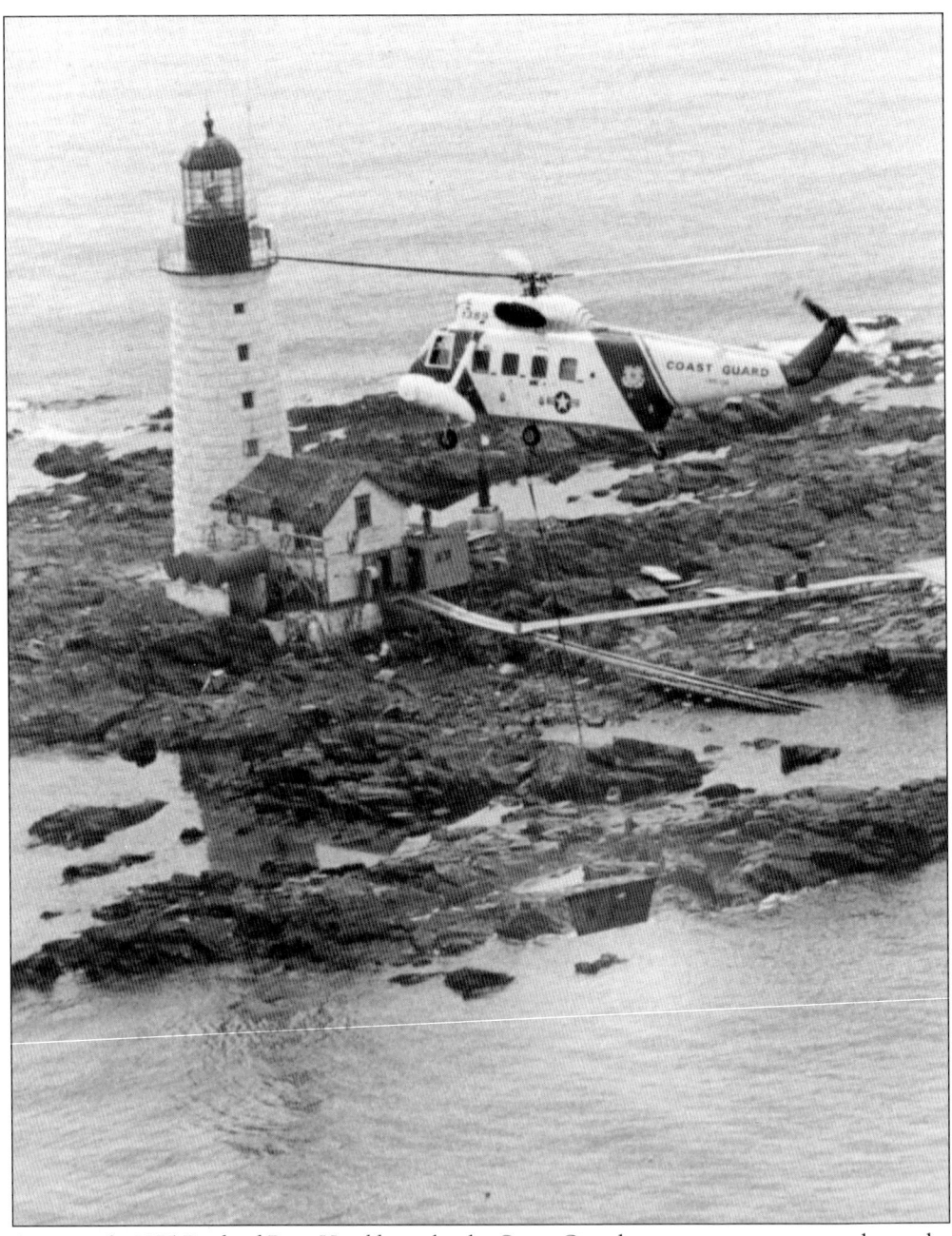

At time of a 1975 *Portland Press Herald* article, the Coast Guard crewmen spent two weeks on the station followed by a week off. The men maintained the equipment and buildings and radioed in weather reports to South Portland every three hours. One of the keepers, 27-year-old Stephen Krikorian, told the *Portland Press Herald* about some of the unusual ways the keepers passed the lonely hours. He picked up a basketball that had washed ashore. "There are 2,448 pimples on this," he said. "I counted 'em. It took a day." The men kept a chart in the house with the heading "House Fly Killings." One of the other crewmen, Ronald Handfield, held the record of 257 fly killings in two months. The keepers were removed for good later in 1975, and the light was automated with a modern DCB 224 optic. This photograph is from 1979. (US Coast Guard.)

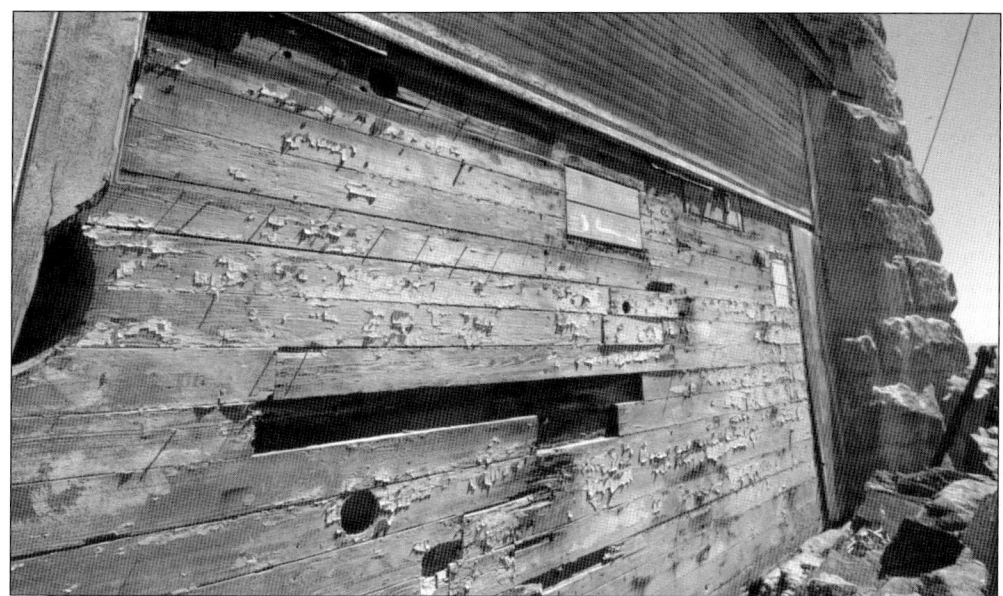

The 1888 wooden boathouse fell into severe disrepair following automation. In June 2004, Maine Preservation named the lighthouse as one of the state's most endangered properties. The lighthouse was made available to a new owner under the guidelines of the National Historic Lighthouse Preservation Act, but there were no applicants. As a result, it was put up for sale via online auction in May 2014. This picture was taken in 2013. (Photograph by the author.)

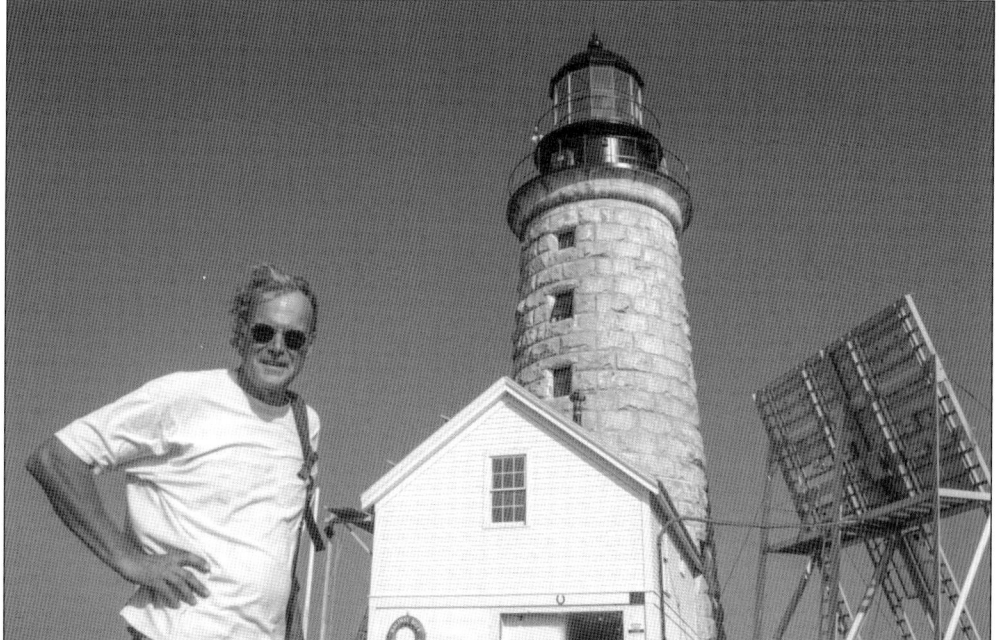

The auction ended in September 2014 with a high bid of $283,000, the most ever paid at auction for a Maine lighthouse. The new owner, Ford Reiche (pictured), is a trustee of Maine Preservation with experience in restoring historic homes. Bob Trapani Jr., of the American Lighthouse Foundation, commented, "Ford was its last hope, really. Thirty years from now, this will be seen as a historic moment." (Photograph by the author.)

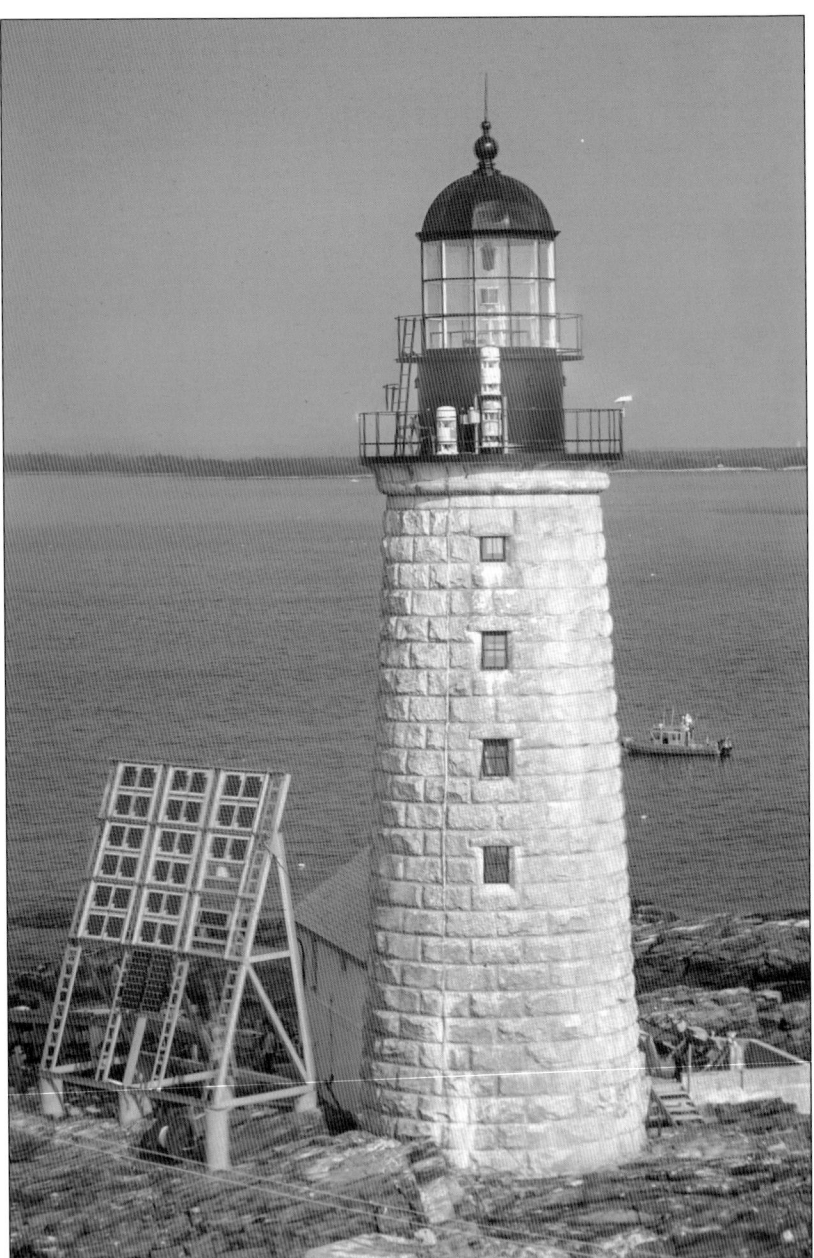

In his first year of ownership, Ford Reiche accomplished the building of an 80-foot boat ramp and the complete exterior and interior restoration of the attached two-story wooden building. In the summer of 2017, the tower was repointed, and the interior was painted. Reiche earned the American Lighthouse Foundation's Keeper of the Light Award in May 2017. The award is "designed to honor those individuals and organizations in the national lighthouse community who have contributed in a significant manner to the preservation of America's lighthouses and their rich heritage." When asked why he took on the project, Reiche told *Preservation* magazine, "If someone could have turned it into a business venture, it would have been saved already. But this is historically important. And it would be tragic not to restore it." He has established a website at www.halfwayrock.com. (Photograph by the author.)

Six
GRAVES

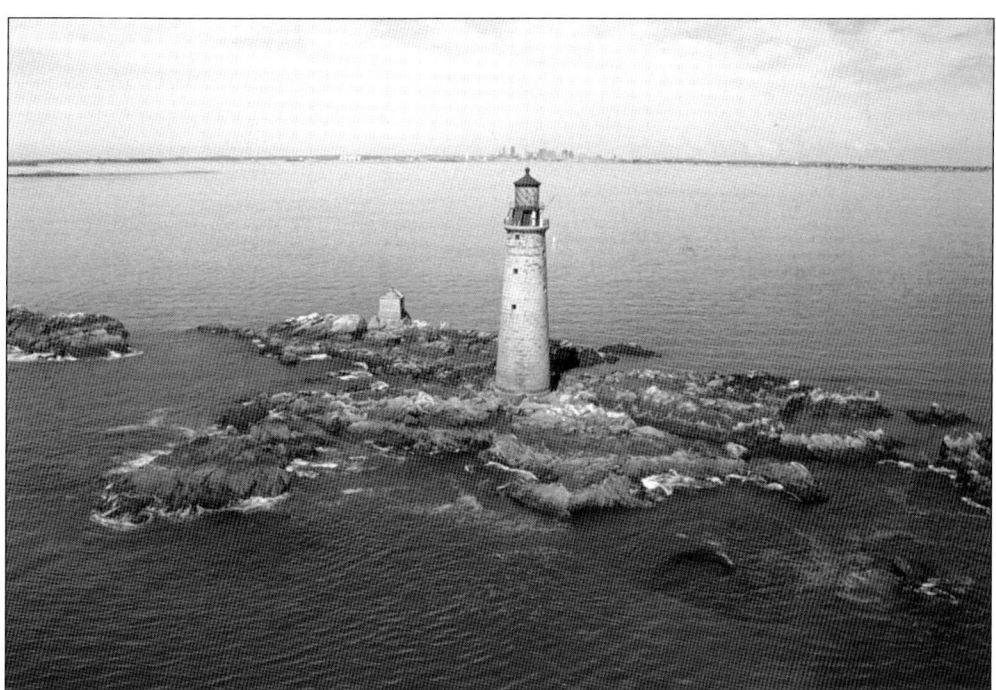

The ledges called the Graves, in outer Boston Harbor, Massachusetts, are not named for a resemblance to gravestones or because of a high incidence of fatal shipwrecks. They were named for Rear Adm. Thomas Graves, who came to the continent from London in 1628 and was an early settler in Charlestown, Massachusetts. As early as 1634, Graves noted the danger the ledges presented to navigation. This photograph is from June 2001. (Photograph by the author.)

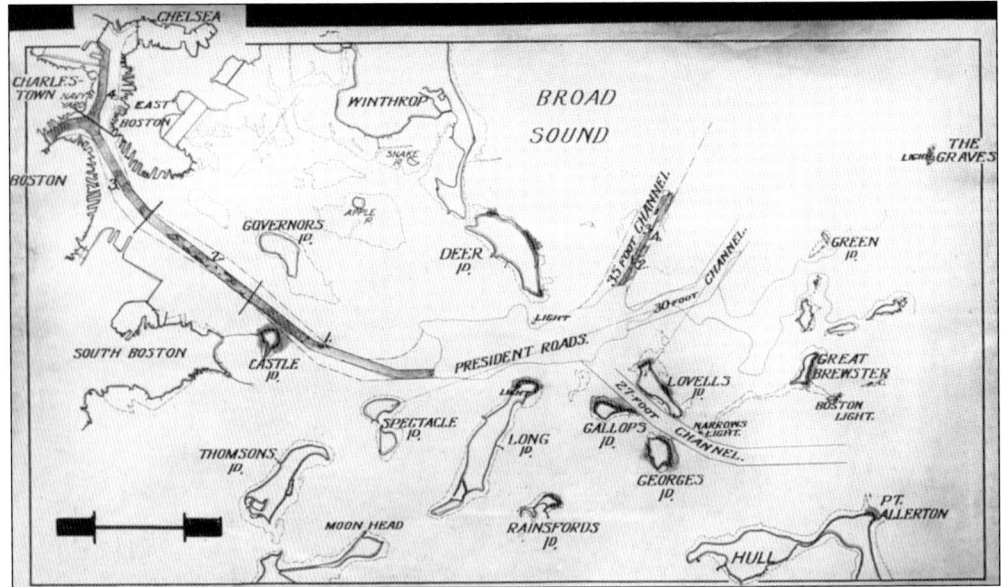

The Broad Sound Channel into Boston Harbor, passing north of the Graves, was improved in the early 20th century so that larger ships could enter the harbor. Before then, the main entrance to the busy harbor was through the Narrows between Point Allerton in Hull and the outer harbor islands. (Dave Waller.)

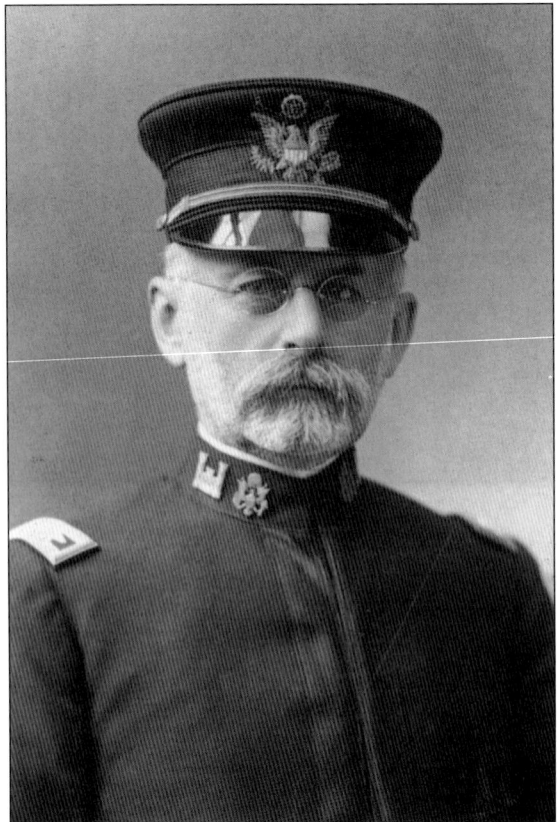

In 1902, Congress appropriated $75,000 for a lighthouse at the Graves. The project ultimately cost $188,000. Construction took place from 1903 to 1905, and Col. William S. Stanton, engineer for the Second Lighthouse District, oversaw the operations. During a long career that began in the 1860s, Stanton was involved in the construction of many lighthouses and forts. (National Archives.)

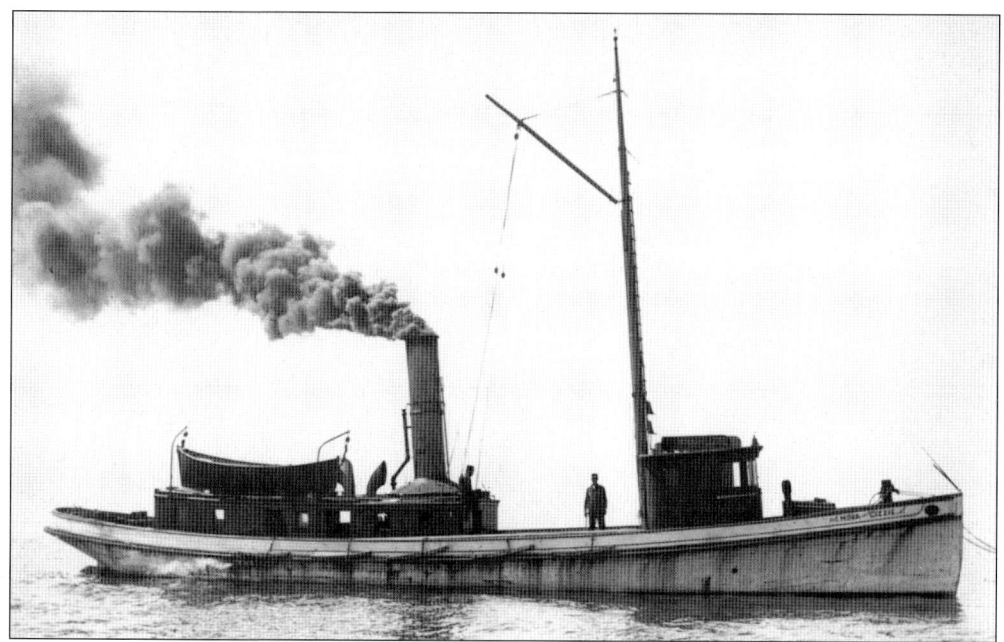

A temporary wharf and quarters for the workers were built at the Lovell's Island buoy depot in the harbor. A small steam vessel, shown here, provided transportation between Lovell's Island and the Graves for workers and materials. Congress appropriated another $113,000 for the lighthouse in April 1904. (National Archives.)

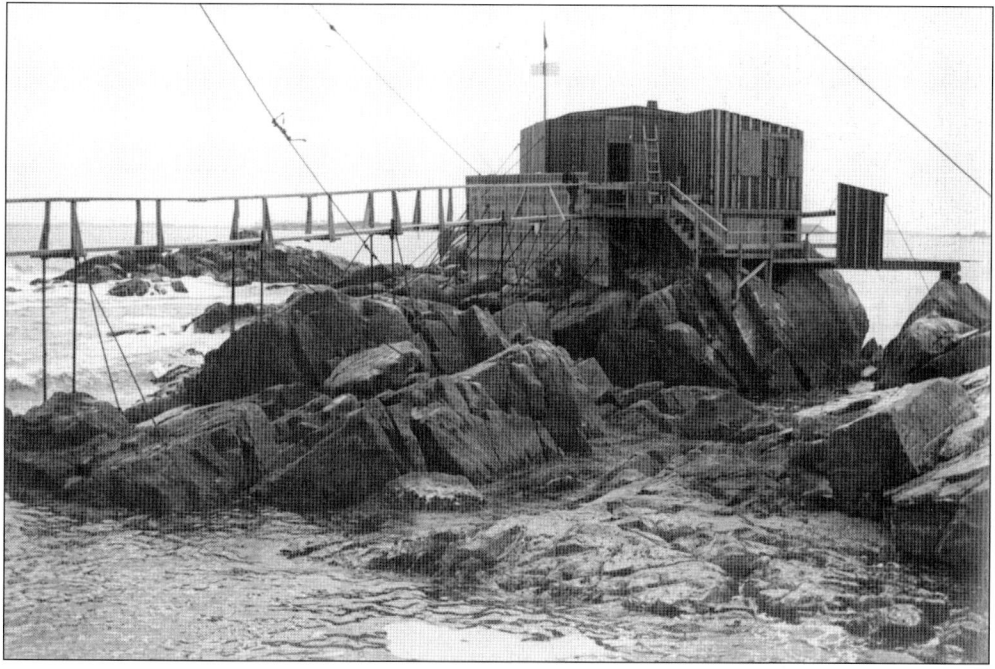

A shanty for the workmen was erected on a high ledge southwest of the lighthouse site and could be accessed by means of a 90-foot walkway. The shanty had living quarters, a storeroom, a blacksmith shop, and a kitchen, and the workers lived there in the summers of 1903 and 1904. (National Archives.)

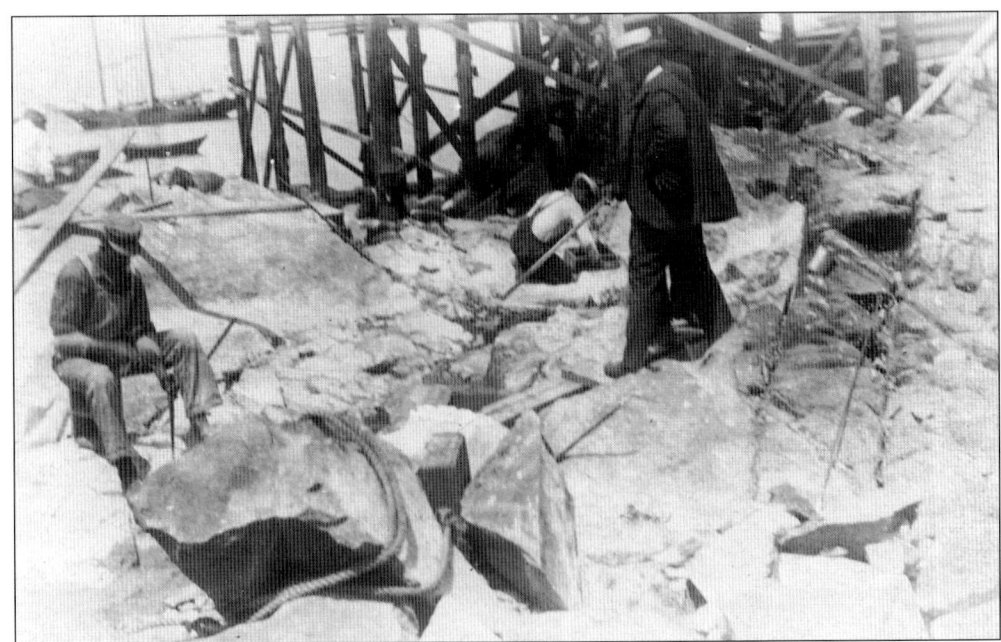

Royal Luther (shown at right), superintendent of the First and Second Lighthouse Districts since 1875, was the superintendent of construction. Luther was a native of nearby Malden, Massachusetts. In his final report on the building of Graves Light, Col. William S. Stanton praises the "excellent management and unremitting care" of Luther. (Dolly Bicknell.)

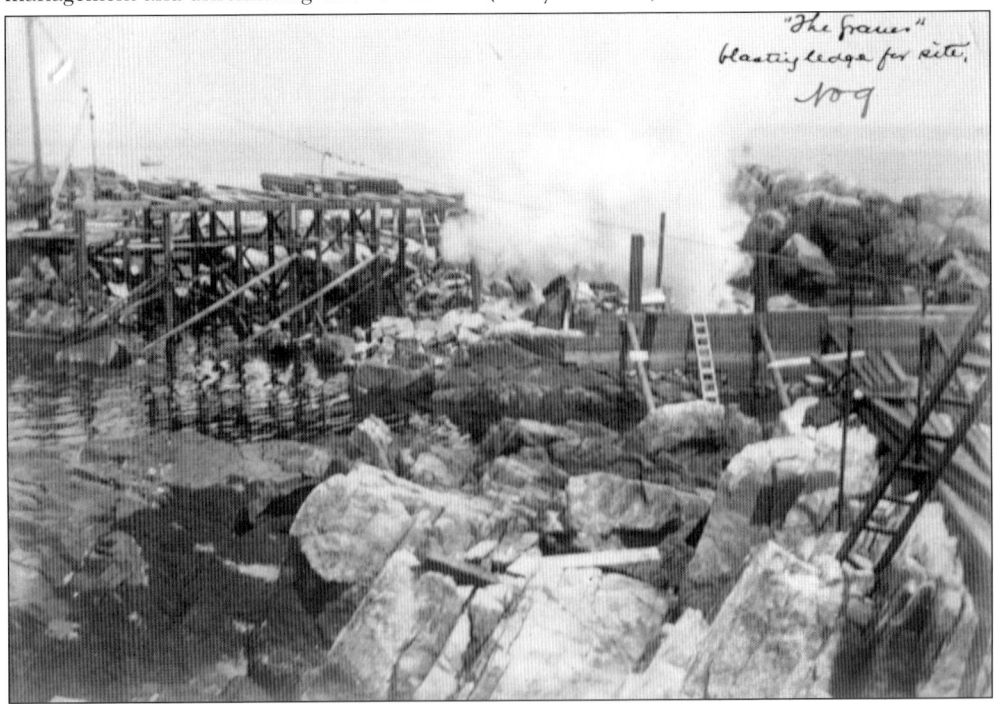

This photograph shows blasting taking place on the ledge in preparation for the laying of the tower's foundation. The plans called for the tower to be built on a foundation that was only three feet above mean low water, with 882 granite blocks laid in 44 courses. (National Archives.)

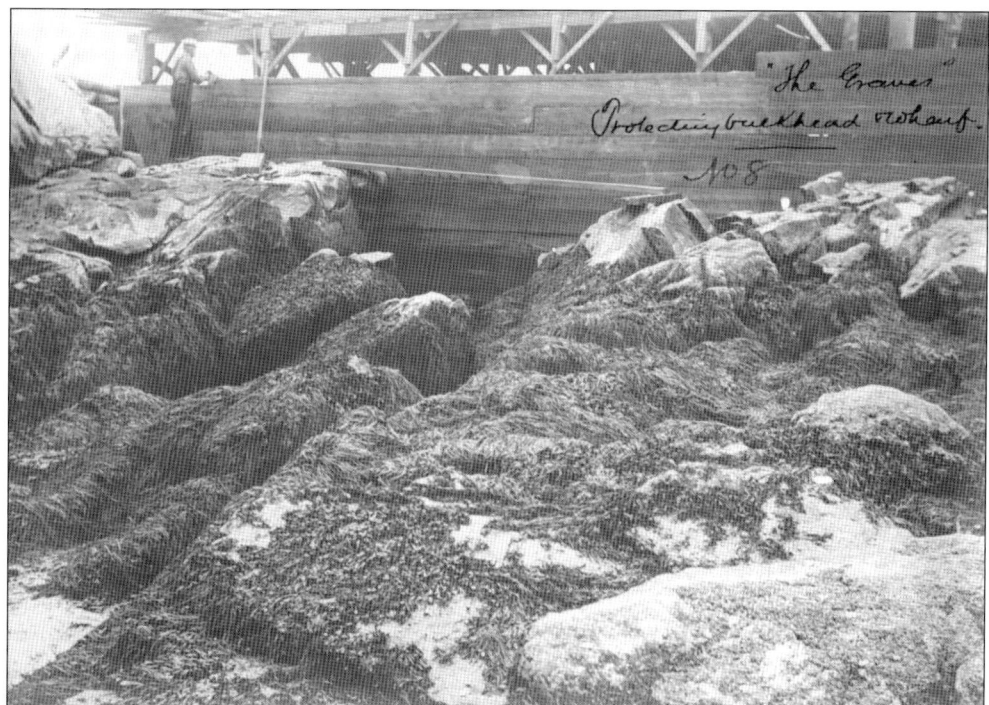

A temporary wharf was built at the ledge along with two bulkheads that protected the site from ocean waves. The bulkheads consisted of yellow pine planks spiked to pine posts that were anchored in the rock with iron bolts. A steam-powered derrick was installed on the wharf. (National Archives.)

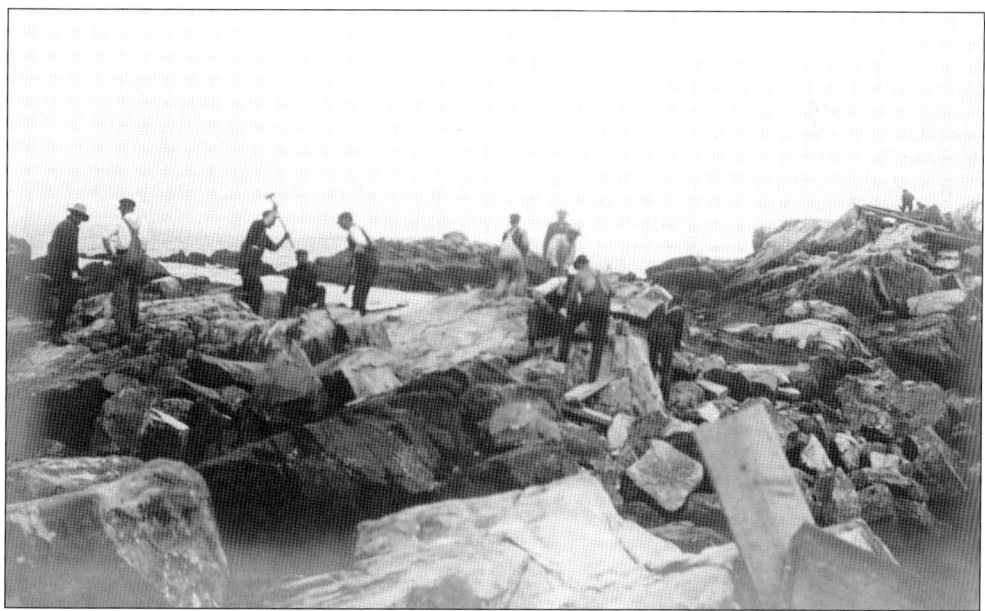

Having the workers living at the site meant constant progress with construction, which was dependent only upon the delivery of materials. The schooner *A.J. Miller* transported the granite to the site beginning on August 11, 1903. (National Archives.)

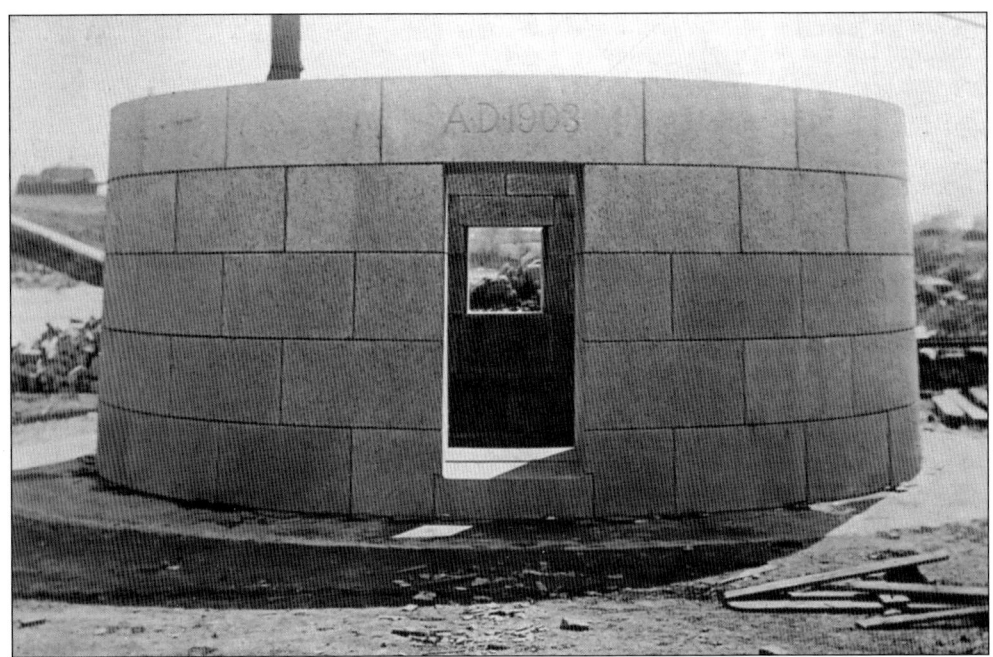

The granite was cut and prepared at a quarry in Rockport, Cape Ann, Massachusetts. Col. William S. Stanton reported that in one instance, when the tide and seas were favorable, one entire course of granite along with a supply of broken stone and sand—amounting to 170 tons in all—was discharged from a schooner in 33 minutes. (National Archives.)

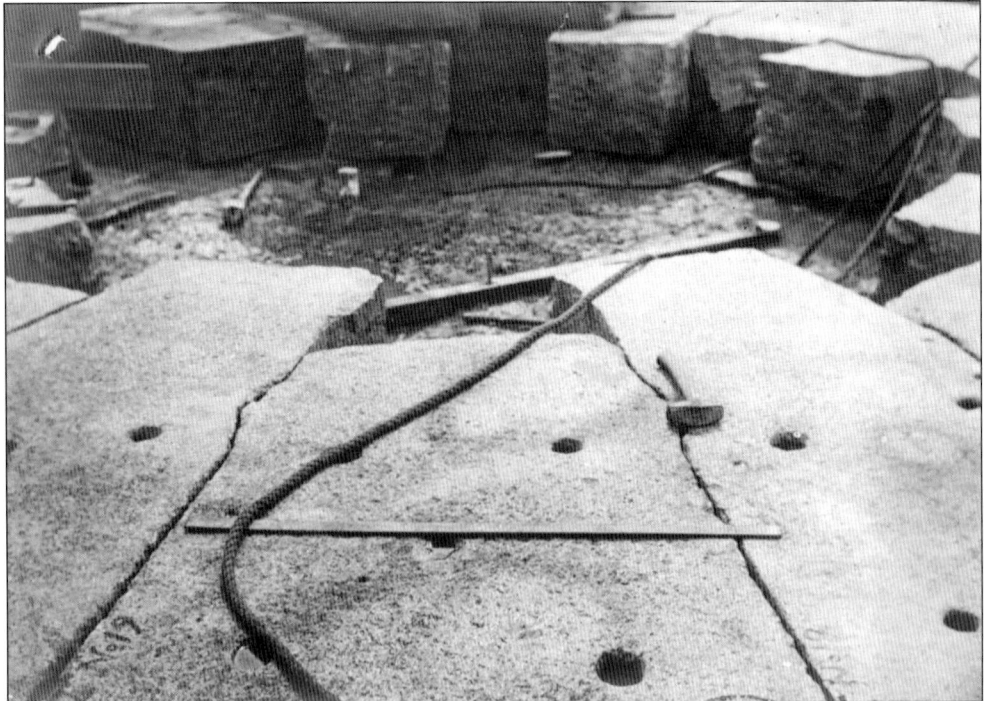

The foundation for the lighthouse tower was laid just four feet above the low tide mark, and the lower granite courses were bolted three feet deep into the ledge. (National Archives.)

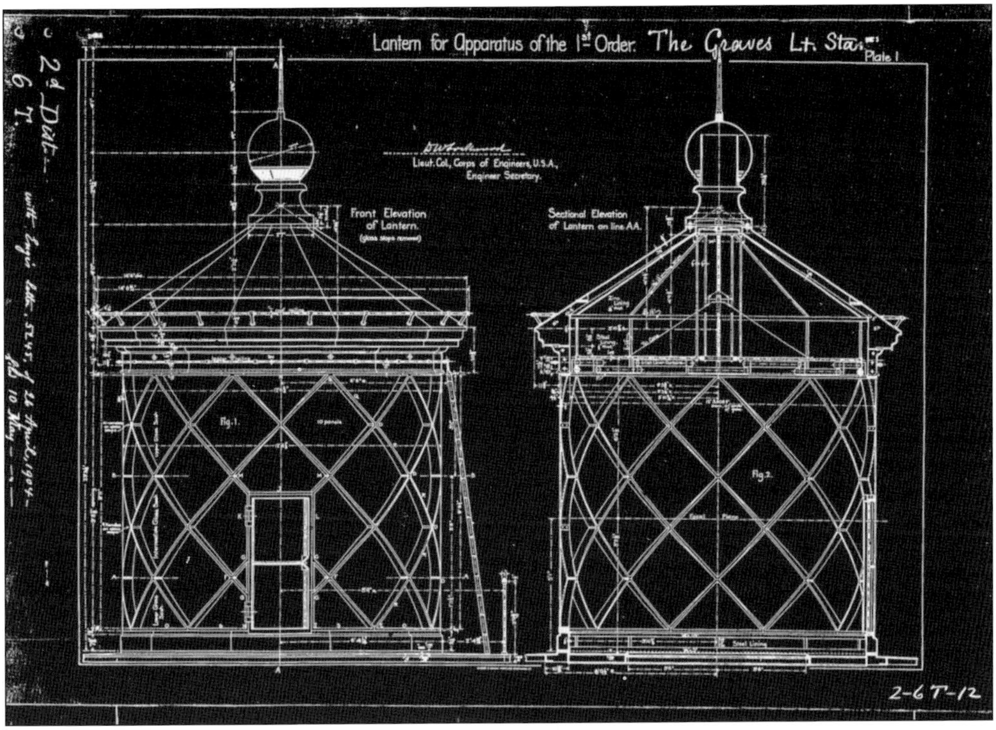

While the tower was under construction, interior ironwork and an exterior ladder for the lighthouse were being prepared in Boston, and interior woodwork was fashioned at a facility in Portland, Maine. These are the plans for the lantern, which was constructed in Milwaukee, Wisconsin. (National Archives.)

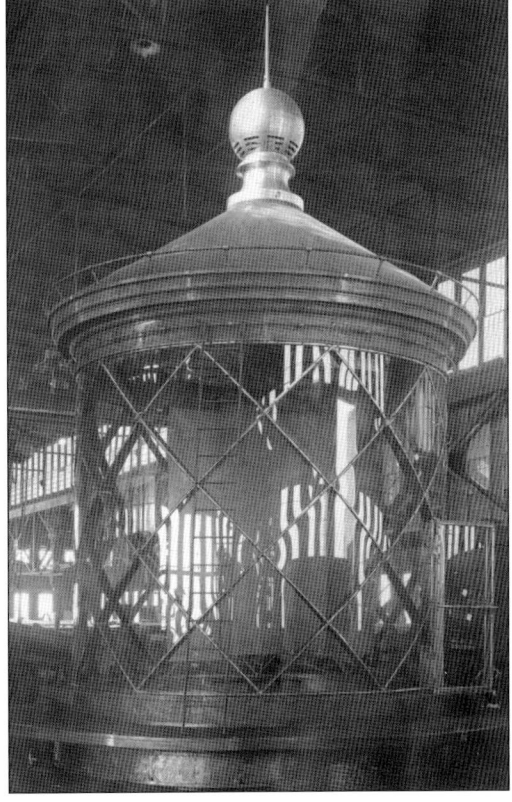

This photograph shows the lantern under construction. The diamond-shaped panes were fairly unusual for an American lighthouse. The lantern was built large enough to accommodate an enormous first-order Fresnel lens that was being created in Paris, France. The lens rotated on a bed of about 400 pounds of mercury. (National Archives.)

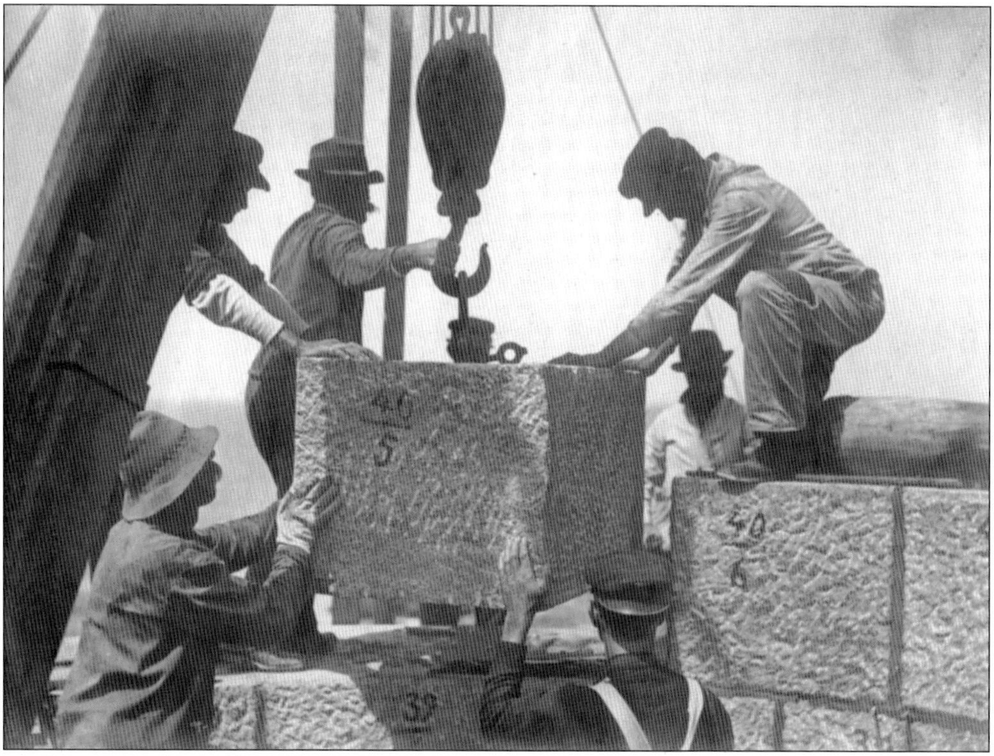

Work continued into the fall of 1903. Each granite block was carefully prepared and numbered at the quarry before being delivered to Graves Ledge. By the time the summer of 1903 was over, the first 42 feet (21 courses) of the tower were completed, the blocks having been put into place with the aid of the hoisting engine and derrick. (National Archives.)

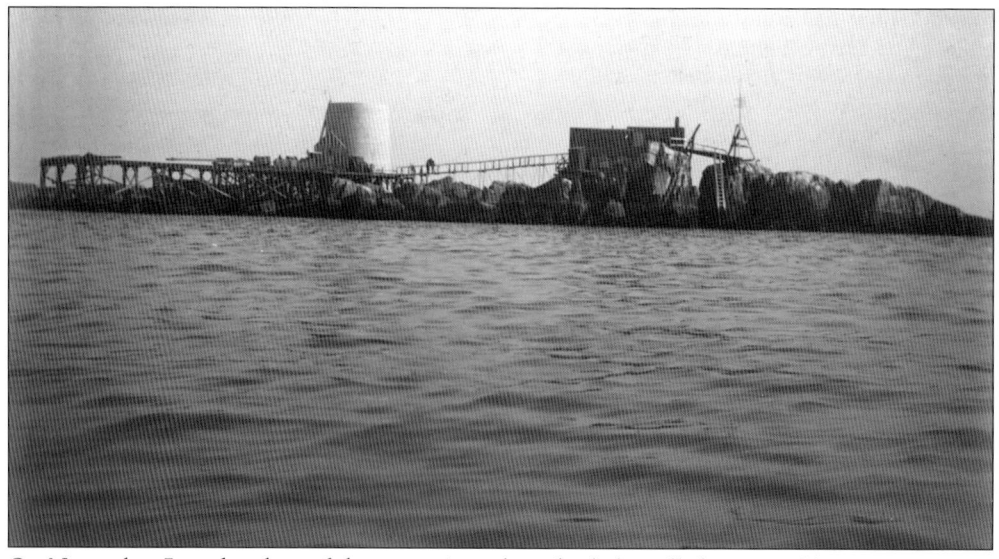

On November 7, at the close of the season's work at the ledge, all the moveable equipment was taken to the depot at Lovell's Island for the winter. The tower is just over 30 feet in diameter at the base, and the lower stones are seven feet thick. The lower 42-foot section of the tower was filled with concrete, with space left for a cistern. (National Archives.)

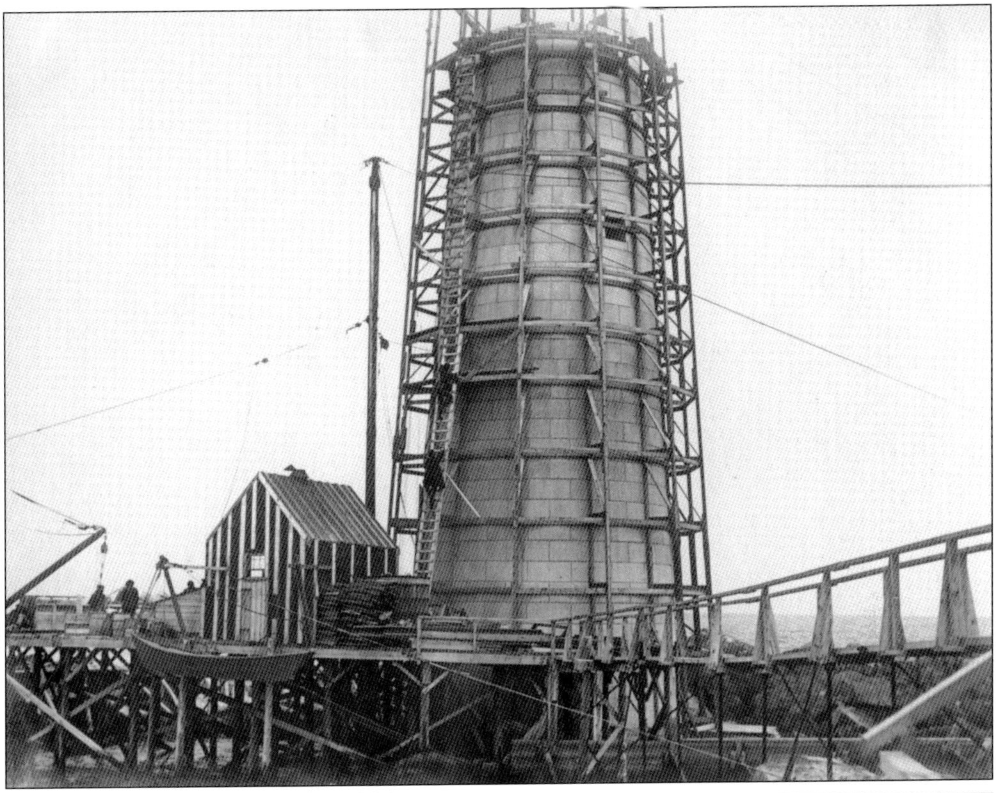

Work recommenced on April 1, 1904. Despite an interruption by a storm late that month, work progressed rapidly until the end of June. By that time, 44 courses of granite had been completed. This brought the granite tower to its full height of 88 feet. During the rest of the 1904 season, the interior stairs, floors, and enameled brick walls were installed. (National Archives.)

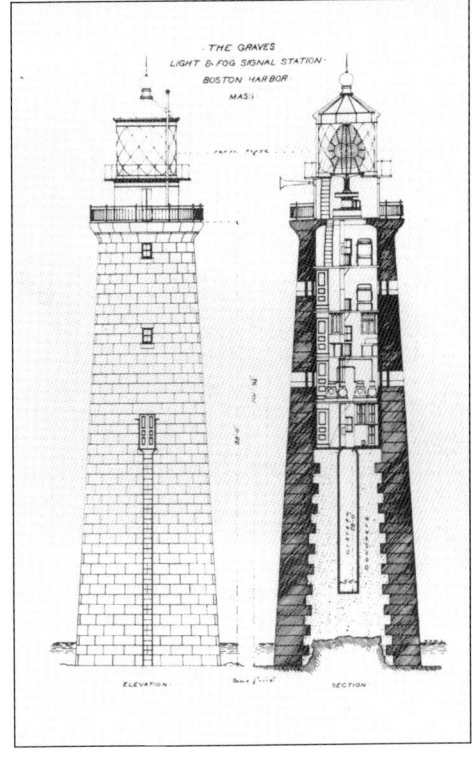

The lantern was delivered in March 1905, and it was installed in May and June. The lens and rotating machinery were in place by the end of July. A fog signal was also installed at the top of the tower; it was a Daboll trumpet operated by compressed air, with compressors and oil engines installed in duplicate. (National Archives.)

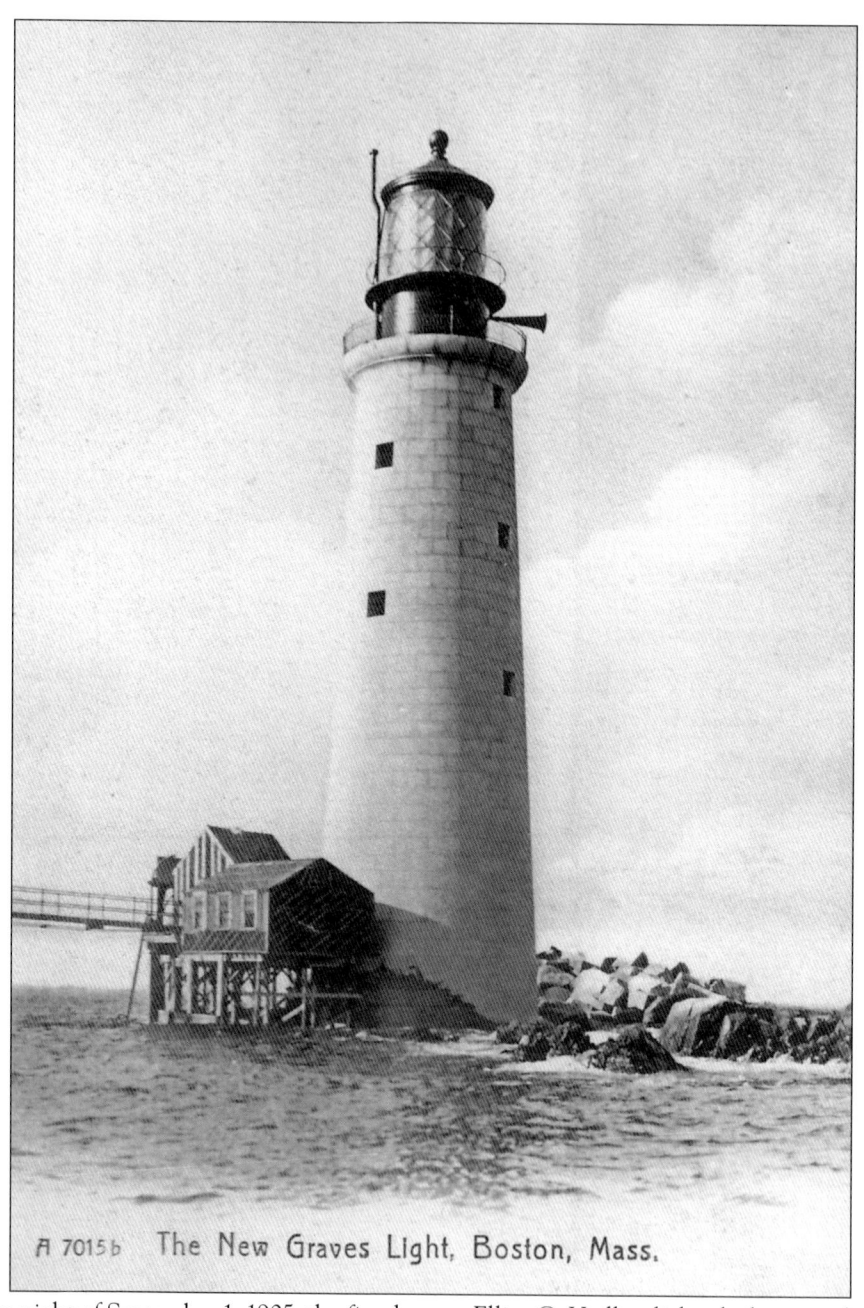

A 7015b The New Graves Light, Boston, Mass.

On the night of September 1, 1905, the first keeper, Elliot C. Hadley, lighted what was then the most powerful lighthouse in the state's history. A 1905 Lighthouse Board report states: "At so exposed a site the height necessary for the lantern above the heavier masses of spray, the consequent geographic range, its location so far seaward, the service of the light to the large commerce of Boston and modern ships of deep draft, make it perhaps the most important light north of Cape Cod." The total height of the tower—lantern included—is 113 feet. The focal plane of the lens, exhibiting a double flash every six seconds, was 98 feet above mean high water. The light was initially rated at 380,000 candlepower. It was later upgraded to 3.2 million candlepower, and it was, for many years, the most powerful light in New England. (Author's collection.)

This 1941 photograph shows visitors climbing the 30-foot ladder to enter the lighthouse. The first story was storage space, the second was the engine room containing the fog signal equipment, and the third was the galley (kitchen). The fourth and fifth levels contained the keepers' beds and a library. (Dolly Bicknell.)

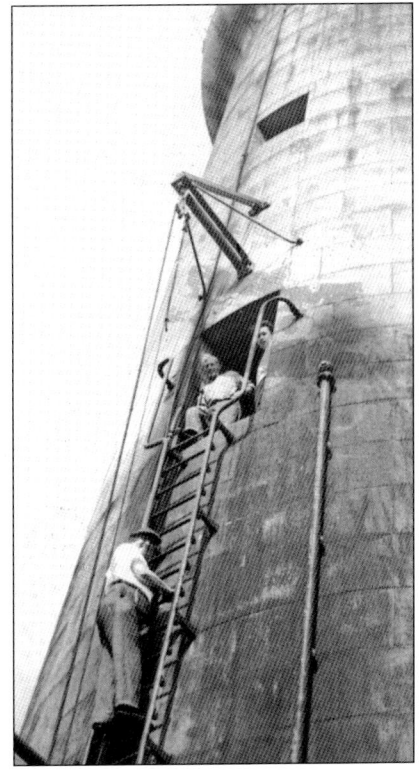

First keeper Elliot C. Hadley described the conditions in storms: "I've looked up at solid water rushing in towards the ledges. . . . I don't know how far up the solid water comes. I've been knocked down by it on the wharf beside the light, and opening a window to look out more than halfway up the tower, I've had as much as three buckets-full dashed in my face." (National Archives.)

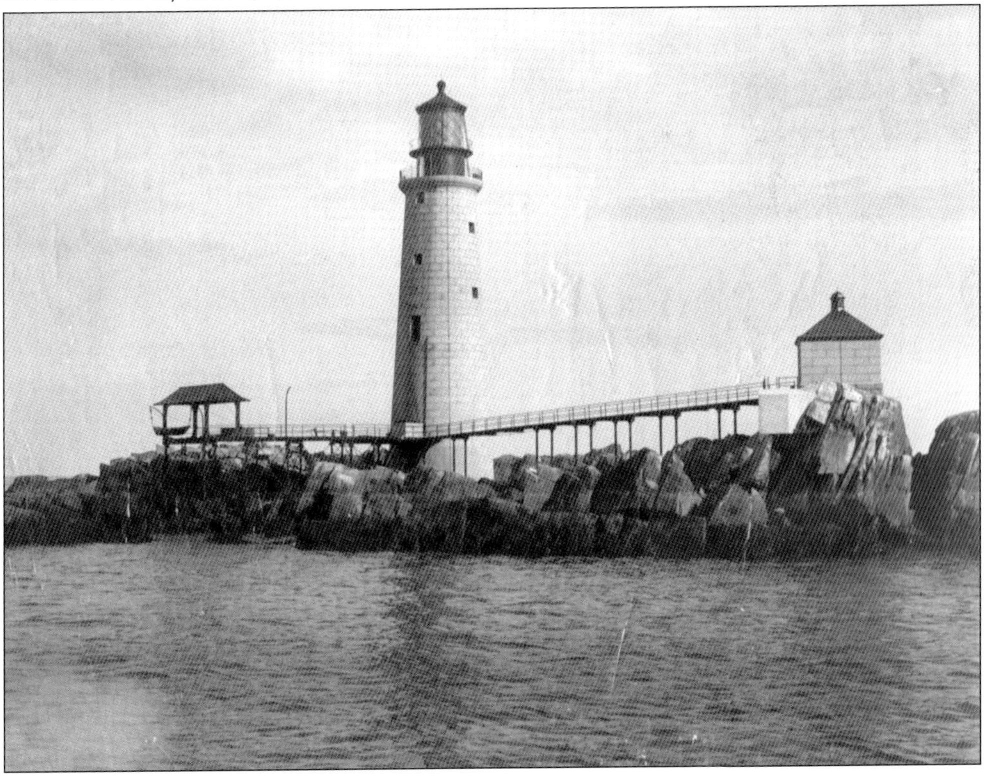

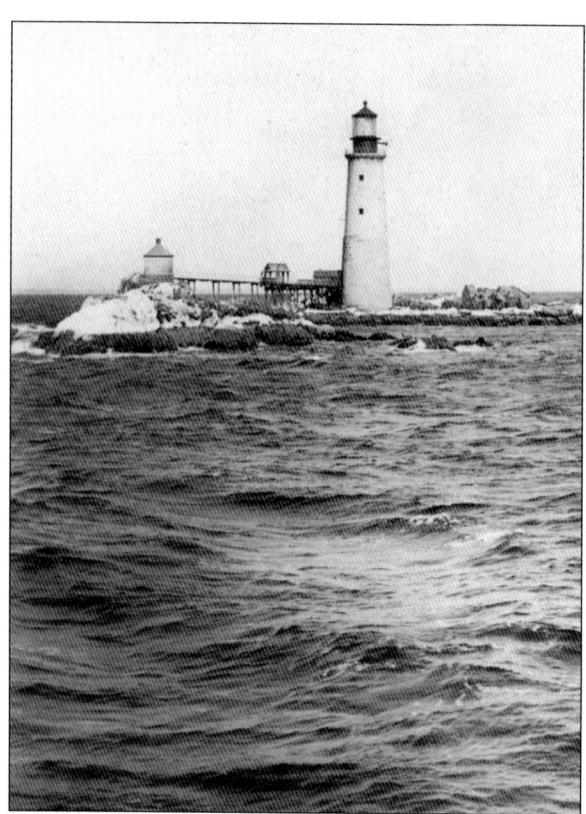

In December 1916, first assistant keeper Harry Whin was alone at the lighthouse and running short on supplies when a ferocious storm struck. Whin had already been on the station for over 70 days and was weeks overdue to be relieved. He was reduced to eating almost nothing but fish and smoking rope and tea leaves in his pipe. (National Archives.)

Pictured here are first assistant keeper George Fitzpatrick (left) and principal keeper Octavius Reamy at a 30th anniversary celebration for Graves Light held on September 1, 1935. By this time, Graves Light was connected to the outside world with radio equipment and a telephone. Two months after the celebration, a storm moved giant three-ton stones and deposited them near the lighthouse. (Dolly Bicknell.)

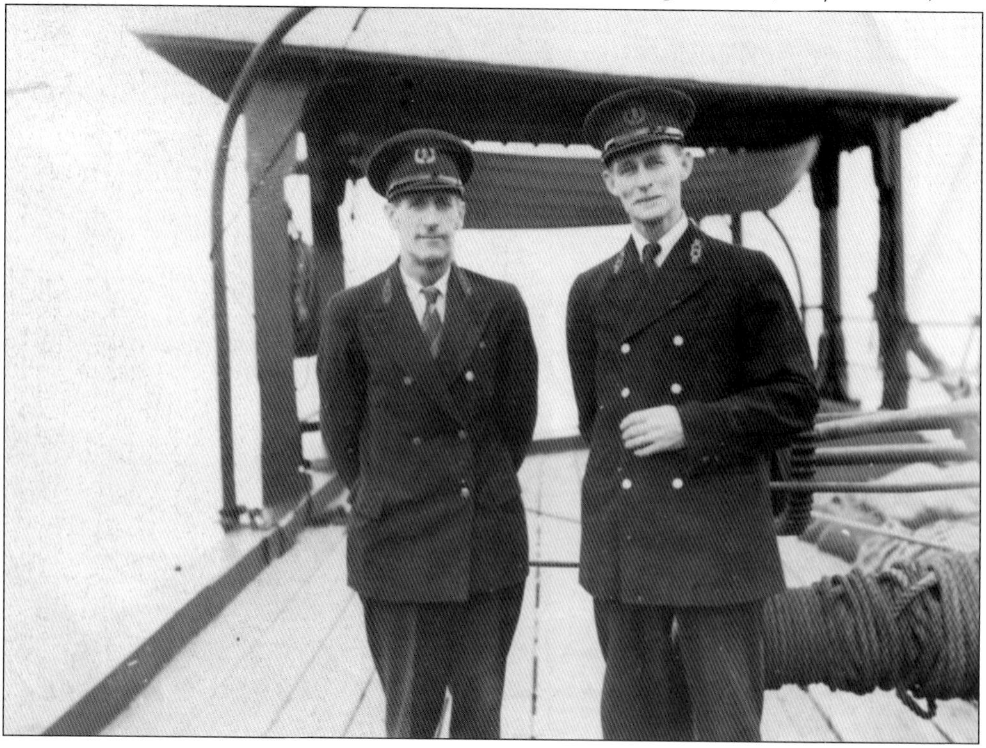

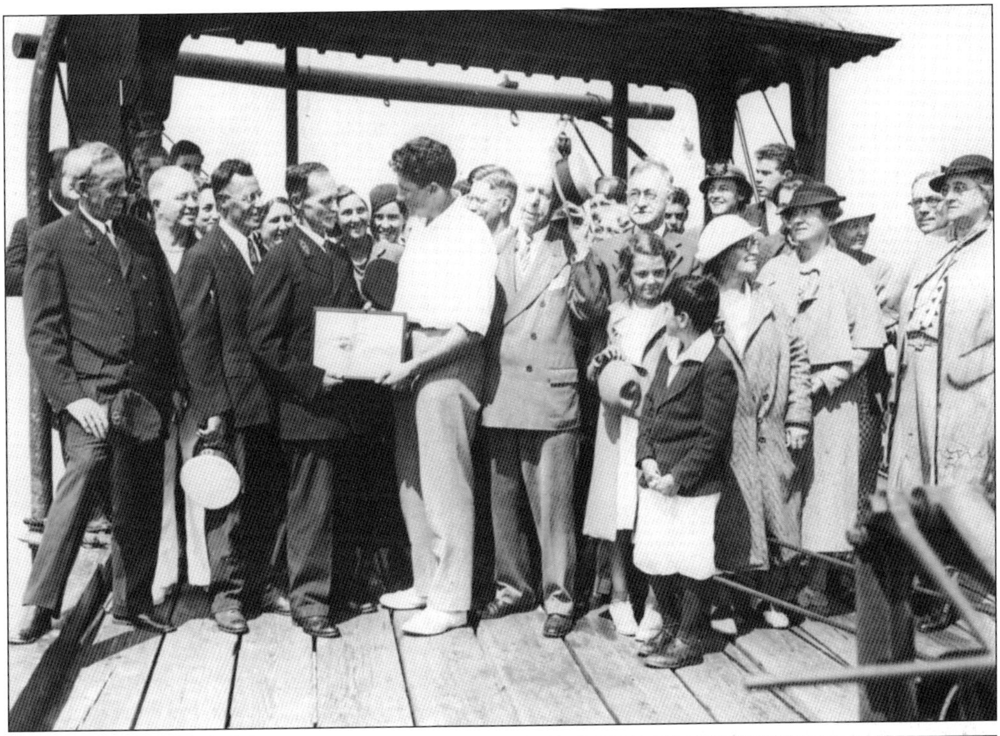

On September 1, 1935, historian Edward Rowe Snow (in the center of the photograph, wearing a white shirt) presents an award to the keepers on the occasion of Graves Light's 30th anniversary. At far left is Maurice Babcock, keeper at nearby Boston Light from 1926 to 1941. (Dolly Bicknell.)

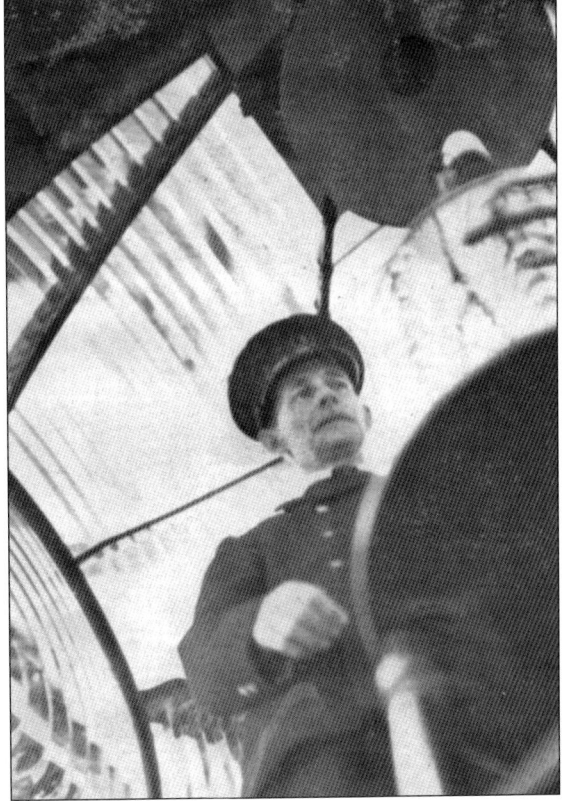

This photograph, taken by historian Edward Rowe Snow, shows keeper Octavius Reamy inside the first-order Fresnel lens at Graves Light in 1935. The lens, manufactured by Barbier, Bénard, and Turenne of Paris, France, is now in storage at the Smithsonian Institution in Washington, DC. The lens produced a double white flash every six seconds. (Dolly Bicknell.)

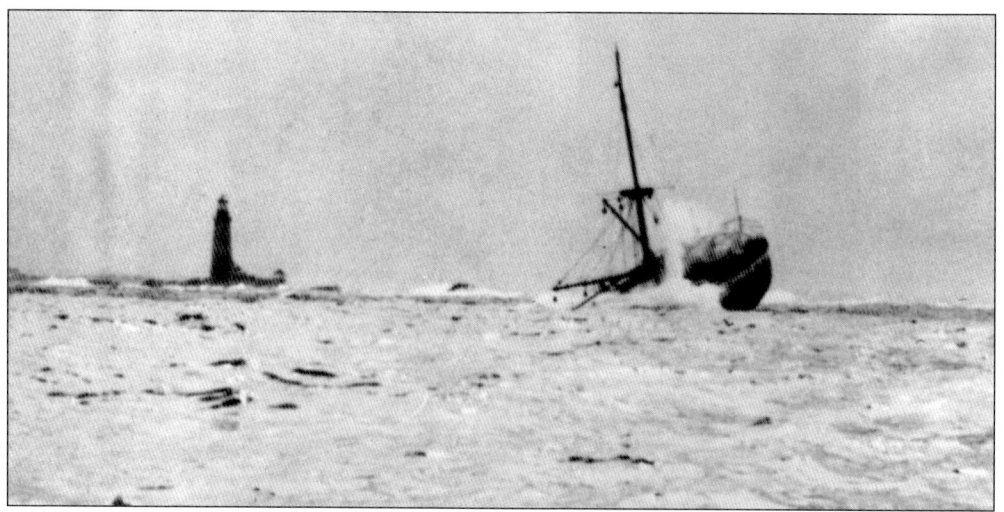

In April 1938, the 419-foot British freighter *City of Salisbury*, recalled as the "Zoo Ship" for its cargo of zoo animals, struck an uncharted rock near the Graves. Most of the animals were rescued, but many monkeys and snakes later died from the effects of the accident. The ship became a tourist attraction for a few months before it finally split in two and sank. (Dave Waller.)

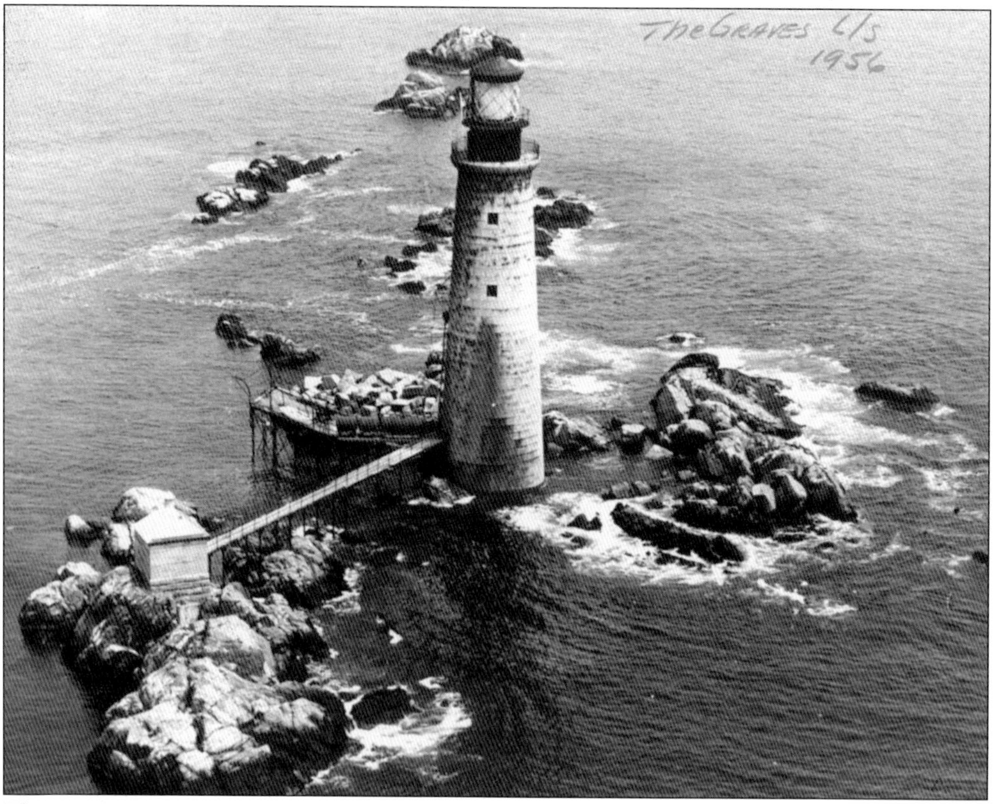

The US Coast Guard took over the management of lighthouses in the United States in 1939. During the Coast Guard era, there were generally three men assigned to Graves Light, with two keepers on duty at all times; each man spent two or three weeks at the lighthouse followed by a week off. (US Coast Guard.)

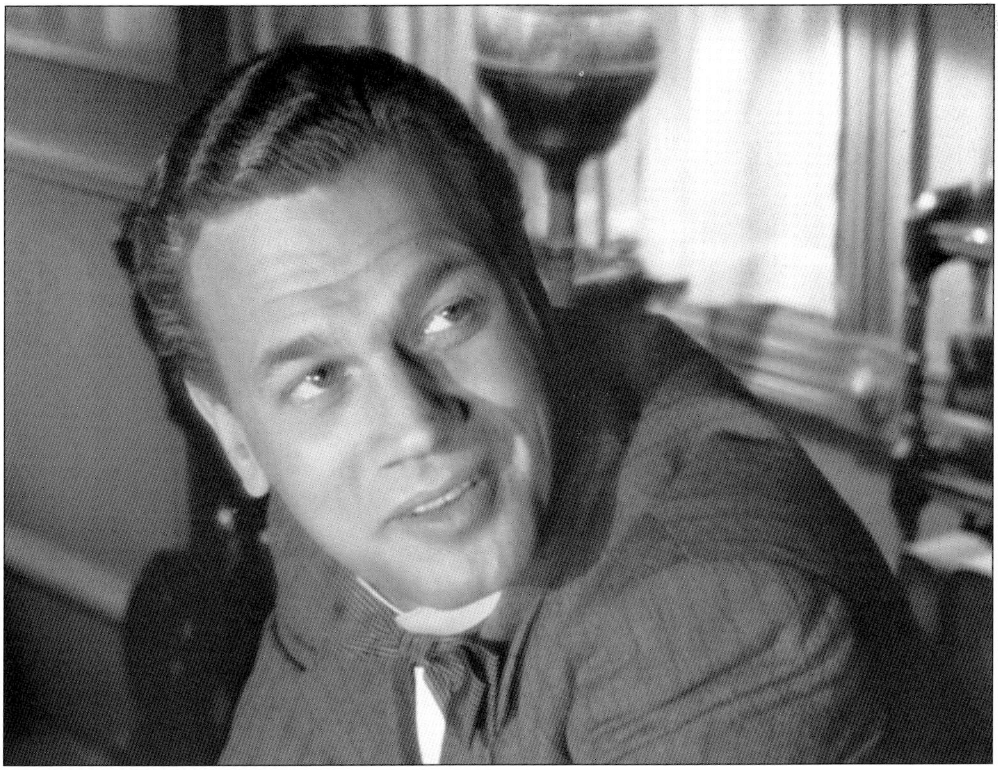

In 1947, the Coast Guard crew had some unusual entertainment when the lighthouse served as a filming location for *Portrait of Jennie*, starring Joseph Cotten (shown here) and Jennifer Jones. The climax of the movie takes place on the ledges around the lighthouse as Cotten's character looks for his lost love, Jennie. (Author's collection.)

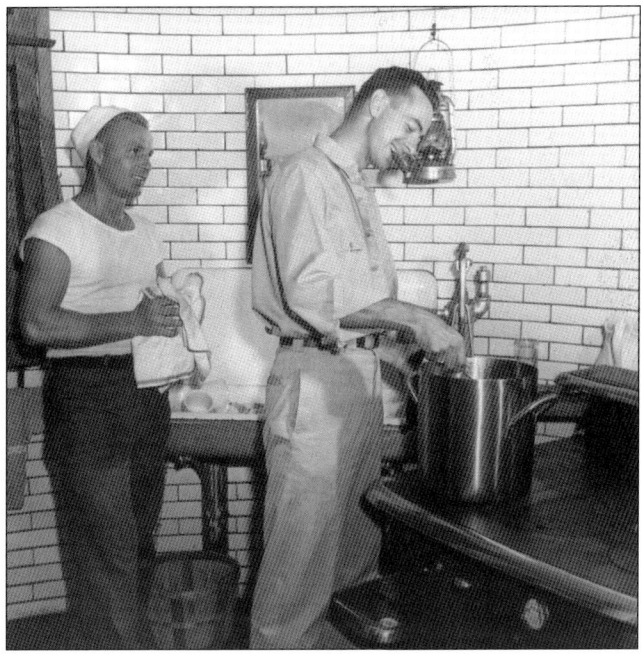

Larry Bowers, a Coast Guard keeper in the early 1960s, later recalled the time he and a fellow keeper got a turkey for Thanksgiving. Neither had prepared one before. "We stuffed the wrong end," said Bowers. "Just couldn't figure out why we couldn't get all the stuffing in. We made mashed potatoes, veggies enough for an army." This picture was taken around 1945. (Photograph by Arthur Griffin; Griffin Museum of Photography.)

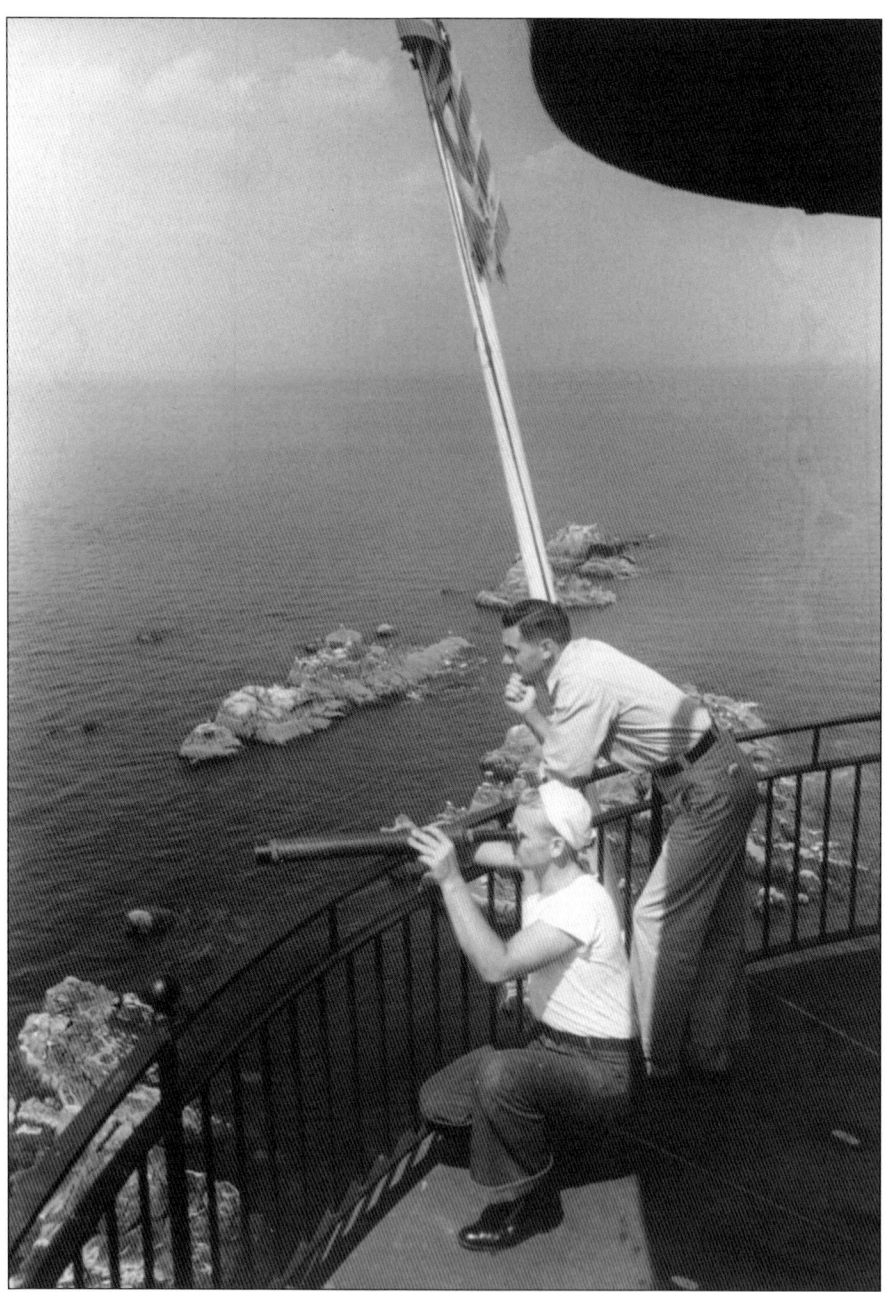

Visits from a buoy tender, which brought water and fuel, were welcomed at the wave-swept location. "Except," according to Larry Bowers, "one time when they pumped fuel into the water tank. No fun on that one. Number two diesel takes a long time to get out of a cistern. We had to pump it dry, and clean it, whitewash it and bleach it. Still didn't help much. We only used that tank in emergencies." Lou Reich, who was stationed at Graves Light in 1965, later recalled, "There was a lot of sanding and painting to be done to keep the iron railings from rusting." The foghorn was hard to forget. "A person can actually get used to sleeping through a night where the fog horn was blasting all night long," said Reich. This picture was taken around 1945. (Photograph by Arthur Griffin; Griffin Museum of Photography.)

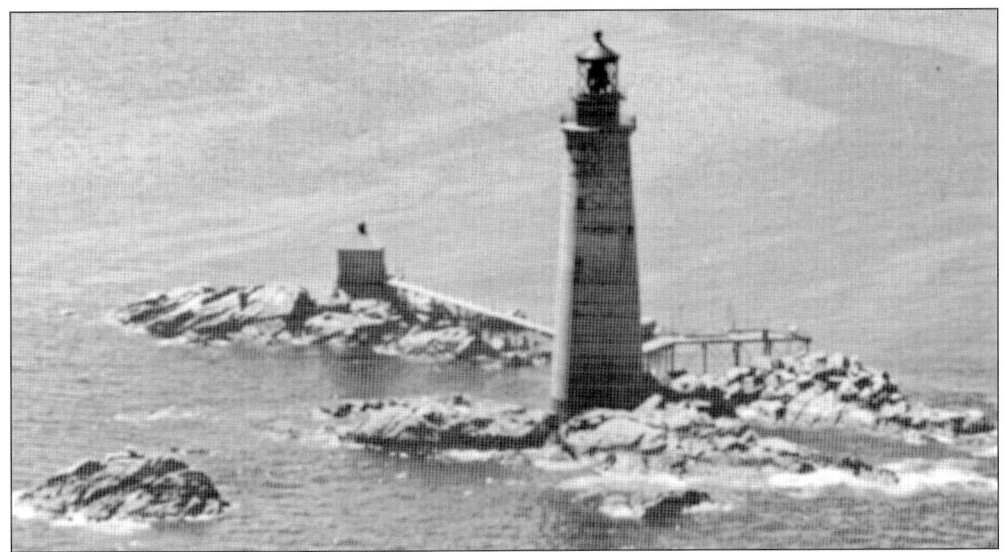

Pedro Marticio, the last Coast Guard keeper at Graves Light, captured this aerial view. "I was there for two tours of duty," he said later. "I closed it down the first time due to a mercury spill, and after the light was decontaminated I went out for another year." The Fresnel lens, replaced by modern equipment when the light was automated in 1976, now sits in storage at the Smithsonian Institution. (Pedro Marticio.)

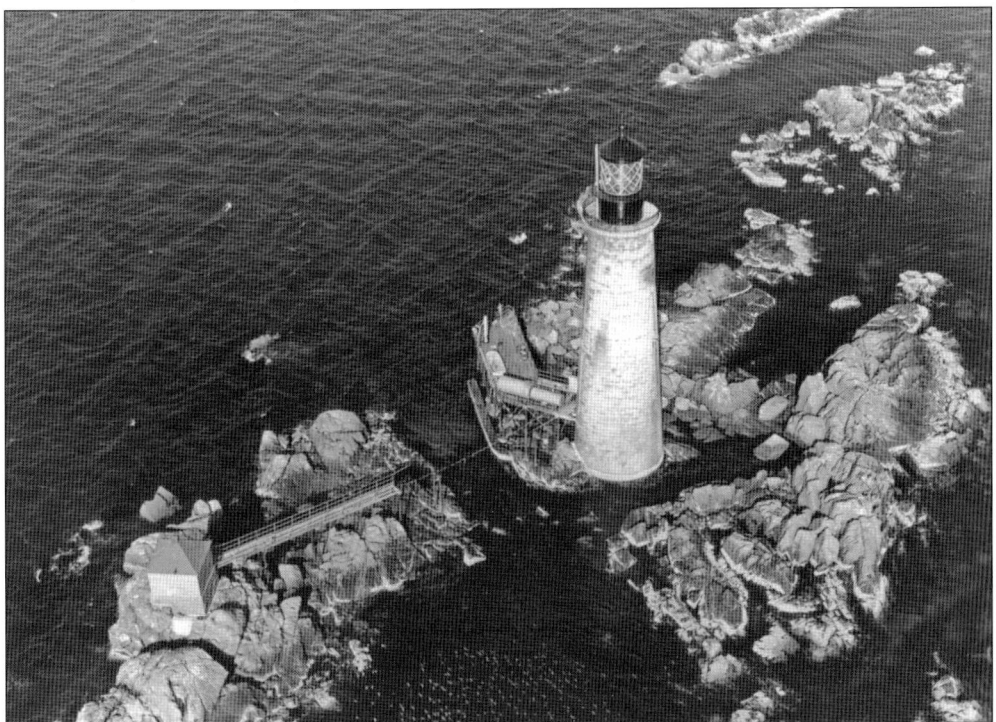

This photograph is from 1974. Over the years, storms destroyed the walkway that led to the station's oil house. For a period beginning in 1983, the light was powered by an emergency generator because of damage to the submarine electrical cable connected to the town of Hull. (US Coast Guard.)

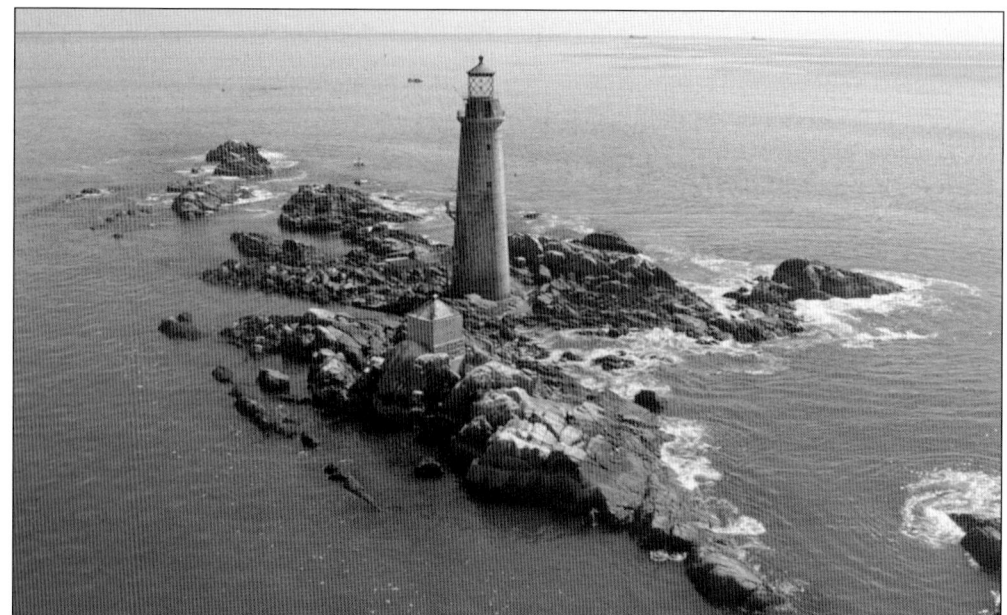

In 1984, four members of the Coast Guard's Aids to Navigation Team Boston had to make an emergency Christmas Eve trip when the light failed and were nearly trapped by rough seas. The officer in charge said, "Four guys almost spent Christmas in a lighthouse instead of at home with their families." The light was converted to solar power in 2001. (Photograph by the author.)

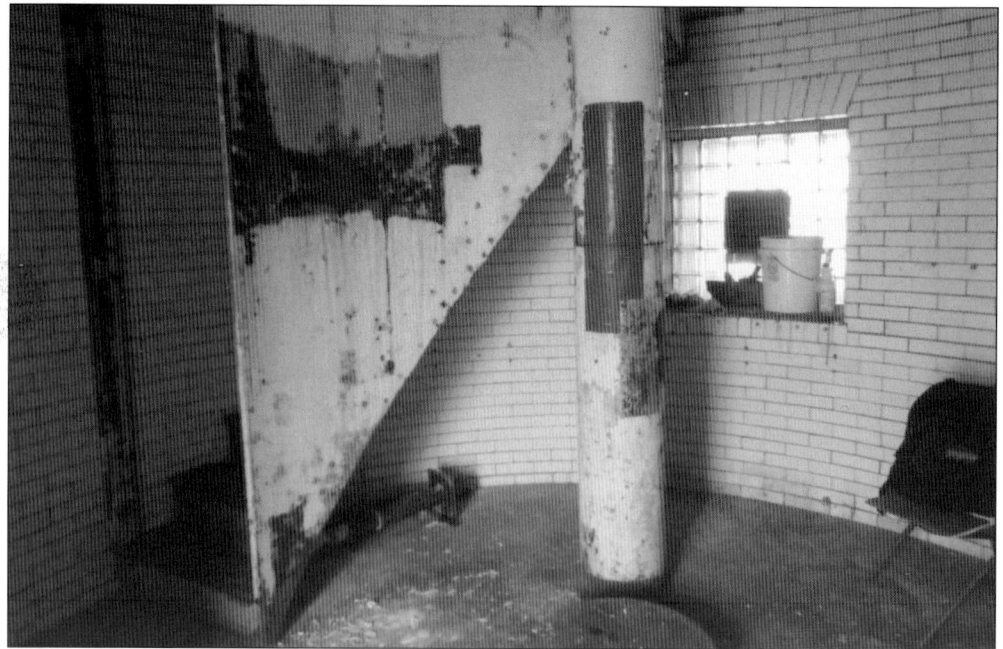

In the years following automation and de-staffing, the interior fell into disrepair. The lighthouse was offered to a suitable new owner at no cost under the guidelines of the National Historic Lighthouse Preservation Act, but there were no takers. As a result, the lighthouse was sold via an online auction in September 2013 (the same year this picture was taken). (General Services Administration.)

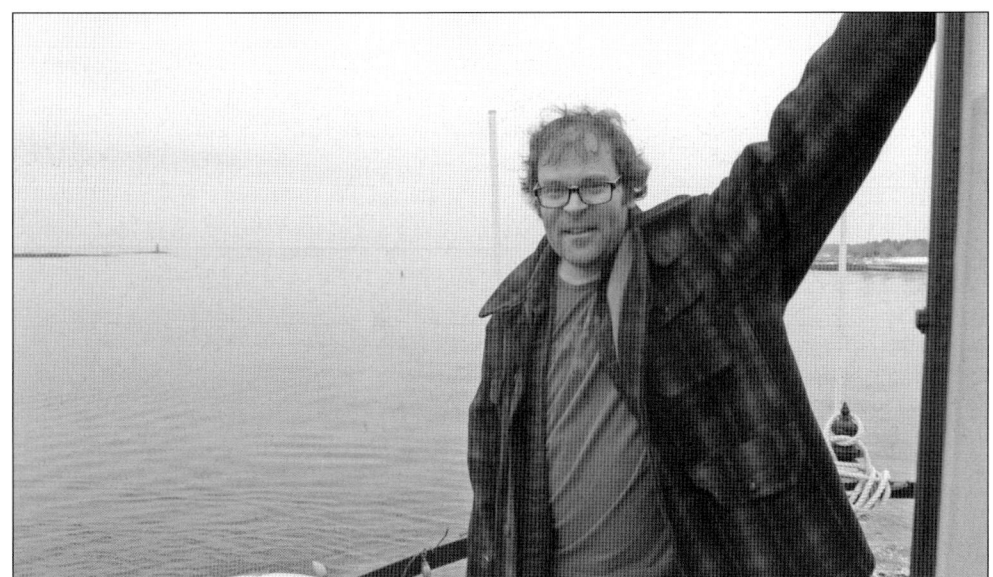

The lighthouse was sold in a government auction in September 2013 to Boston businessman David Waller, shown here. The selling price was $933,888, more than twice the highest amount that had previously been paid for a lighthouse at auction. After Waller bought the lighthouse, restoration began in 2014. (Photograph by the author.)

The work completed in the first year of David Waller's ownership included the repair of damaged granite blocks at the lighthouse base; the sealing and repainting of the walls and ceilings of all seven levels; the replacement of glass block windows with reproductions of the original casement windows; the cleaning and polishing of the interior glazed brick walls; and much more. (Dave Waller.)

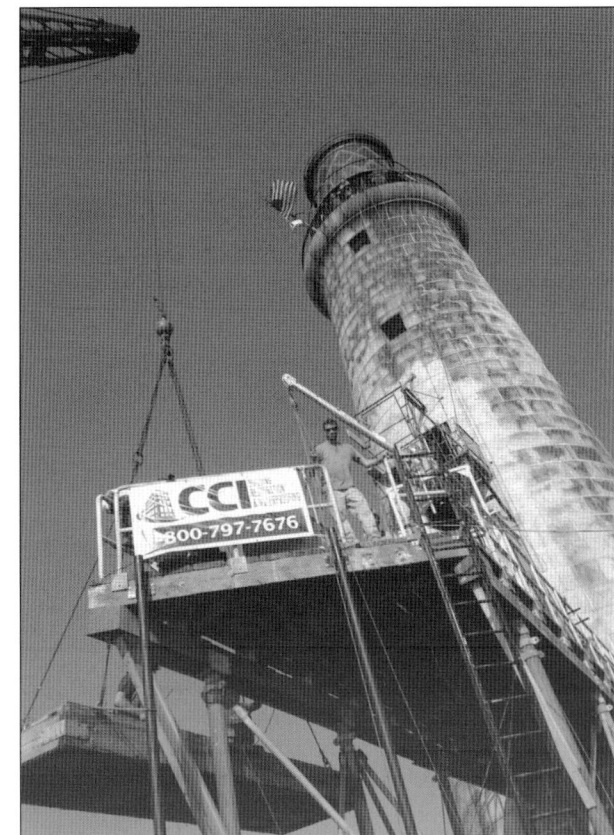

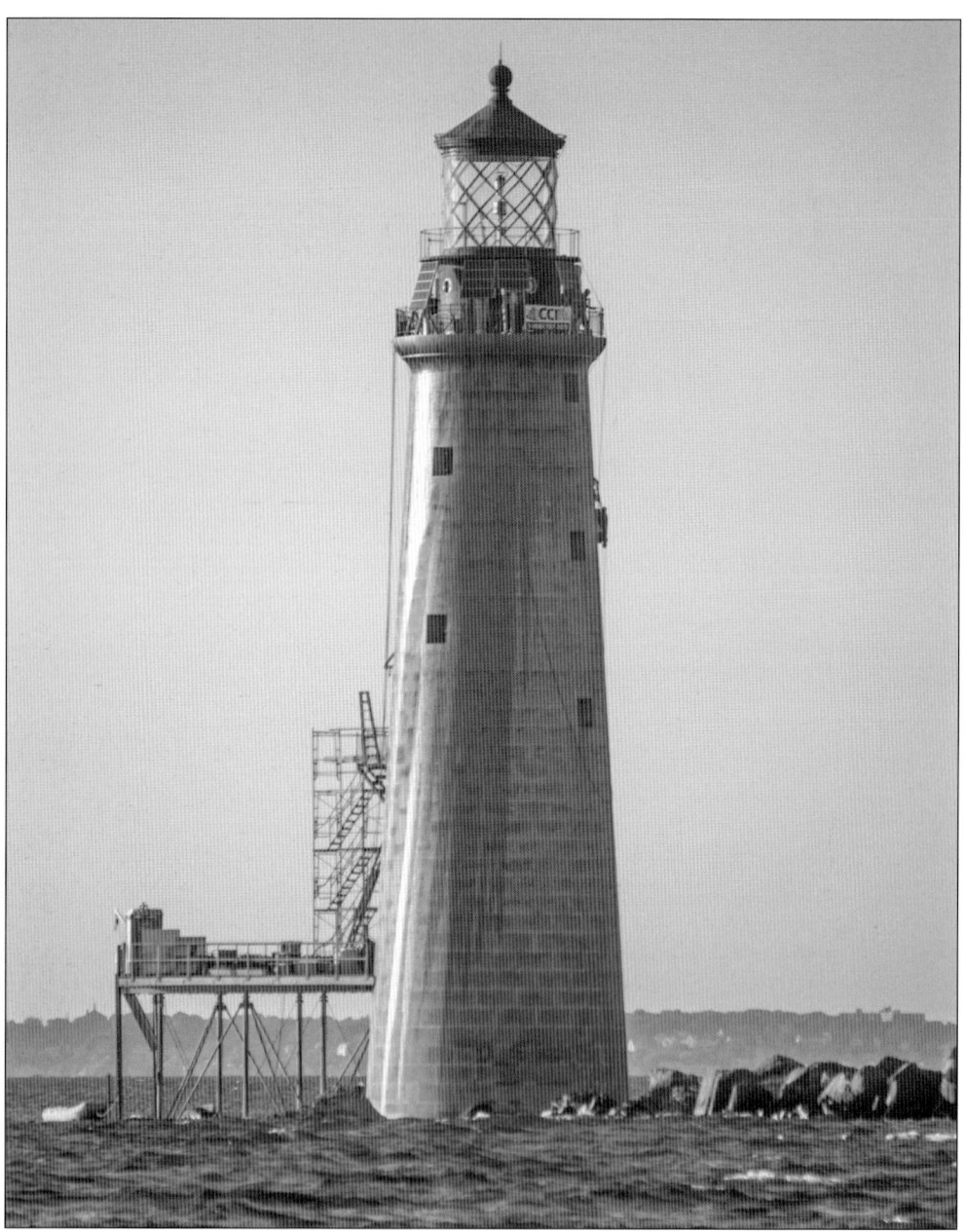

The tower was power-washed in 2014, which left it looking like new. Work has progressed with further restoration of the lighthouse. Among many other improvements, owner Dave Waller has had a new bathroom installed with working plumbing and a water treatment system. Also, with Graves' old Fresnel lens in storage at the Smithsonian Institution, Waller and friends have set about creating a new first-order lens using pieces collected from around the world. The "Frankenstein lens" is on exhibit in the level below the lantern. "The best part of fixing up The Graves hasn't been the fabulous sunsets, discovering the dramatic history, or even watching those cute baby seals," says Waller. "It's the wonderful people we've met along the way." Among the many people on the "Graves Light team" is Bobby Sager, the Boston philanthropist who is the owner of Minot's Ledge Light. (Photograph by the author.)

Seven
Ram Island Ledge

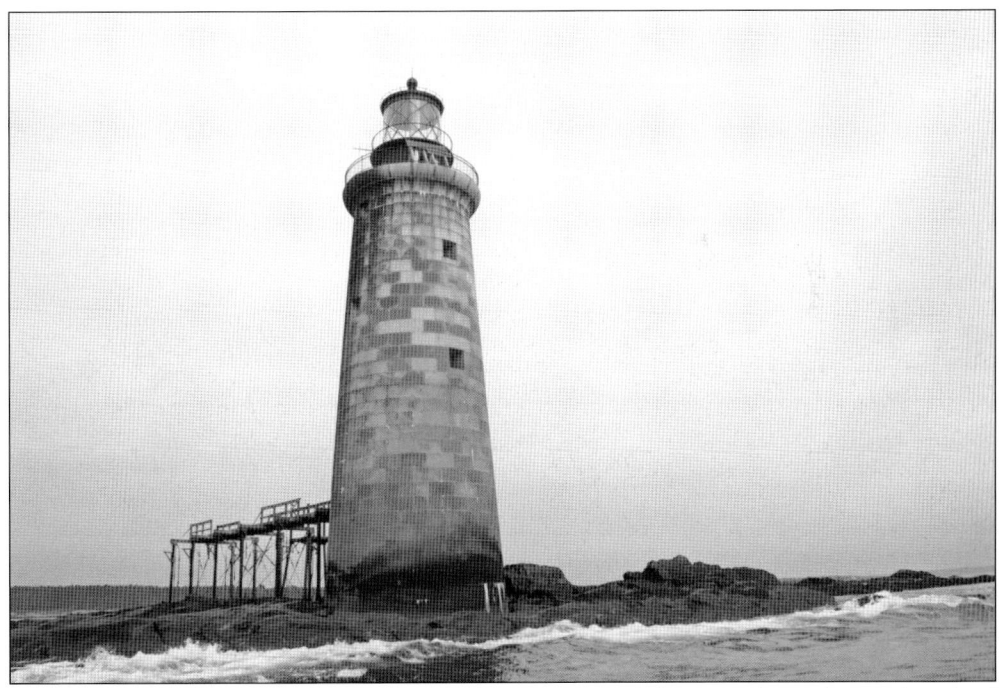

Ram Island, on the easterly approach to Portland Harbor and about a mile northeast of Portland Head, is surrounded by dangerous ledges. As early as 1855, an iron spindle was erected as a navigational aid on Ram Island Ledge, which extends to the south of Ram Island. The marker was helpful in the daytime, but in bad weather and at night, it was virtually invisible. (Photograph by the author.)

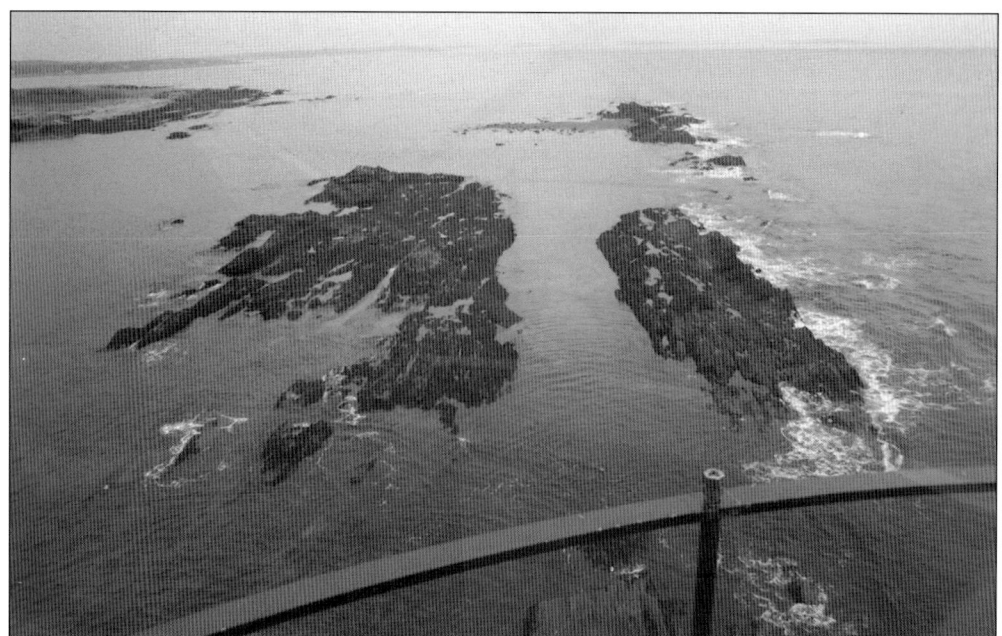

Local tradition held that Ram Island Ledge, described as a "jagged disarray of hungry monsters" by historian Herbert Milton Sylvester, claimed a vessel every seven years. On just one day, May 27, 1866, there were four wrecks. Many fishing boats and schooners struck the ledges over the years, often while trying to make Portland Harbor in bad weather. This is a view of Ram Island Ledge from the top of the lighthouse. (Photograph by the author.)

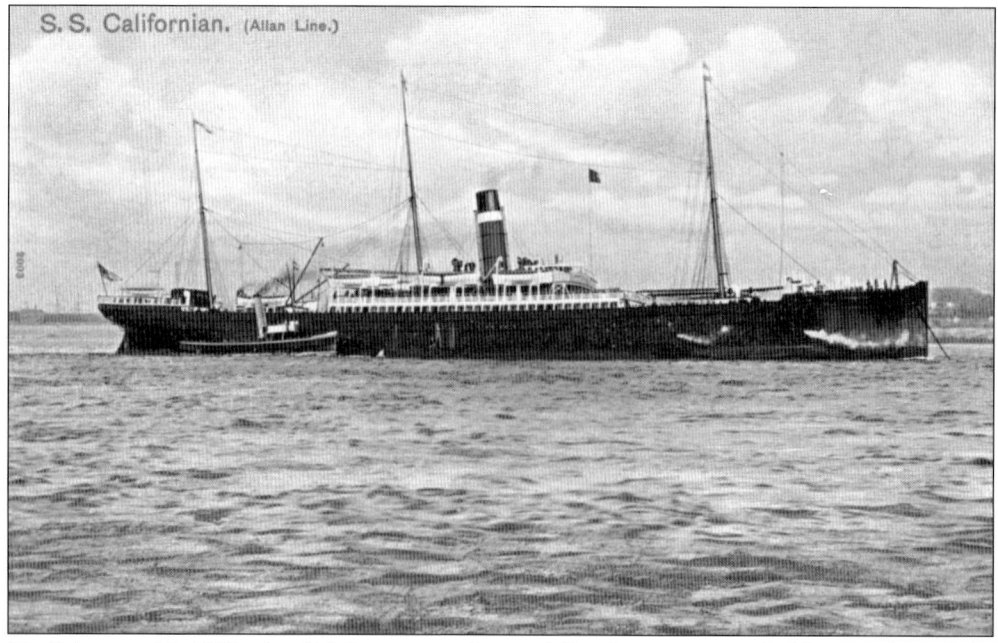

On February 24, 1900, the 400-foot transatlantic Allan Line steamer *Californian*, bound for England from Portland with a crew of 96 plus 21 passengers, went aground at the outer end of Ram Island Ledge in a snowstorm. There was no loss of life, and the steamer was refloated six weeks later. (Author's collection.)

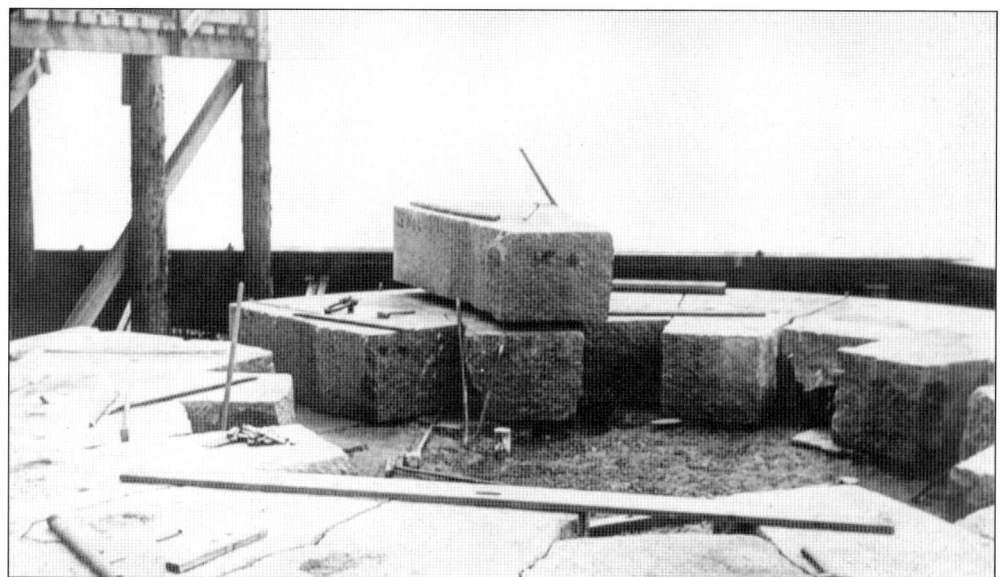

In June 1902, Congress appropriated $83,000 for the building of a lighthouse on the ledge. An additional appropriation of $50,000 was later made. The Bodwell Granite Company provided granite blocks from a Vinalhaven quarry. The giant blocks were brought to Central Wharf in Portland, numbered to indicate their positions, and then ferried to the ledge, which had been leveled to three feet above mean low water. (Dolly Bicknell.)

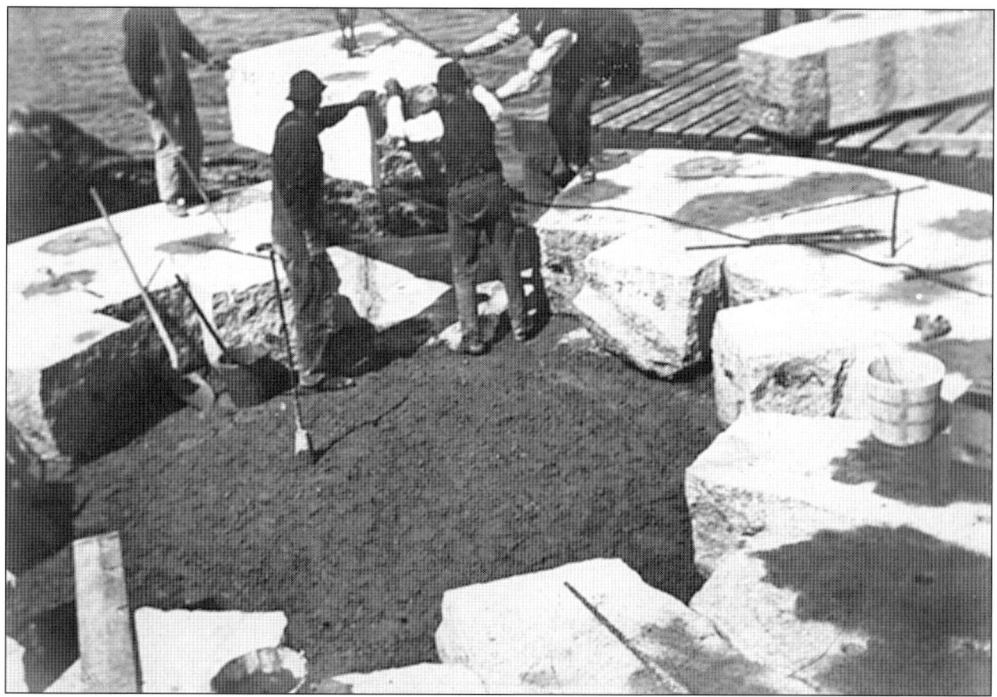

By June 30, 1903, the ledge was leveled and construction began on the tower's foundation. A platform for materials, a hoisting engine, and a derrick were built on the ledge, and temporary quarters were set up for the workers on Ram Island about 600 yards from the work site. A small steamer provided transportation between the ledge and Portland. (Dolly Bicknell.)

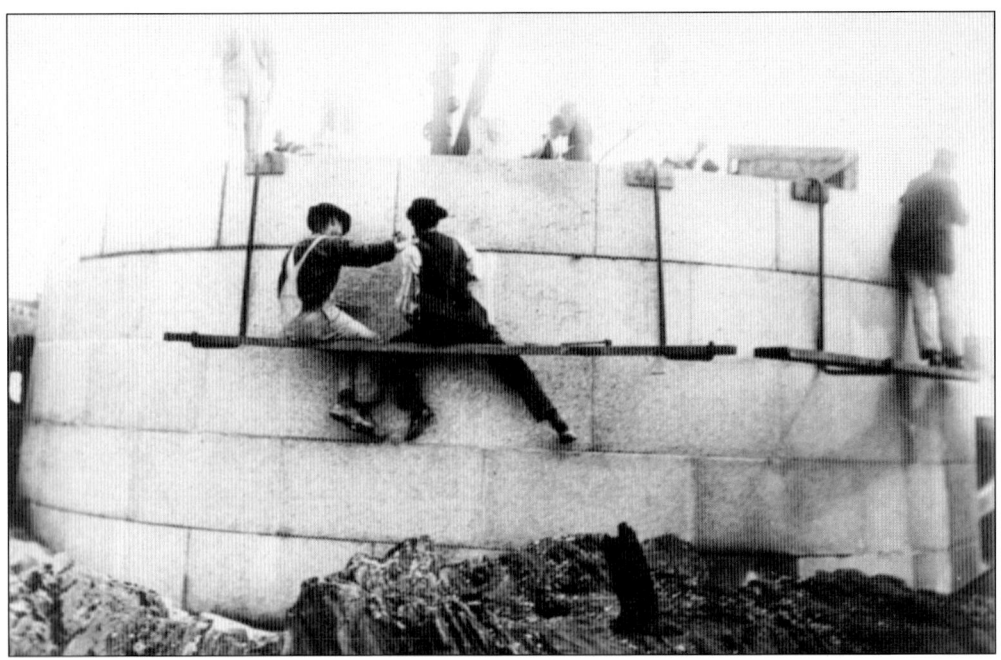

The first stones were laid in July 1903. Two months later, the *Kennebec Journal* reported that the lighthouse was "assuming definite shape, and climbing skyward at an astonishing rate of speed, considering the nature of the work, and extremely rough and dangerous spot where it is located." (Jim Claflin.)

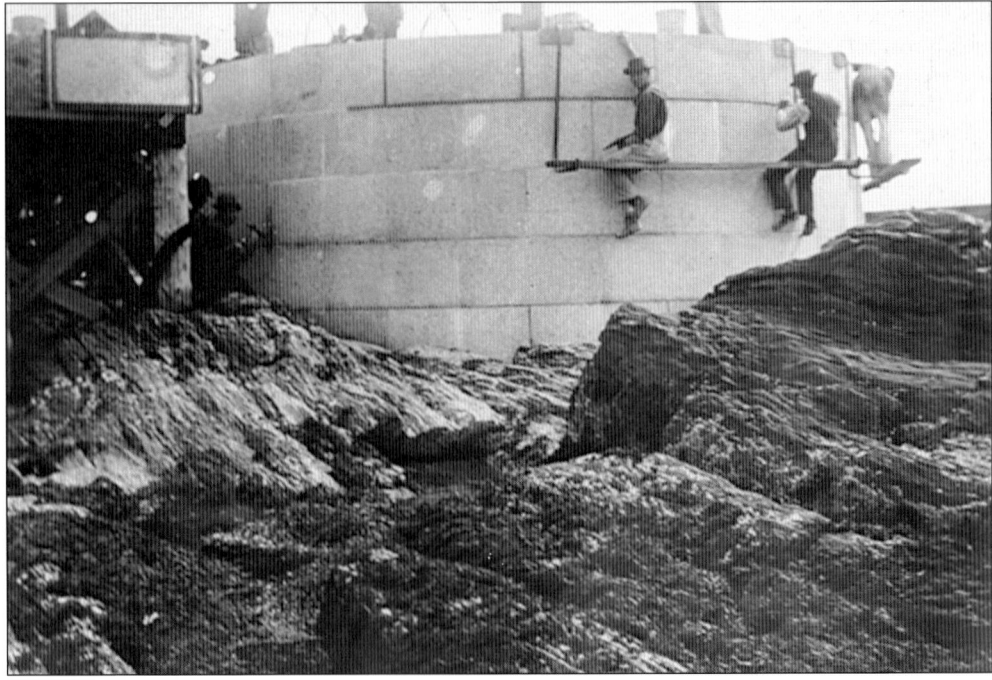

The stones near the base weighed four tons each, and the upper stones weighed about three tons each. The stones on the lowest course were each secured with four iron bolts extending three feet into the ledge and eight feet into the blocks. (Jim Claflin.)

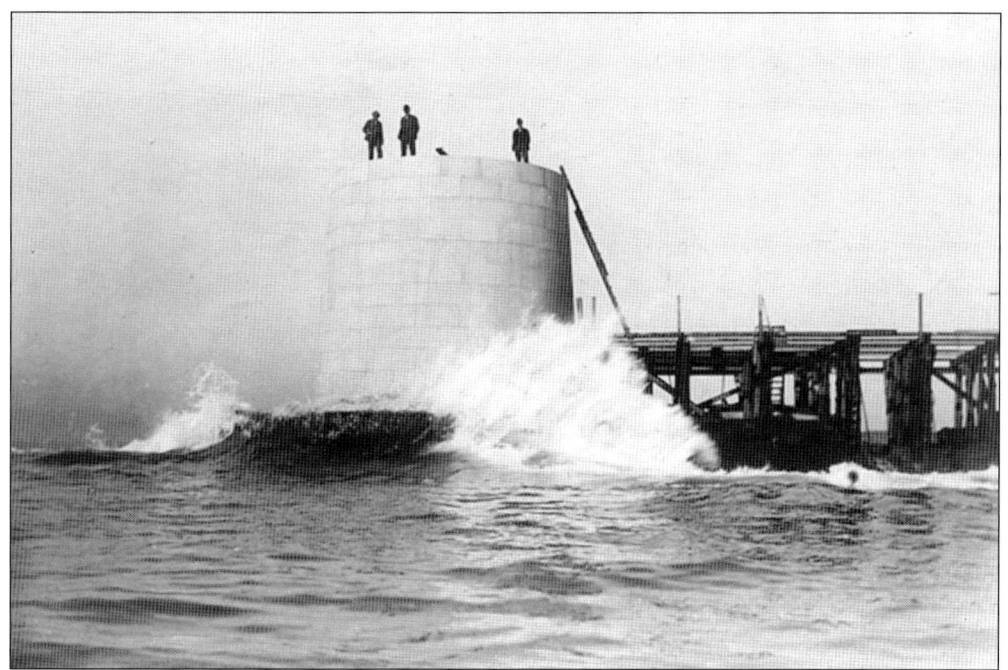

By the end of September 1903, the tower had reached 16 courses and 32 feet. Another appropriation of $33,000 was needed to complete the project, which cost $166,000 in all. The final tally of blocks used was 699 in 35 courses. The interior walls were lined with enameled bricks. (Dolly Bicknell.)

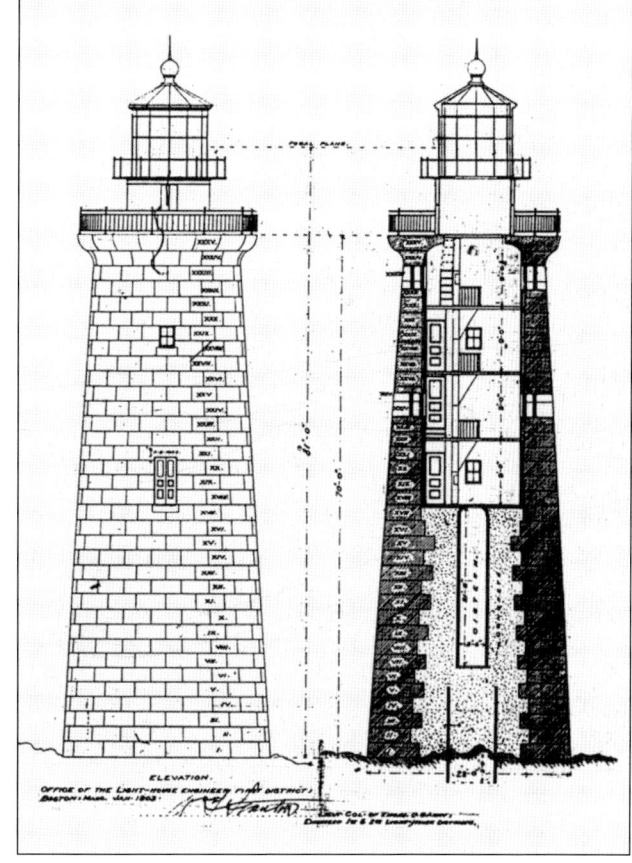

The interior ironwork and exterior ladder were manufactured at a machine shop in Boston, and the interior woodwork was prepared in Portland. Entry to the tower was achieved by climbing a ladder to the first level. The next level was the galley, followed by three more levels with space for equipment and living quarters for the keepers. (US Coast Guard.)

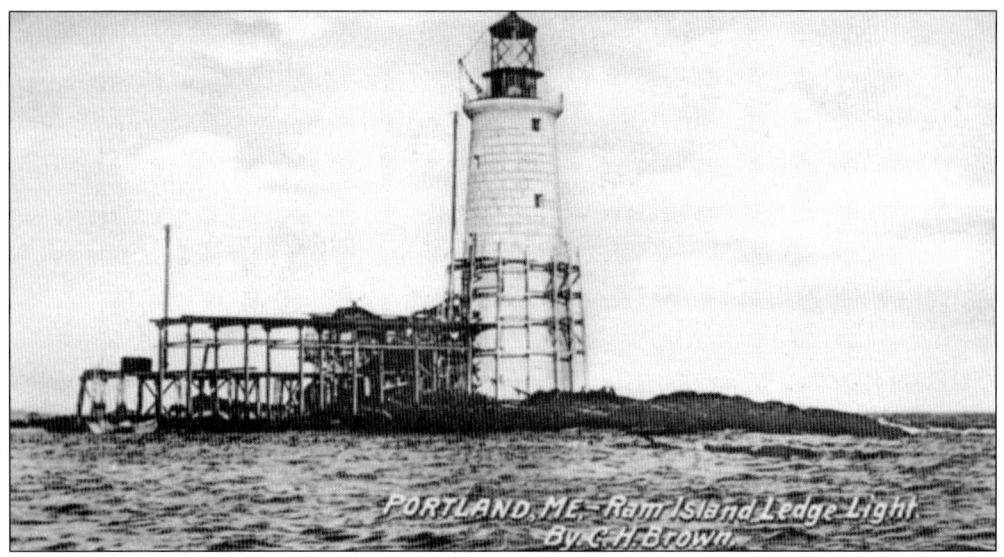

A 26,000-pound lantern manufactured in Atlanta, Georgia, was placed on the tower and fitted with a third-order Fresnel lens from Paris. With the lantern, the lighthouse reached a height of 90 feet, with the light 77 feet above mean high water. The tower is a slightly shorter sibling of Graves Light in outer Boston Harbor, which was built almost at the same time. (Author's collection.)

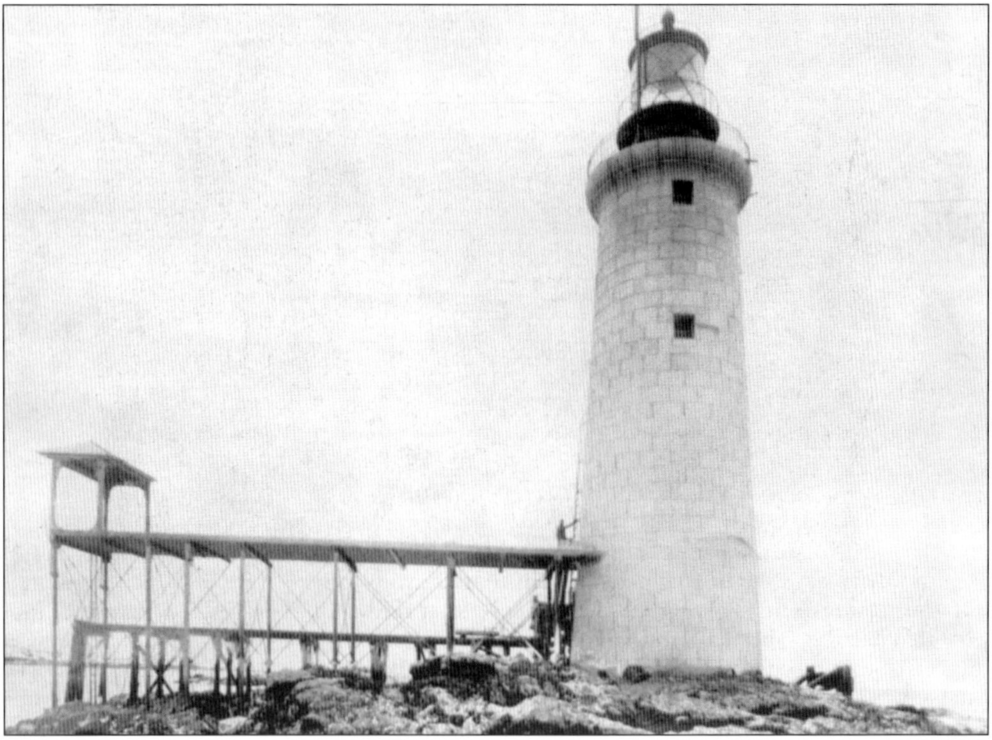

In the predawn hours of January 12, 1905, the schooner *Leona* struck a ledge near Ram Island in a snowstorm. The crewmen launched a lifeboat and managed to stay afloat for a few hours until the construction workers at the ledge saw one of their flares. The workers directed the lifeboat to a cove near the lighthouse and then helped the men get safely ashore. (Author's collection.)

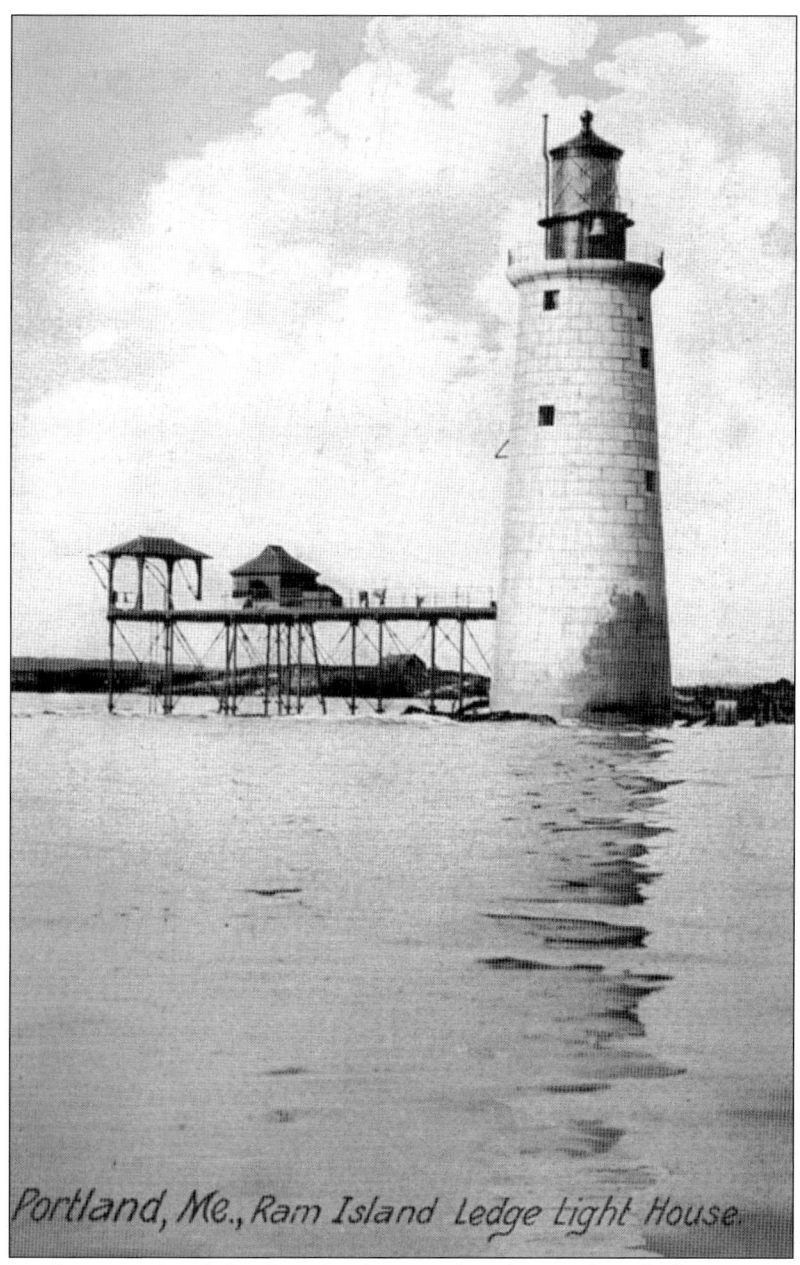

Portland, Me., Ram Island Ledge Light House.

The kerosene lamp was first lighted on April 10, 1905, with two white flashes every six seconds. On the night of its first lighting, Capt. Sumner N. Dyer at the Cape Elizabeth Life-Saving Station reported that the light was "strong and brilliant." The light's flashing characteristic was produced by a clockwork mechanism that rotated the lens, which floated on a bed of mercury. The keepers had to wind the mechanism every 90 minutes. An iron pier was also built extending to the west with a fog bell tower at its end. The bell went into operation on August 28, 1905, with automatic striking machinery producing a blow every 10 seconds. The first principal keeper was William C. Tapley, formerly at Saddleback Ledge Light and Deer Island Thorofare Light. Tapley served until 1929. There were three keepers assigned to the station; each keeper stayed for two weeks, with daily 12-hour shifts, followed by a week of shore leave. (Author's collection.)

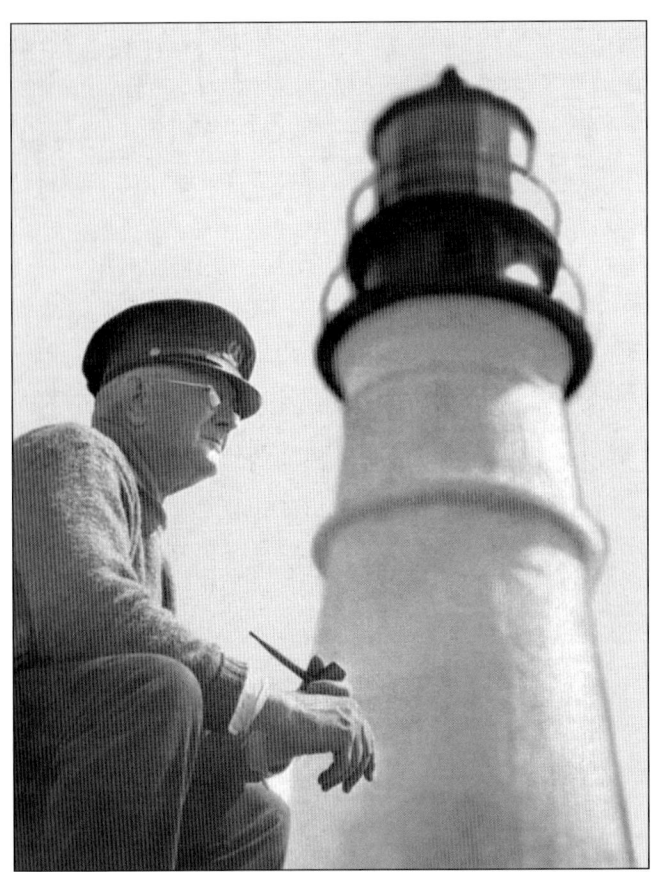

Around 1915, one of the assistants was Robert Thayer Sterling, who later served many years at Portland Head Light and moonlighted as a writer. In his book *Lighthouses of the Maine Coast and the Men Who Keep Them*, he writes, "I have always fancied living in a lighthouse because I know it is the best kind of house for a poet to live in." (American Lighthouse Foundation.)

According to the historian Peter Dow Bachelder, Ram Island Ledge became a popular destination for adventurous tourists during the summer. Picnickers, curiosity seekers, and fishing parties were not uncommon. One enterprising visitor bragged to keeper William Tapley that he earned $500 each summer by gathering the sea moss that was plentiful on the rocks. (Maine Lighthouse Museum.)

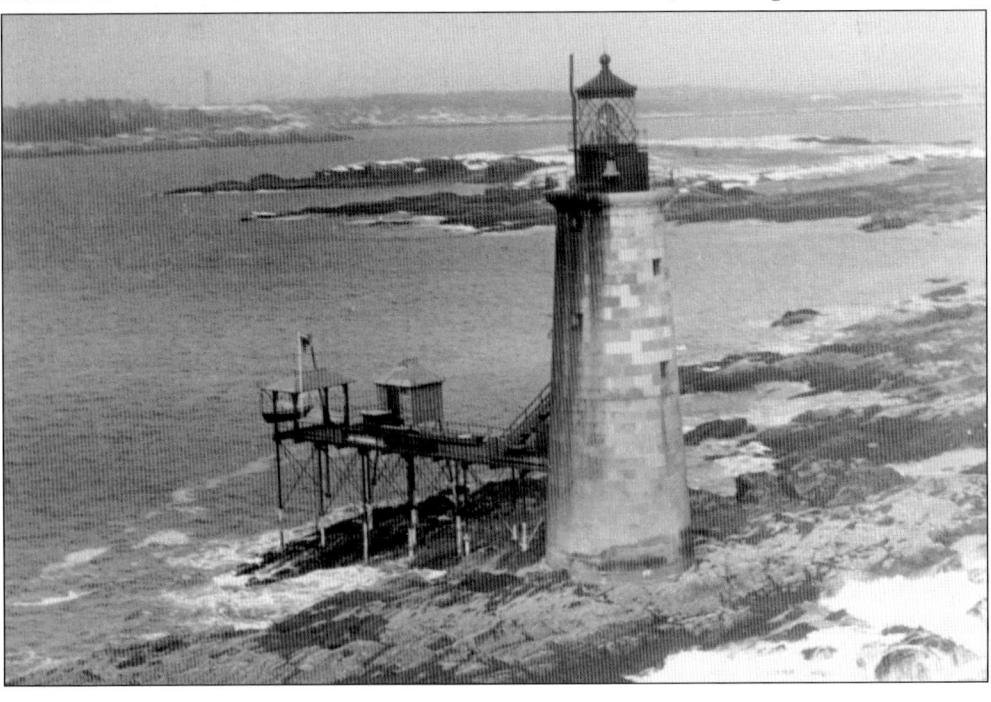

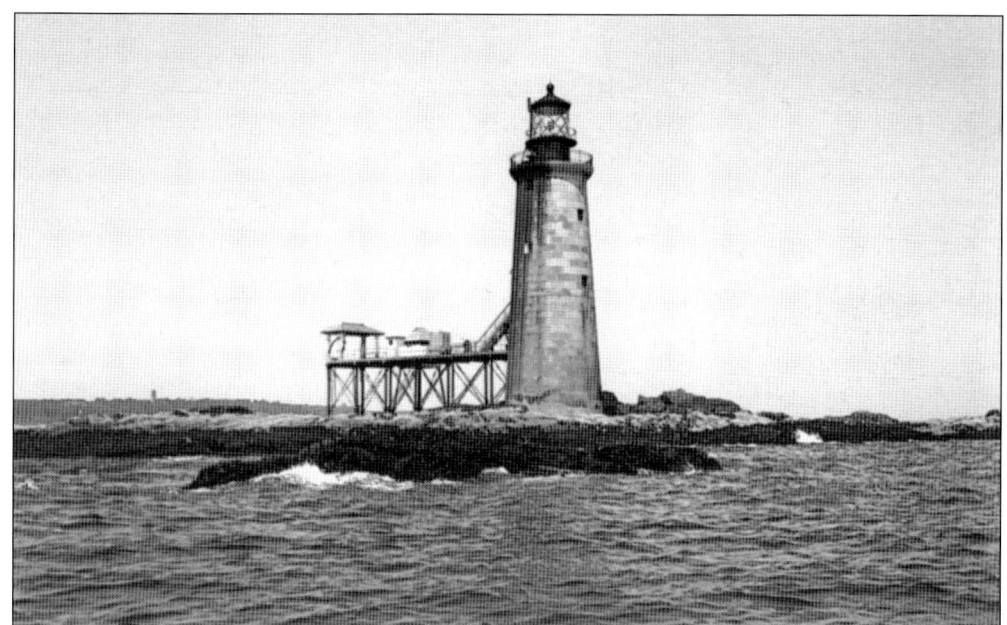

Joe Johansen was an assistant keeper for the Coast Guard in 1949 and 1950. He later told an interviewer about his life at Ram Island Ledge: "In the winters the nights were kind of long because you split the watch. . . . You usually stood watch in the galley because that's where your only source of heat was: a kerosene stove, which we used for cooking and heat." (Author's collection.)

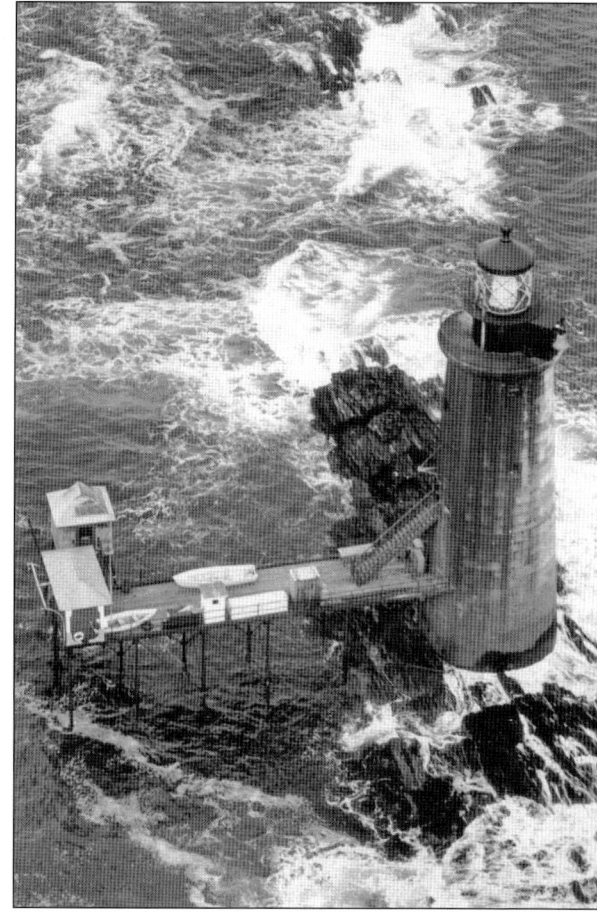

When Joe Johansen was an assistant keeper at Ram Island, the lens still turned on a mercury bed, and the rotating mechanism had to be manually wound every 90 minutes. Occasionally, the man on watch might fall asleep and miss a winding. "That was really a ding on your record," said Johansen. The station was converted to electricity (via a submarine cable) in 1958 and to solar power in 2001. (US Coast Guard.)

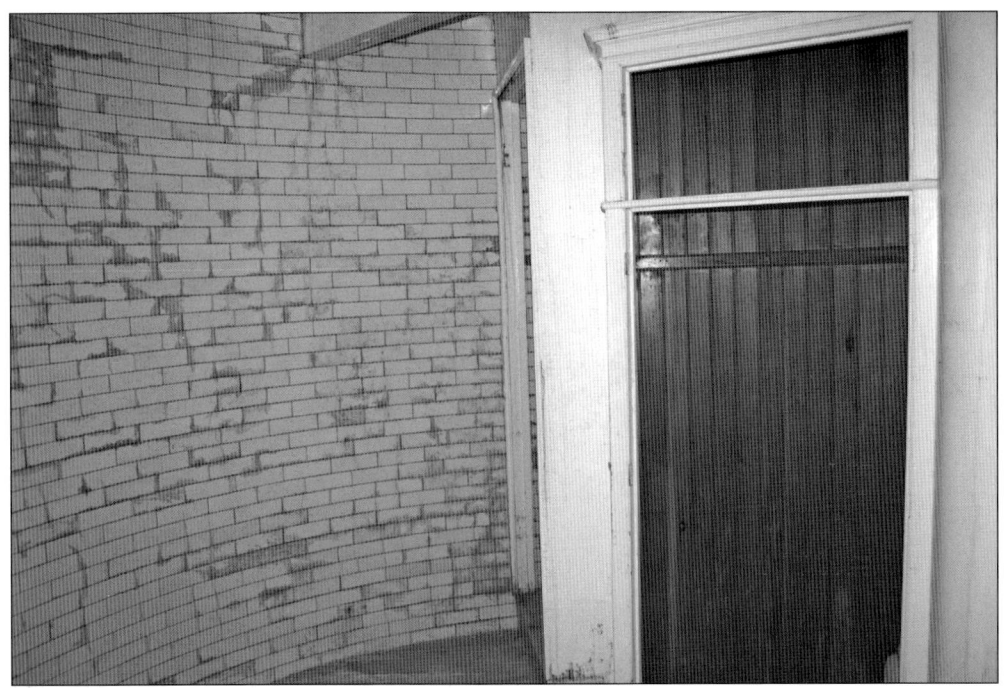

The condition of the lighthouse's interior deteriorated following automation and de-staffing in 1959. This 2006 photograph shows the enameled brick walls on one of the levels in the tower. In 2009, the lighthouse was made available to a suitable new steward under the guidelines of the National Historic Lighthouse Preservation Act of 2000. (Photograph by the author.)

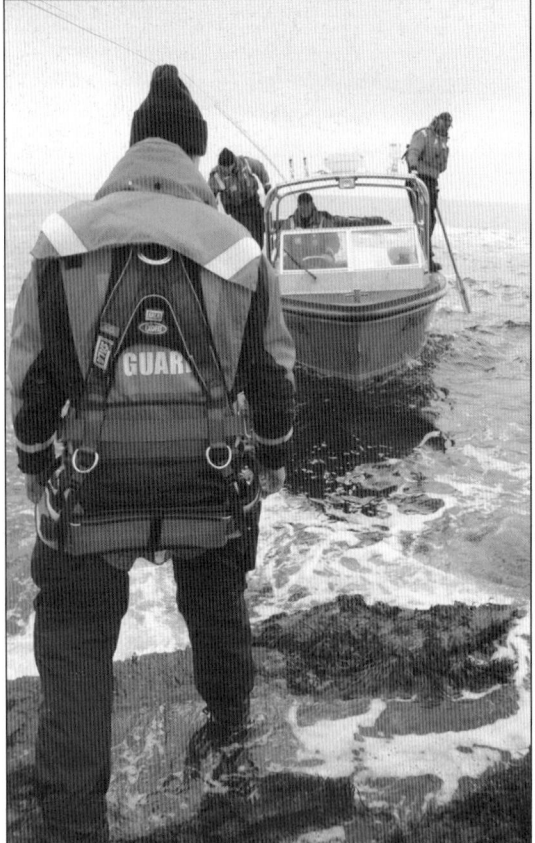

This photograph was taken during a February 2006 visit by the Coast Guard's Aids to Navigation Team South Portland. Because there were no applicants for the lighthouse under the National Historic Lighthouse Preservation Act, it was put up for auction to the general public in the summer of 2010. (Photograph by the author.)

Here, Coast Guard Aids to Navigation personnel ascend the ladder to the doorway of the lighthouse. On September 14, 2010, Ram Island Ledge Light was sold to Dr. Jeffrey Florman of Windham, Maine, for $190,000. According to news reports, Florman and a local real estate developer flipped a coin to see which one would drop out of the bidding. (Photograph by the author.)

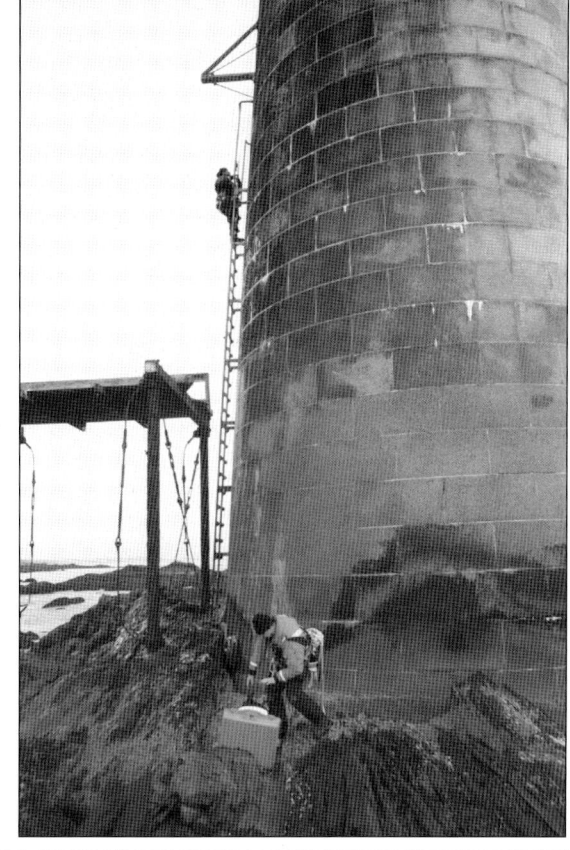

This is Bob Trapani Jr. during a site visit in February 2006. Trapani is a lighthouse technician and executive director of the American Lighthouse Foundation. Today, the modern 300-millimeter optic at Ram Island Ledge exhibits two white flashes every 10 seconds. A fog signal is operated as needed by mariners via VHF radio. (Photograph by the author.)

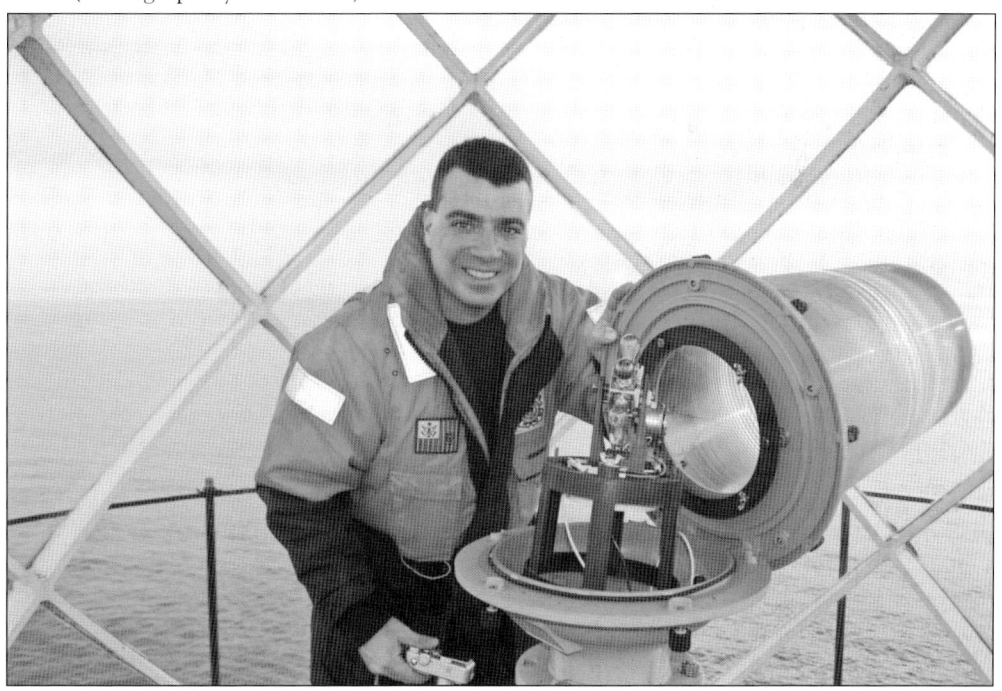

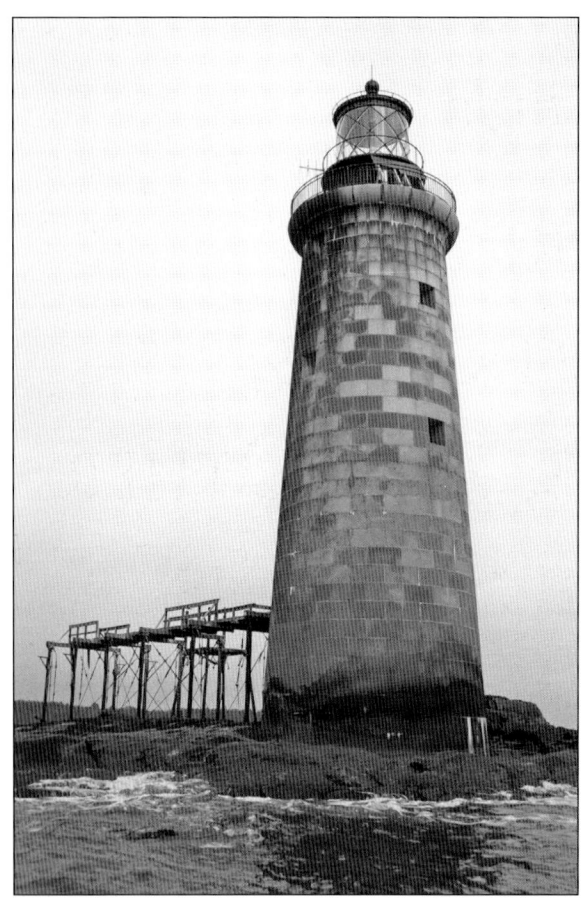

The pier at Ram Island Ledge Light is dilapidated, meaning access is only possible by pulling a boat up to the ledge and disembarking on the rocks. There has been discussion of the possibility of removing the old pier and building a new one. The lighthouse tower itself is structurally sound, but much work will be needed in the interior. (Photograph by the author.)

Portland Head Light in Cape Elizabeth, Maine, is said to be the most visited lighthouse in the world, with well over a million visitors each year. From Portland Head, it is possible to see as many as six other lighthouses, including Ram Island Ledge Light just about a mile offshore. (Photograph by the author.)

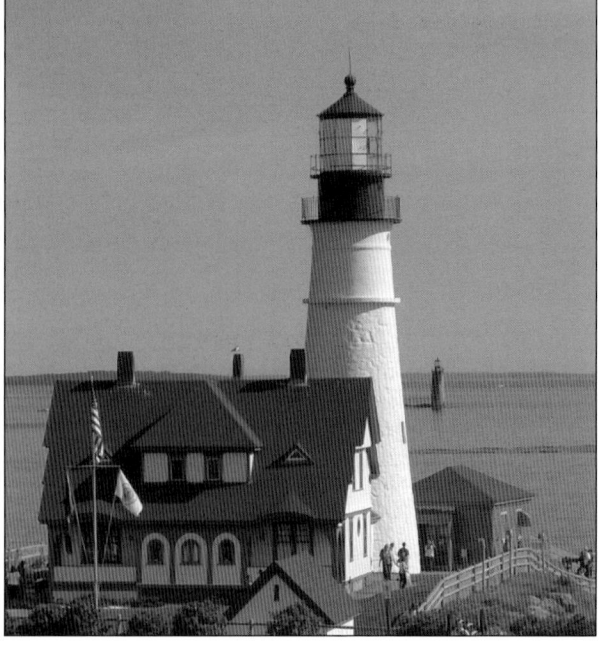

Eight
"Sparkplug" Lighthouses, Lightships, and Other Remote Stations

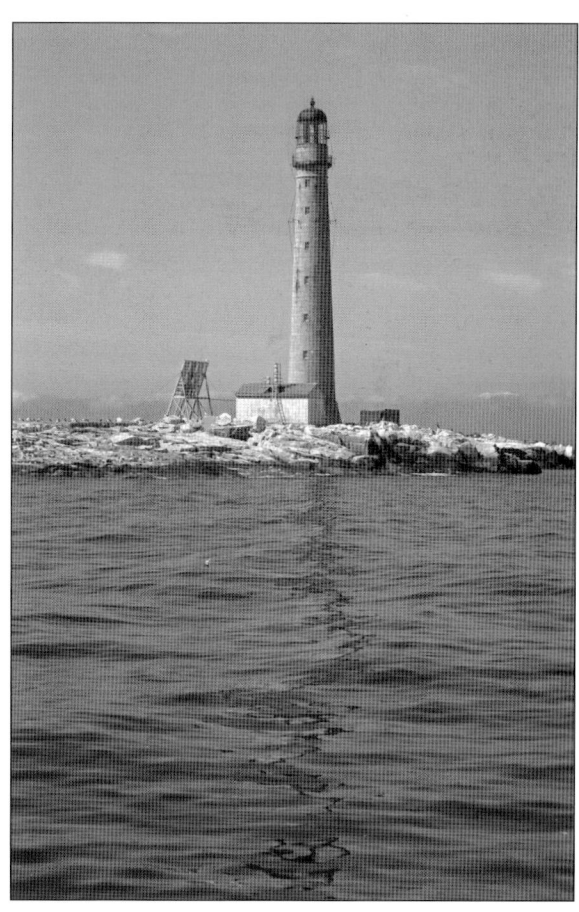

Although its architecture does not fit the usual description, and its keepers lived in a separate keeper's house rather than in the tower itself, some might classify Boon Island Light as a wave-swept lighthouse. The small island, which is only about 14 feet above sea level at its highest point, is several miles away from the towns of York and Kittery in southern Maine. (Photograph by the author.)

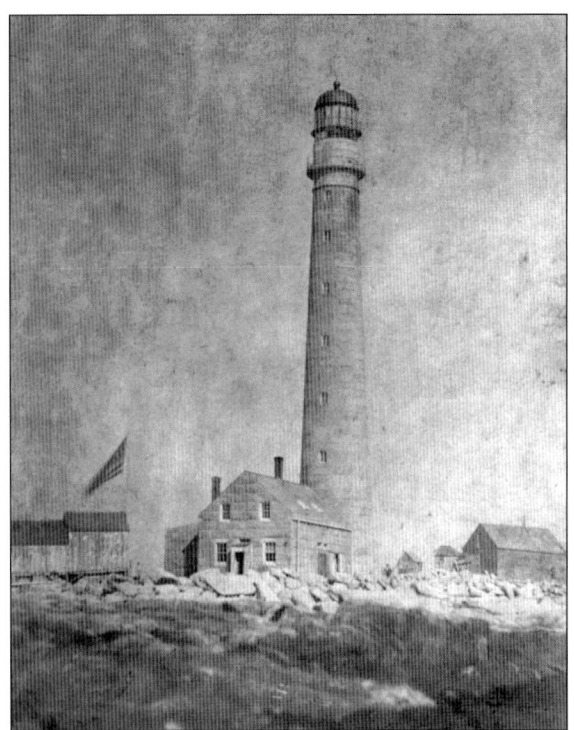

The first lighthouse at Boon Island was built in 1811, and the extant tower was built in 1854. At 133 feet tall, it is the tallest lighthouse in the New England region. About 1,800 tons of granite from a Biddeford, Maine, quarry was used in the tower, and it was lined with 70,000 bricks. This is a c. 1859 photograph. (National Archives.)

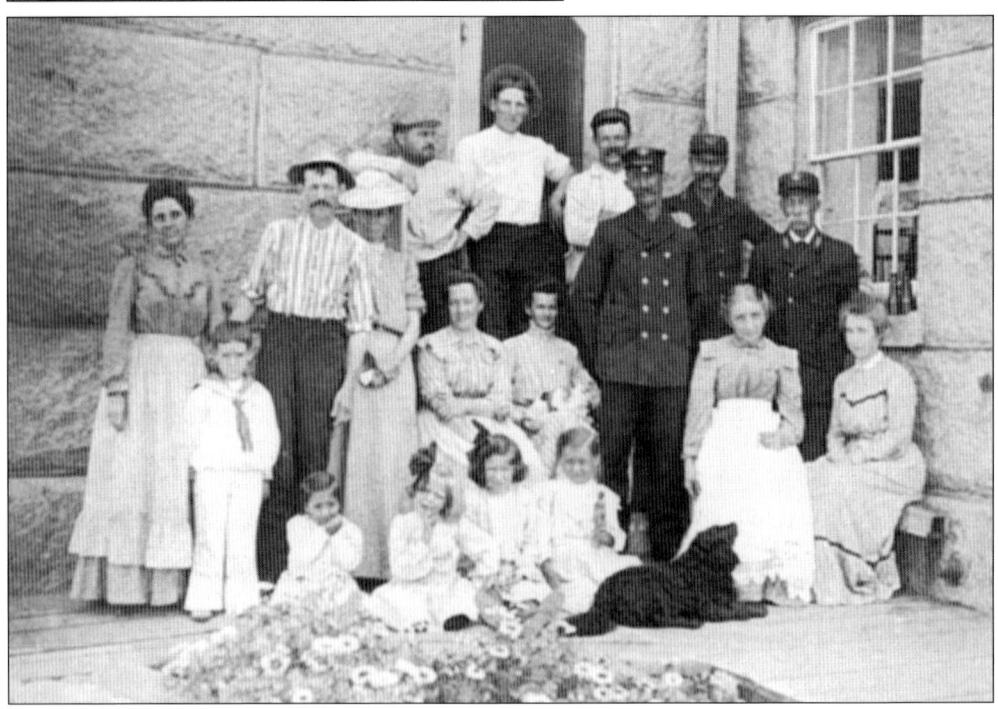

Boon Island was a family light station until the late 1800s. Later, the families were often on the island in summer, as shown in this image from the early 1900s. There was no soil on the rocky island. The families brought soil in the spring so they could have a flower garden, but it would inevitably be washed away in winter. (William O. Thomson.)

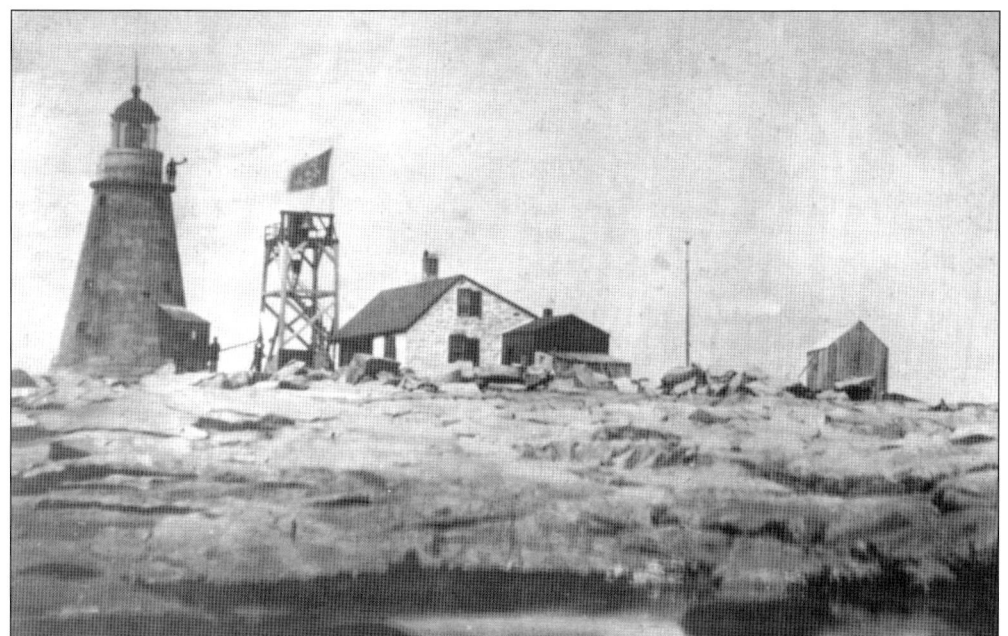

Another lighthouse that many people might classify as wave-swept is Mount Desert Rock Light. Located more than 20 miles from the nearest port at Mount Desert Island, it is one of the most dramatically isolated of all United States lighthouses. George Putnam, for many years the commissioner of the Bureau of Lighthouses, regarded Mount Desert Rock as the most exposed light station in the United States. This is a c. 1859 image. (National Archives.)

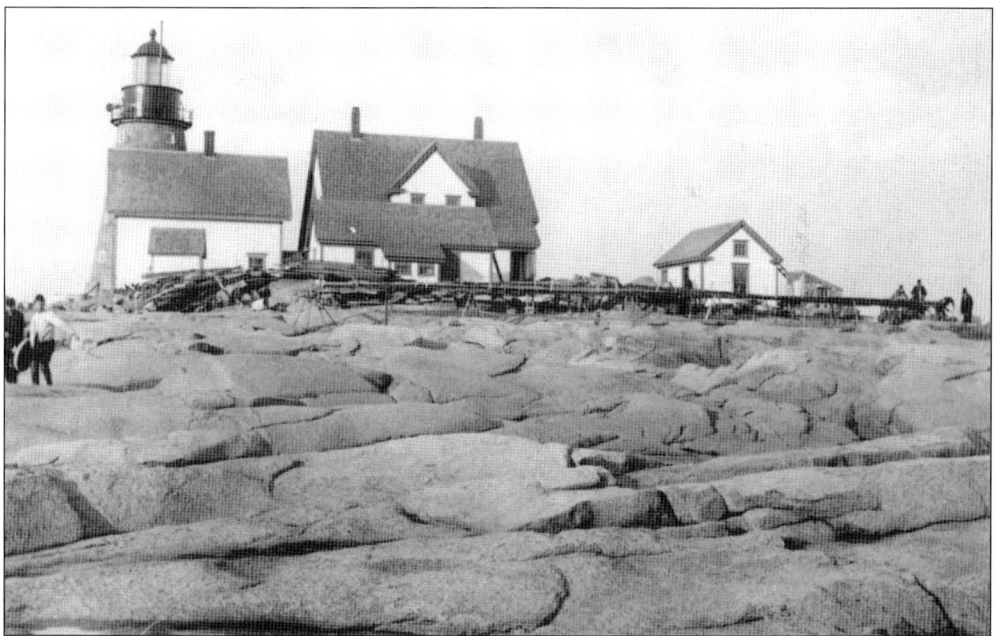

The current 58-foot conical granite tower replaced the original small stone tower at Mount Desert Rock in 1847. Noted architect Alexander Parris designed the new tower, which was very similar to his 1839 granite tower at Saddleback Ledge. Few keepers stayed more than a few years at the rugged and remote station. (National Archives.)

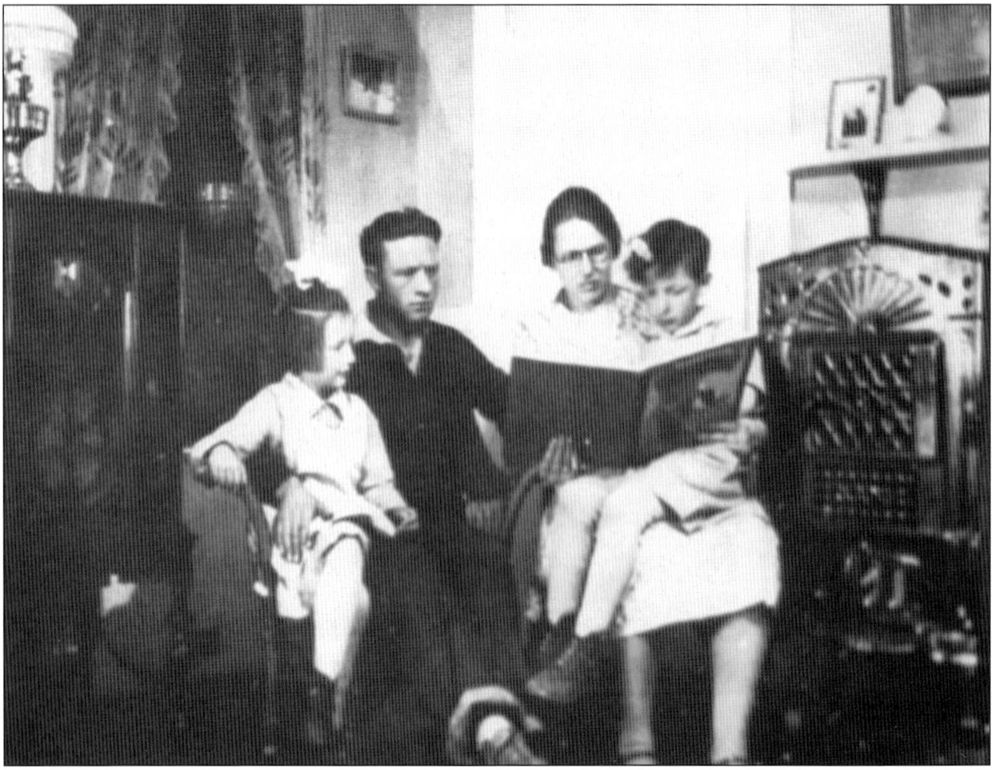

George York was a keeper at Mount Desert Rock from 1928 to 1936. His children, Wilbur and Shirley, passed the hours on the small island playing tag, sailing their toy boats in a freshwater pool, or playing with their pet chickens. "Of course," Wilbur later said, "it didn't take much to amuse me, because I didn't know any better." (Maine Lighthouse Museum.)

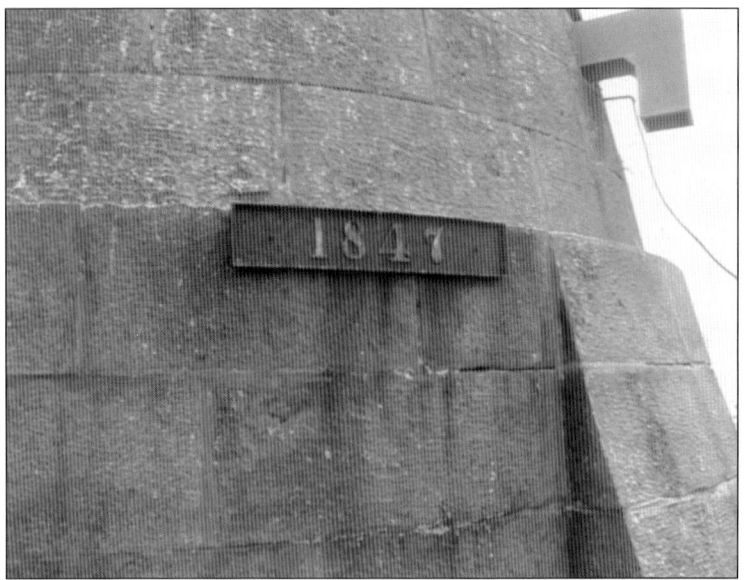

Mount Desert Rock Light's sturdy granite construction has weathered countless severe storms. Today, the light station is used by Bar Harbor's College of the Atlantic as a whale-watching station. The college's Allied Whale program compiles and maintains catalogs for the whale population of the North Atlantic. (Photograph by the author.)

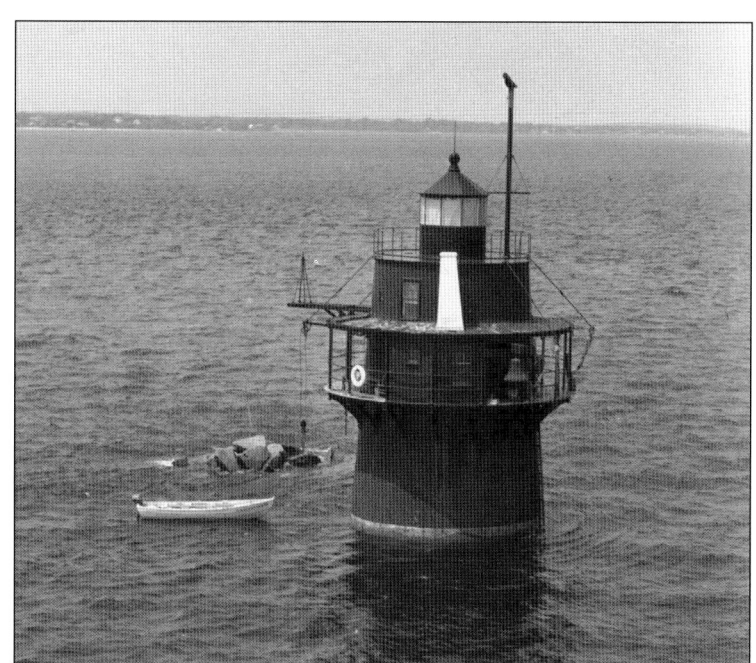

Duxbury Pier Light—built in 1871 and known fondly to locals around Plymouth, Massachusetts, as "Bug Light" or simply "The Bug"—occupies an important niche in lighthouse history as the first offshore cast-iron caisson lighthouse in the United States. This type of lighthouse became a preferable lower-cost alternative at exposed offshore locations. (US Coast Guard.)

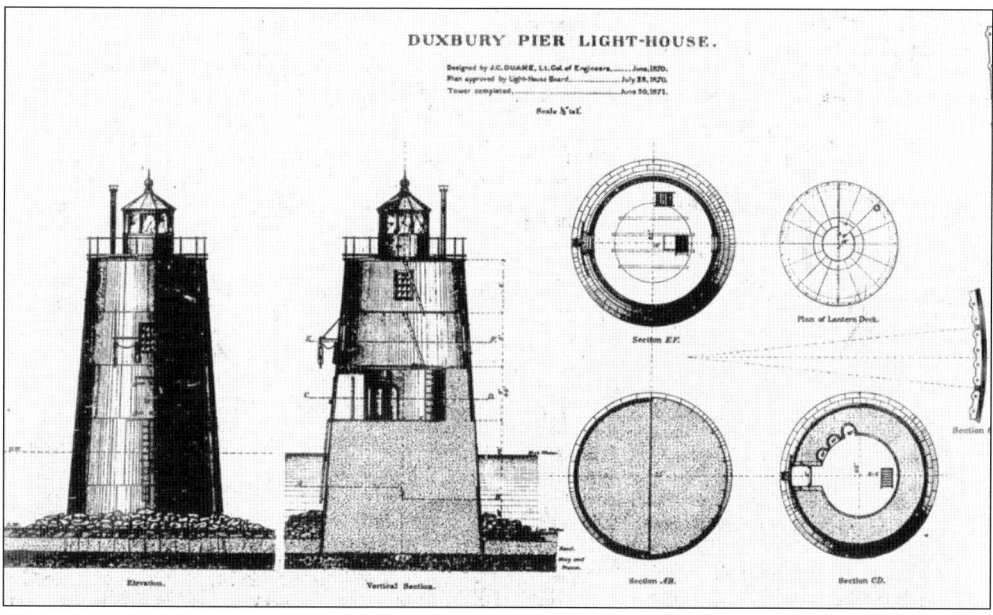

The caisson lighthouse type used a cast-iron cylinder, which was usually sunk into the seabed and filled with concrete to form a foundation. Duxbury Pier Light, 47 feet in height, contained three levels below the lantern, including two that served as living quarters. To protect the structure, 100 tons of stones were placed around the base in 1886, and another 175 tons were added in 1890. (US Coast Guard.)

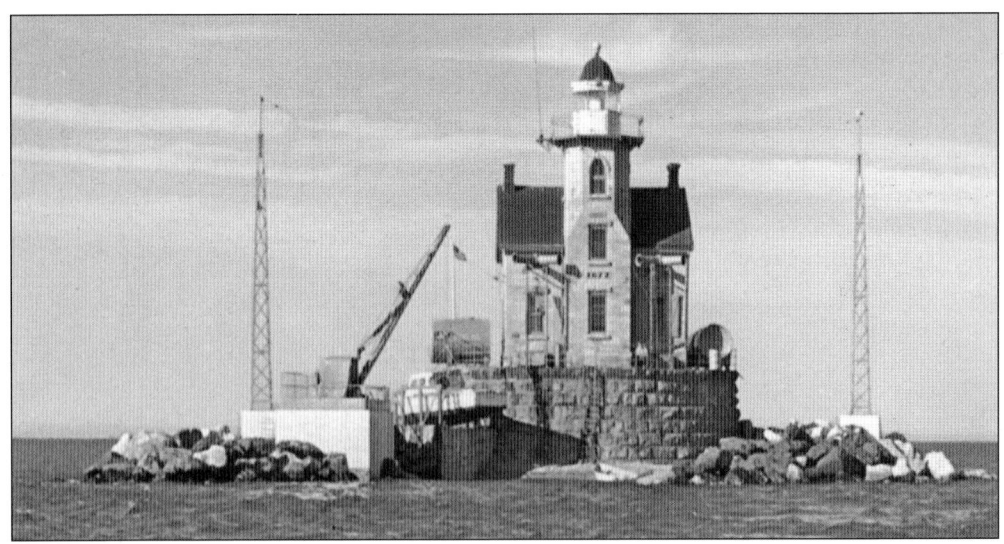

Stratford Shoal Light, near the Connecticut/New York border in Long Island Sound, was one of the last masonry lighthouses built at an offshore location before the switch to near-exclusive construction of lighthouses on cast-iron caissons. Completed in 1877, it is very similar to Race Rock Light, which was built about the same time in Fishers Island Sound. (Author's collection.)

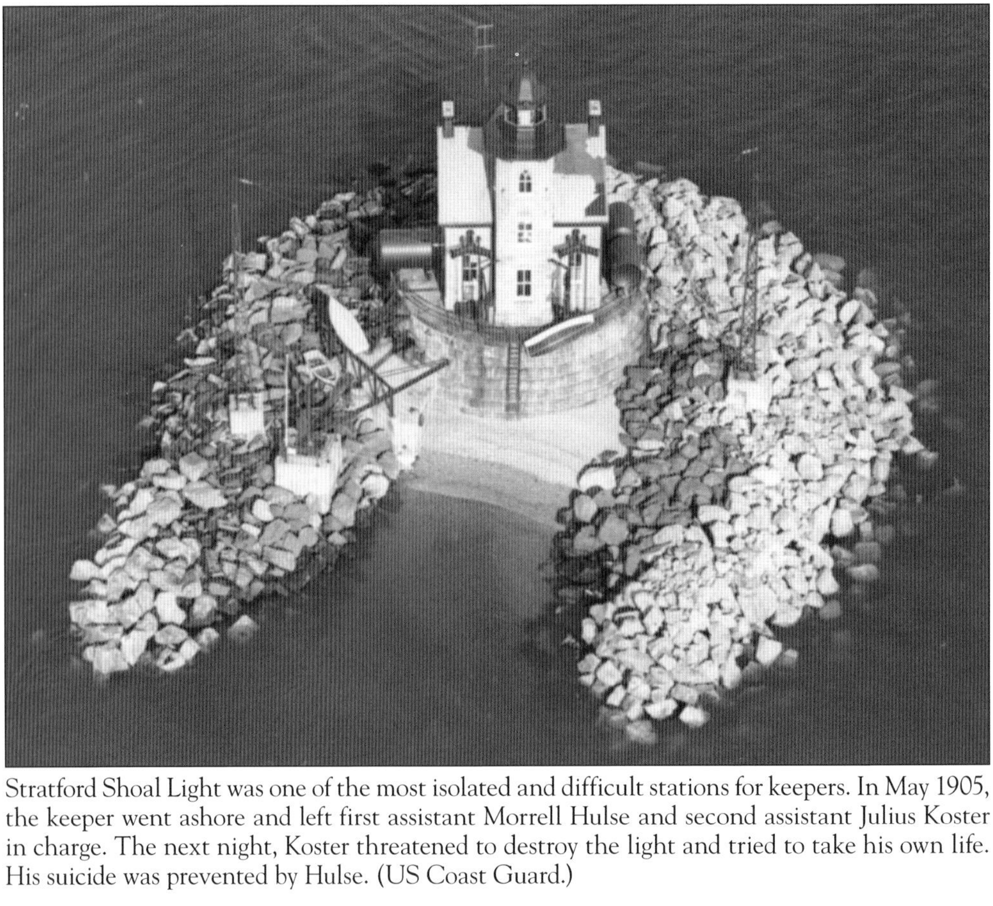

Stratford Shoal Light was one of the most isolated and difficult stations for keepers. In May 1905, the keeper went ashore and left first assistant Morrell Hulse and second assistant Julius Koster in charge. The next night, Koster threatened to destroy the light and tried to take his own life. His suicide was prevented by Hulse. (US Coast Guard.)

Southwest Ledge Light, which went into service on January 1, 1877, at the entrance to the harbor of New Haven, Connecticut, is an architecturally unusual lighthouse. Built atop a cast-iron caisson, it is eight-sided, with Second Empire detailing and a mansard roof topped by an octagonal lantern. The interior contains three stories. It is identical to Ship John Shoal Light in Delaware Bay. (Author's collection.)

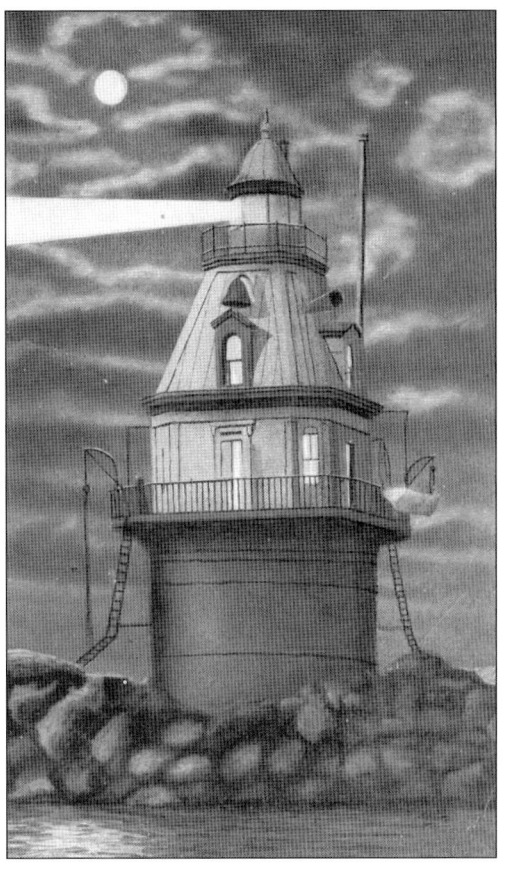

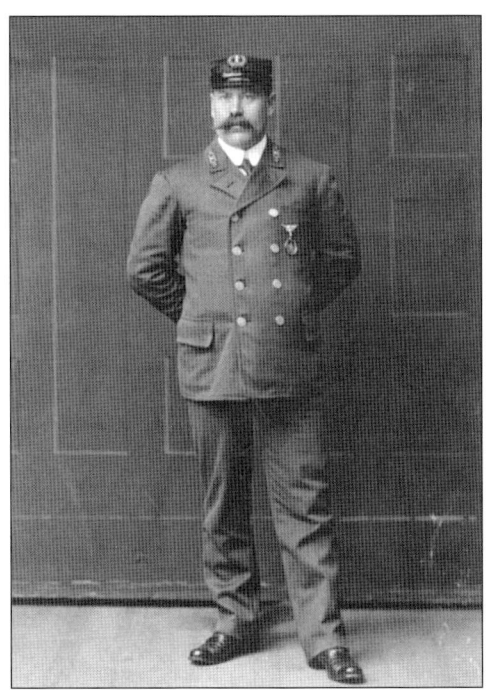

Southwest Ledge Light was a rough assignment for keepers, and the isolation and poor conditions apparently led assistant keeper Nils Nilson (pictured) to become despondent and violent. On one occasion, Nilson chased keeper Jorgen Tonnesen around the lighthouse with a fire ax. In January 1908, not long after this episode, Nilson took his own life while onshore. (*Lighthouse Digest*.)

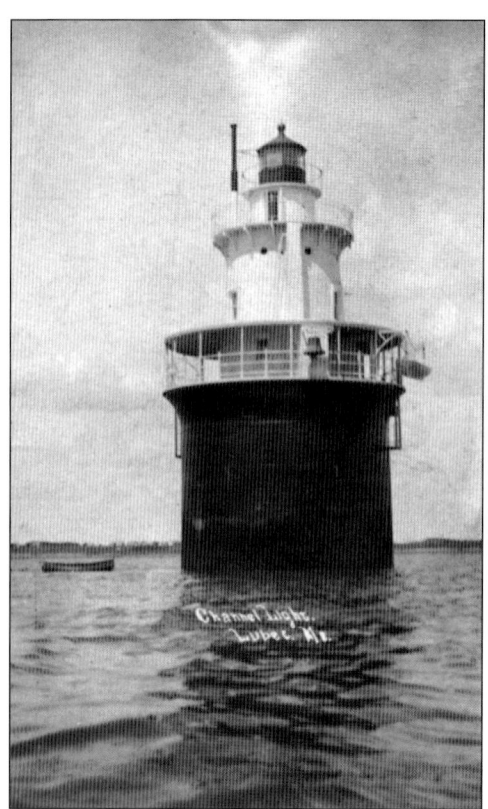

In the southern United States, screwpile lighthouses were built in many offshore locations and constructed atop piles that were screwed into the substrate. In northern locations, where ice floes were sometimes a problem, caisson lighthouses were more practical. Caisson lighthouses were, at first, likened to coffee pots, but their typical shape eventually earned them the nickname "sparkplug lights." This is Maine's Lubec Channel Light, completed in 1890. (Author's collection.)

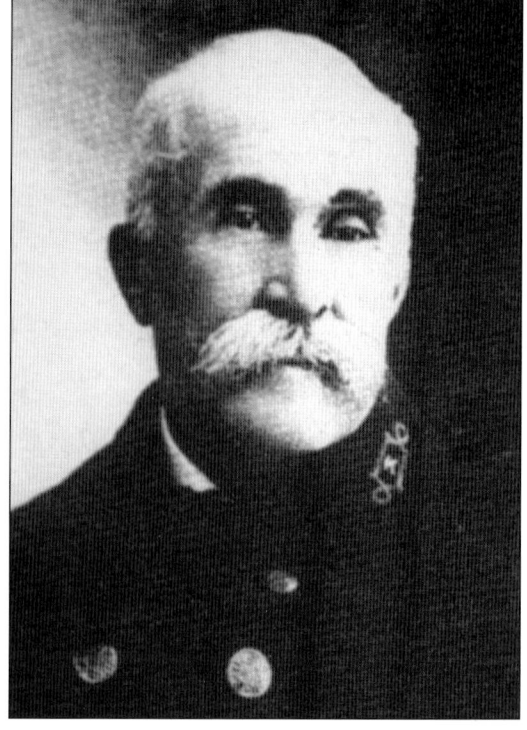

Two male keepers staffed Lubec Channel Light, which was located offshore between Lubec, Maine, and Campobello Island, New Brunswick. The first principal keeper was Frederick W. Morong (pictured). Keeper Nathaniel Alley was alone one day in 1939 when he was overcome by gas from the coal stove. He was found and taken to Lubec for medical treatment, but he soon died. (Maine Lighthouse Museum.)

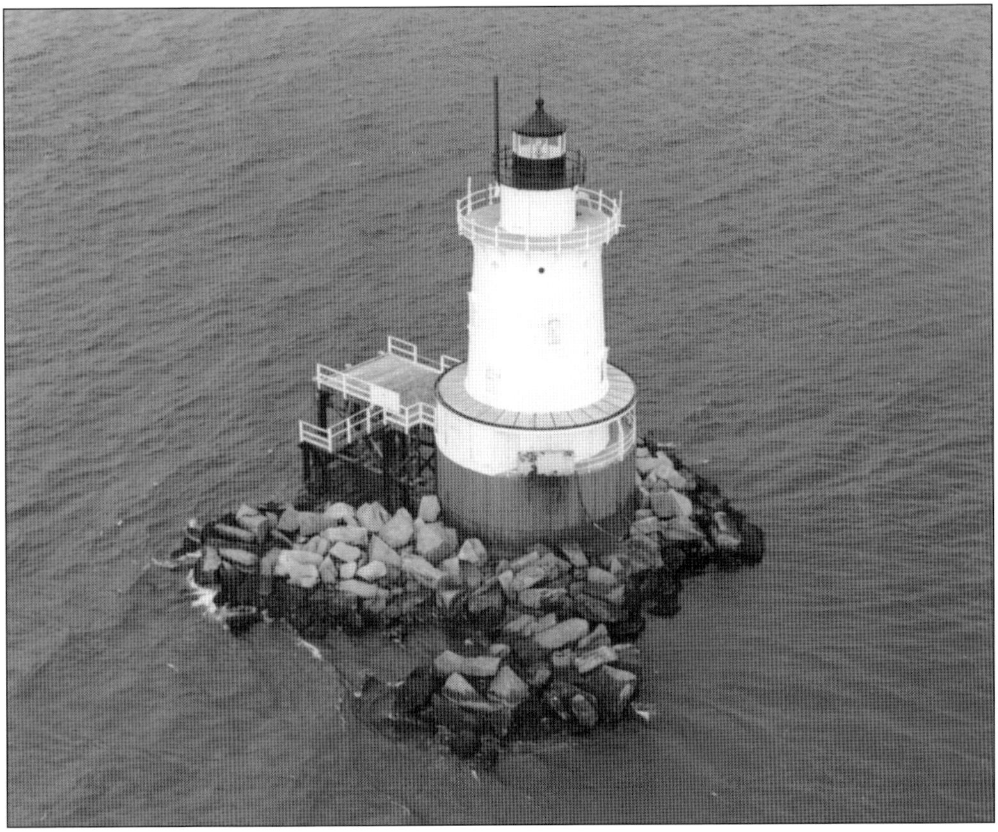

Conimicut Light, completed in 1883 near the entrance to the Providence River in Rhode Island, is another typical "sparkplug light." In March 1905, keeper Daniel MacDonald's two sons were playing near the base of the tower. Three-year-old Melton fell into the freezing water. Easing himself down until he was waist-deep, six-year-old Leslie extended a pole and pulled his little brother to safety. (US Coast Guard.)

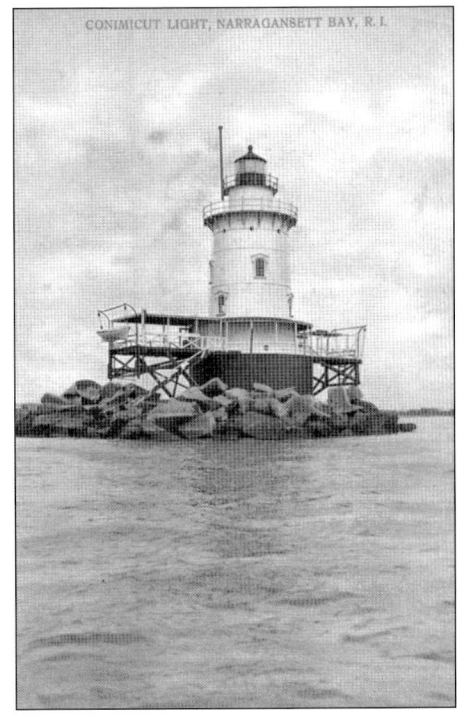

Like many offshore lighthouses, Conimicut Light was the scene of a tragedy in June 1922. Keeper Ellsworth Smith went to do some errands, leaving his wife and two young sons at the lighthouse. His wife, Nellie, who had reportedly grown despondent after a year of lighthouse life, poisoned herself and their two sons. Nellie and one son died; the other son survived. (Author's collection.)

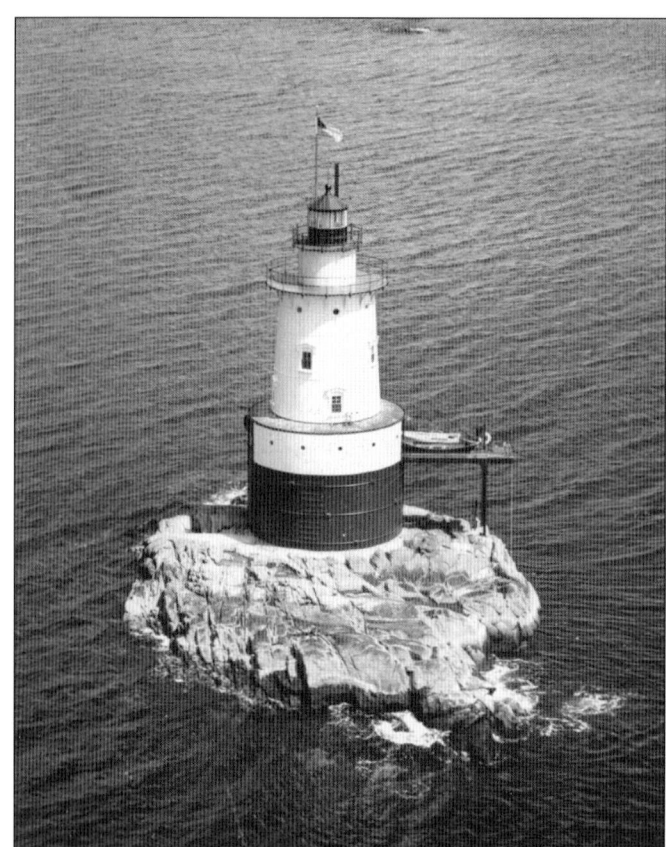

Sakonnet Point Light, near Little Compton, Rhode Island, is another "sparkplug light," but in this case, the cast-iron caisson was bolted to a rocky ledge. The base was completed in 1883, but severe weather delayed progress. Work continued through most of the following year, and the lighthouse went into operation on November 1, 1884. The combined height of the caisson and tower is 66 feet. (US Coast Guard.)

Two keepers weathered the great hurricane of September 21, 1938, inside the Sakonnet Point Light. Keeper William Durfee wrote later: "The first sea that came along was the one that caused the most damage. That sea, when it hit the tower, sounded like a cannon. And it hit with such a force as to knock me off my feet." (US Coast Guard.)

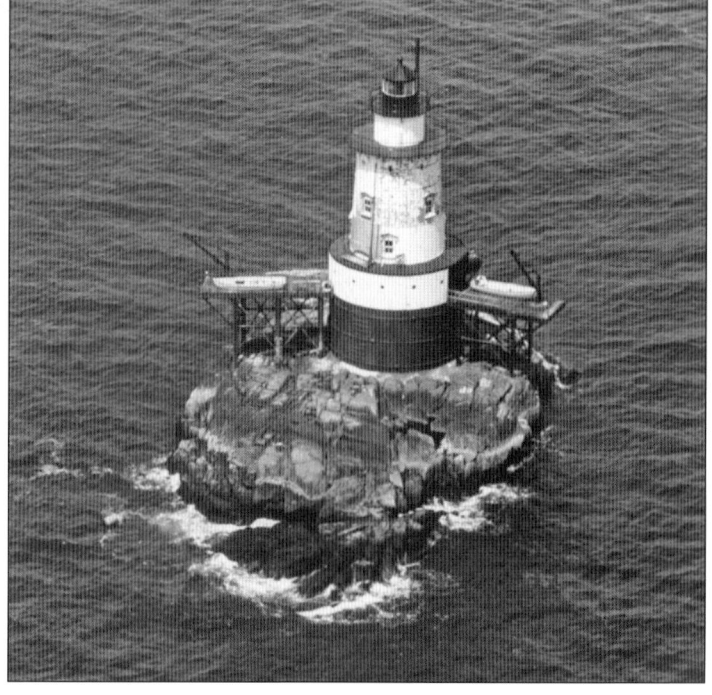

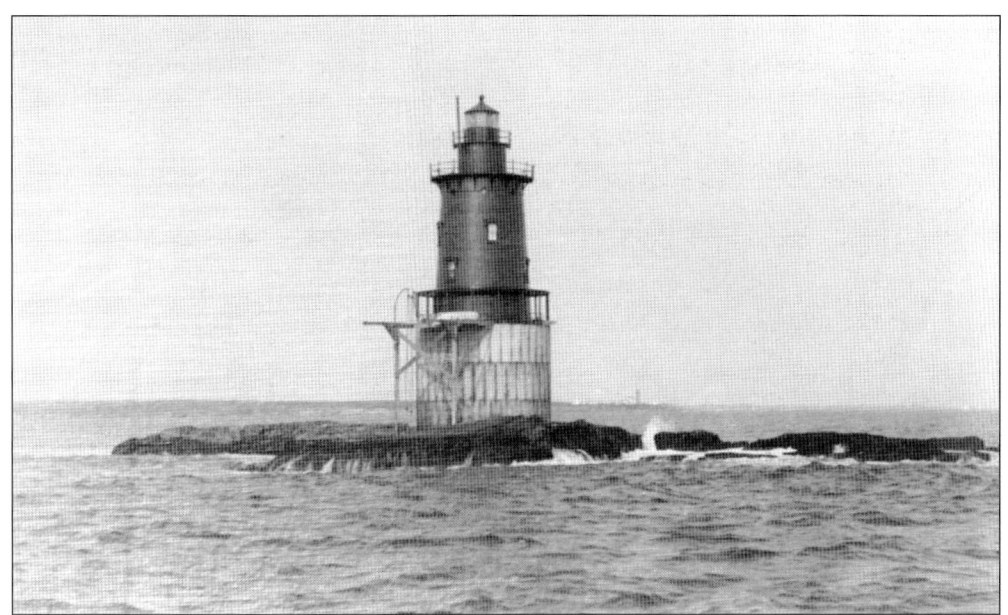

Whale Rock Light, built in 1882 at the mouth of the west passage of Narragansett Bay, was another of Rhode Island's "sparkplug lights." When construction was completed, the *Narragansett Times* reported, "The carpenters are glad to have finished work at so rough a place. The seas at times this summer made clean sweeps over the rock, and on one occasion carried the master mechanic overboard." (National Archives.)

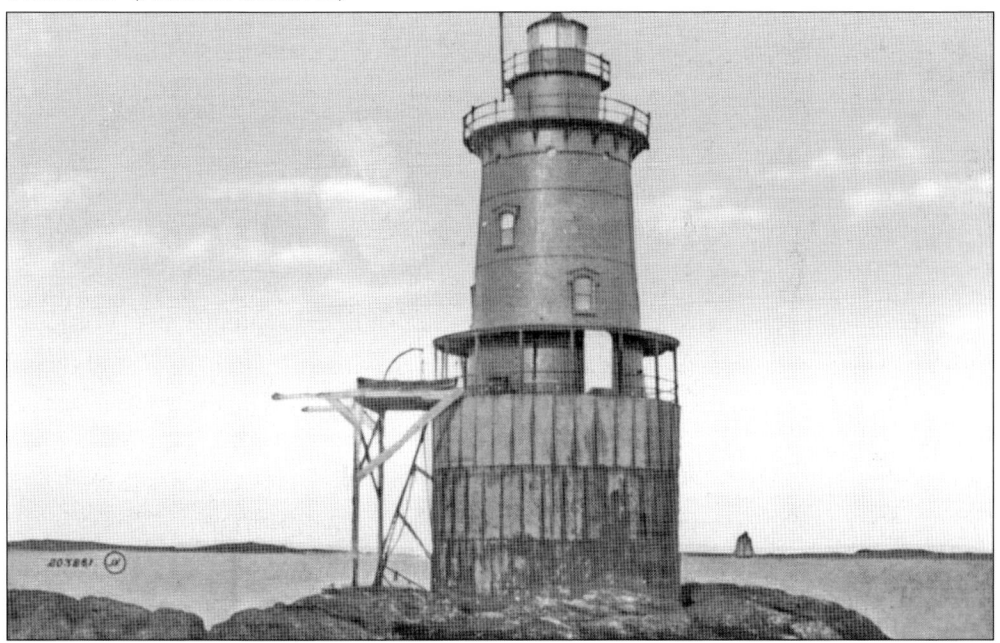

Judson Allen, principal keeper, and assistant keeper Henry Nygren had a violent clash in August 1897. Allen went up to the lantern to tend the light and turned around to see Nygren rushing at him with a knife. Allen escaped with his life, and Nygren was apprehended and brought ashore in irons the next day. Officials of the Lighthouse Board soon dismissed him from government service. (Author's collection.)

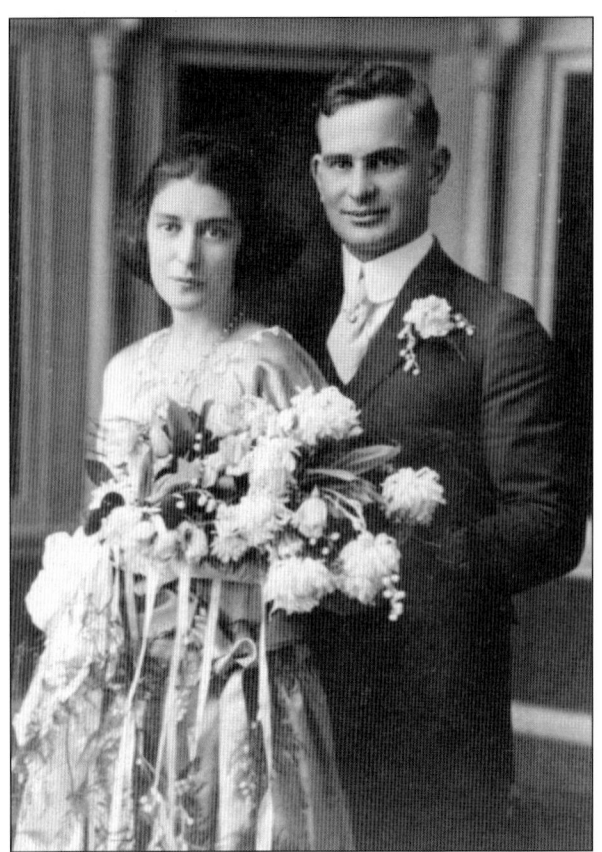

Walter Eberle, pictured here with his wife, Agnes, became the second assistant at Whale Rock in 1937. Born in Iowa in 1898, he had lied about his age when he enlisted in the US Navy at 15. Eberle entered the US Lighthouse Service in 1937 and was assigned to Whale Rock—a welcome assignment since it was relatively close to the family's home in Newport. (Dorothy Roach.)

Walter Eberle was alone at the lighthouse when a devastating hurricane struck on September 21, 1938. Dan Sullivan, the principal keeper, phoned the Eberle family early the morning and told them, "The light is gone." Many days passed before the seas calmed down enough to get a boat out to Whale Rock. The lighthouse and 40-year-old Walter Eberle, father of six, were gone. (Author's collection.)

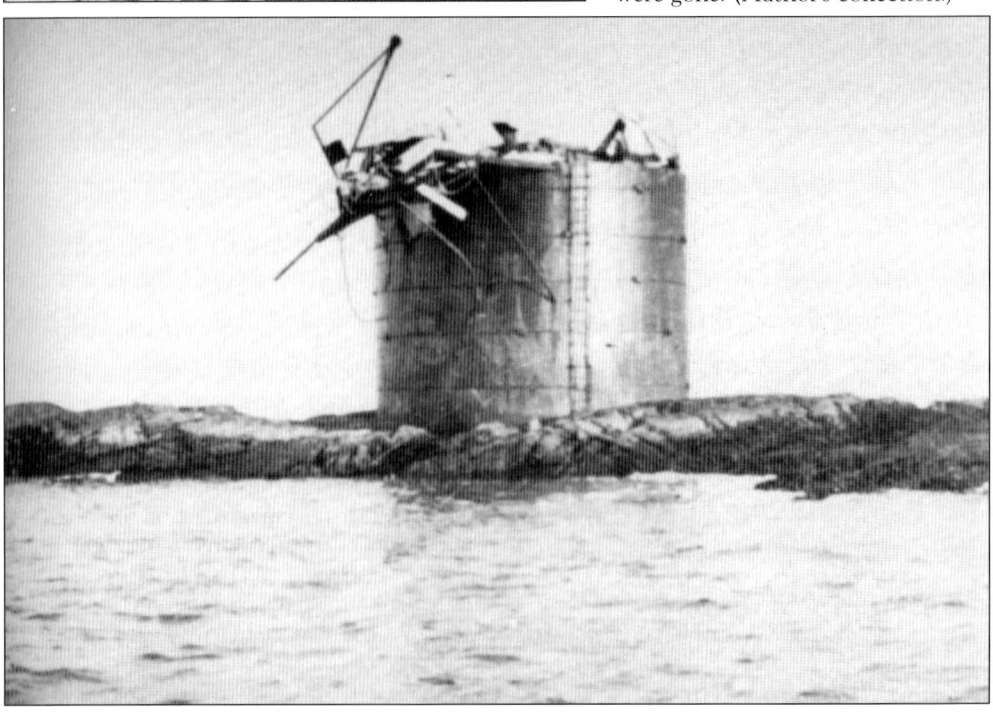

The west passage of Rhode Island's Narragansett Bay, the most direct route from the south to Providence, was bustling with vessels carrying coal and other freight in the late 19th century. In many ways, Plum Beach Light, completed in 1899 in the west passage, is a fairly typical offshore "sparkplug light," but the method of its construction was an innovation. (Author's collection.)

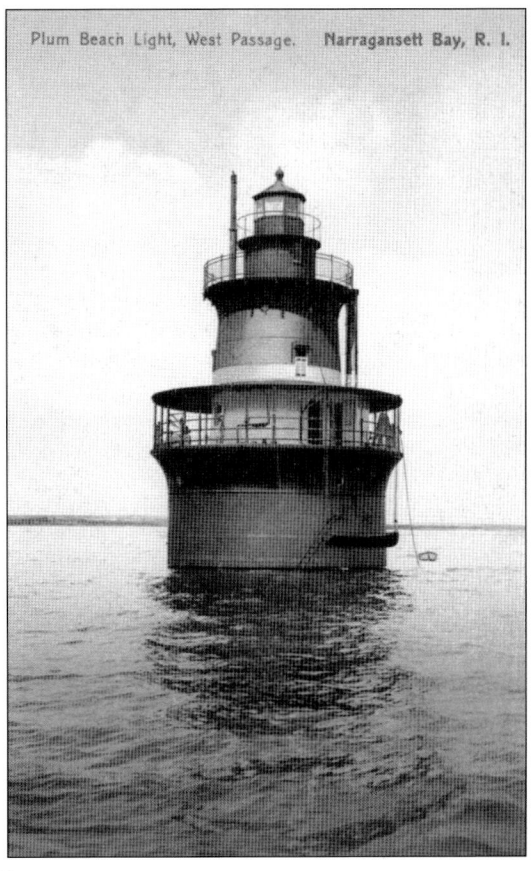

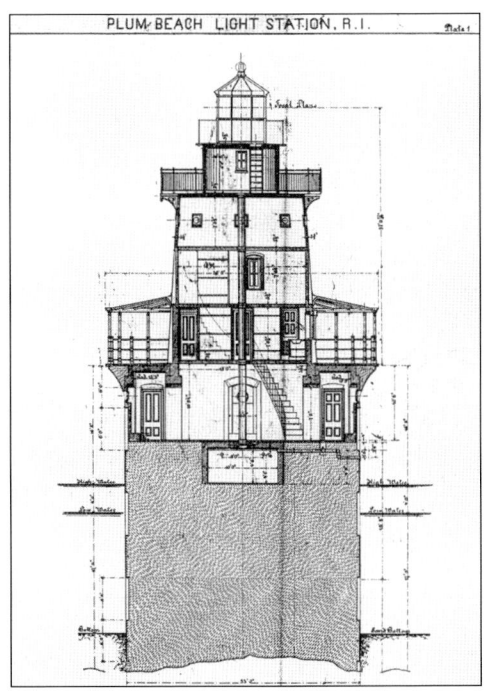

Plum Beach Light was one of only about a dozen lighthouses in the United States built using the pneumatic caisson method. Simply put, a caisson is sunk underwater with an airtight chamber at the bottom, into which air is supplied. As soil is excavated and removed by workers inside the chamber, the caisson is gradually sunk into the ground. (US Coast Guard.)

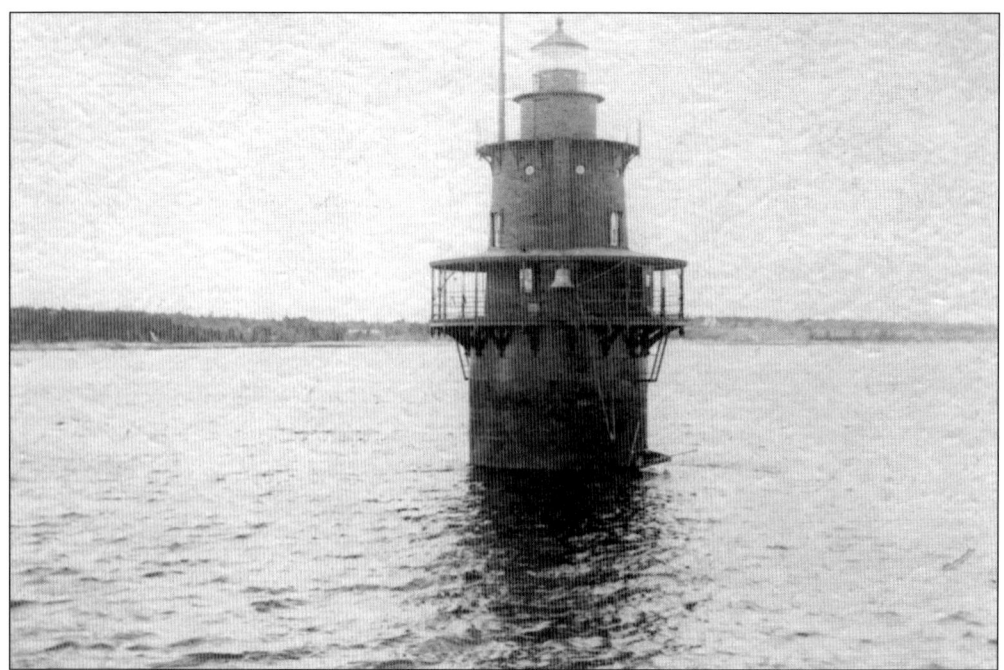

Crabtree Ledge, a mile off Hancock Point in Maine's Frenchman Bay, went into service in January 1890. It was a typical cast-iron "sparkplug light." Two keeper brothers, Leon and Chester Brinkworth, drowned in a 1916 accident. The light was discontinued in 1933, and the lighthouse fell over in a winter storm in 1950. (National Archives.)

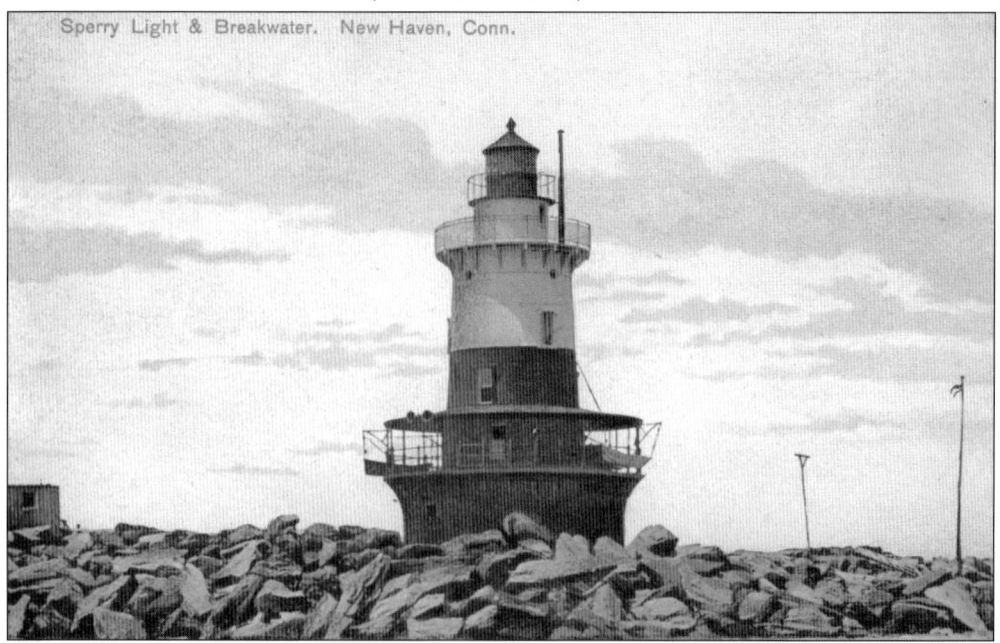

The Outer Breakwall Light in New Haven, Connecticut, also known as Sperry Light, was completed in 1900. One of the keepers, Samuel Armour, drowned in January 1907 while trying to row ashore in rough seas. The lighthouse was dismantled and replaced by a skeleton tower in 1933. (Author's collection.)

Greens Ledge Light in Norwalk, Connecticut, which was completed in 1902, was among the last of the cast-iron caisson lighthouses built in New England. On March 2, 1910, principal keeper John Kiarskon left the lighthouse in the station's only boat. He never returned. Eleven days later, the lighthouse tender *Pansy* landed at Greens Ledge and found assistant Leroy Loughborough nearly starved to death. (Author's collection.)

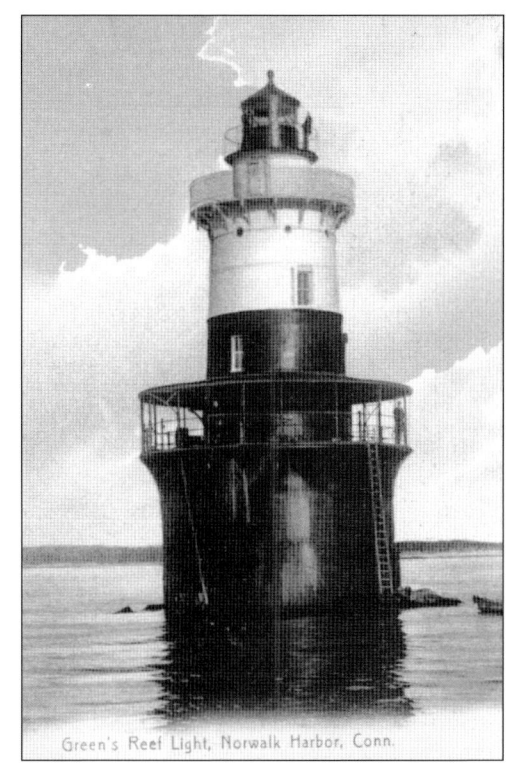

Over the years, especially after the September 1938 hurricane, Greens Ledge Light developed a tilt, and the keepers complained that the vibrations from the station's generators caused all the furniture to move to one side of the tower. They solved the problem by only having furniture on one side. This picture of the light was taken in the 1940s. (Photograph by Andrew J. Simso; Sarah DeMaria.)

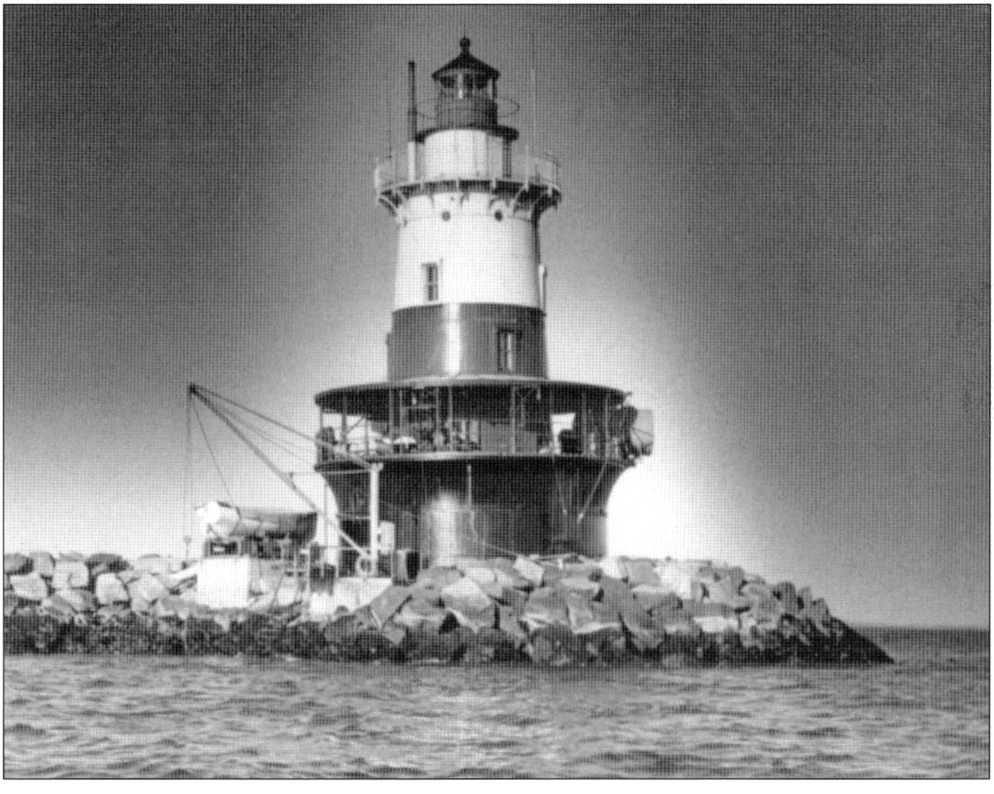

Cape Cod had a classic wave-swept granite lighthouse that no longer exists. Bishop and Clerks Light stood almost three miles south of Point Gammon in West Yarmouth. The 65-foot tower was completed in 1858. The keepers lived inside the tower. From 1892 to 1919, the keeper was Charles Hinckley, who, with a height of four feet, nine inches, was regarded as the shortest lighthouse keeper in the world. (National Archives.)

Bishop and Clerks Light was converted to automatic acetylene gas operation in 1923 and discontinued in 1928. By 1952, the tower was tilted to one side and was missing many blocks, and the Coast Guard decided to raze the structure. It was demolished using dynamite in September 1952; a small lighted beacon now marks the spot. (Dolly Bicknell.)

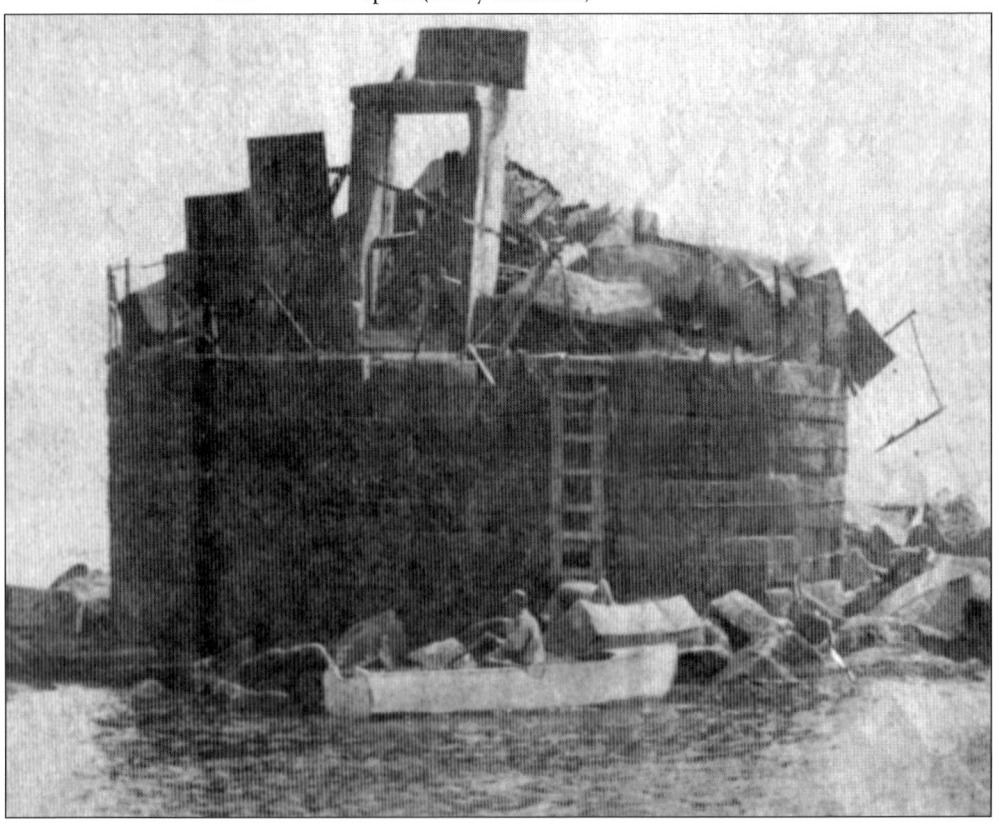

New London Ledge Light, built at the mouth of Connecticut's Thames River in 1909, marked an unusual departure from the offshore caisson lighthouses that were prevalent in the early 1900s. The lighthouse is said to owe its distinctive Second Empire style to the influence of the wealthy homeowners on the local coast, who wanted a structure in keeping with the elegance of their homes. (Author's collection.)

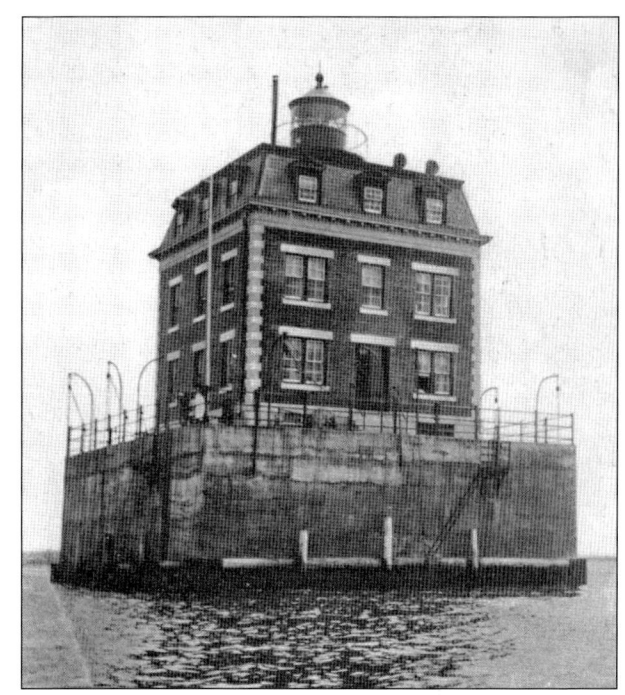

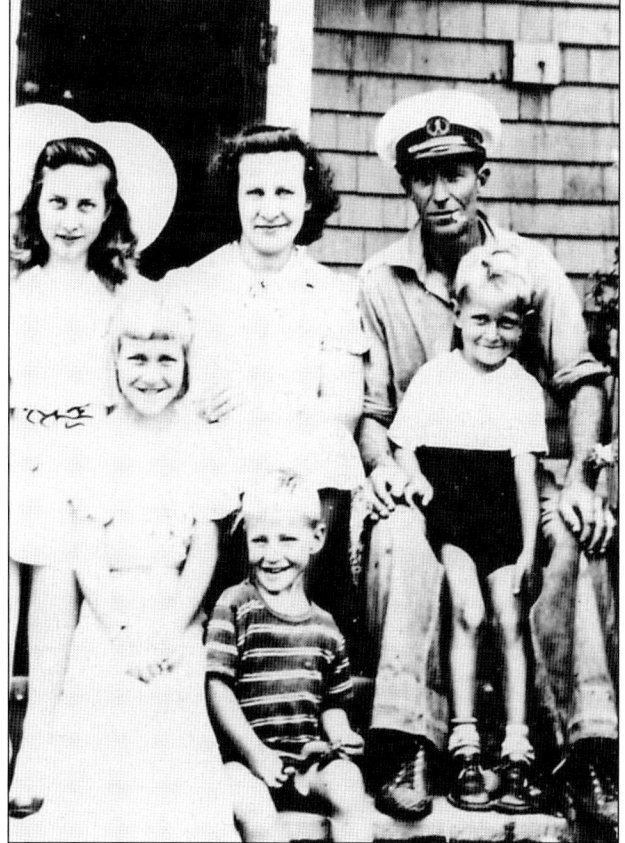

Howard B. Beebe, shown here with his family, was keeper of New London Ledge Light during the hurricane of September 21, 1938. "It washed out everything," he later said. "We moved to the lantern. It was a three-story building. Waves were coming through the second floor. I've seen waves before, in the Bay of Fundy, but I never saw them like that." (Barbara Gaspar.)

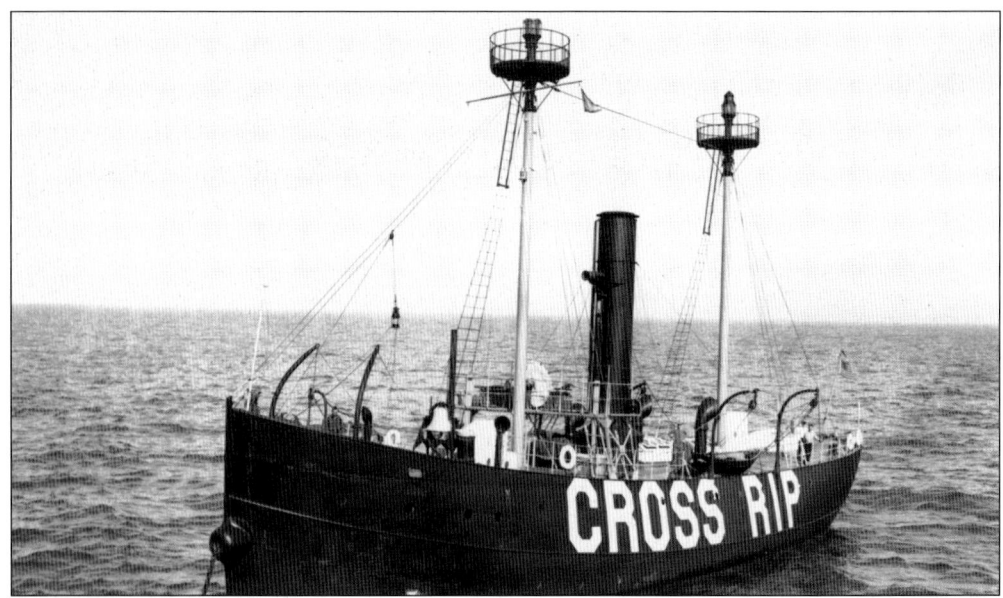

Lightships were utilized at locations where it was impossible or impractical to build a lighthouse, often because the water was too deep. Lights were mounted on one or two tall masts, and the vessel was anchored in place. After the early 1800s, lightships used mushroom anchors—invented by engineer Robert Stevenson—weighing three or four tons. (Wikimedia Commons.)

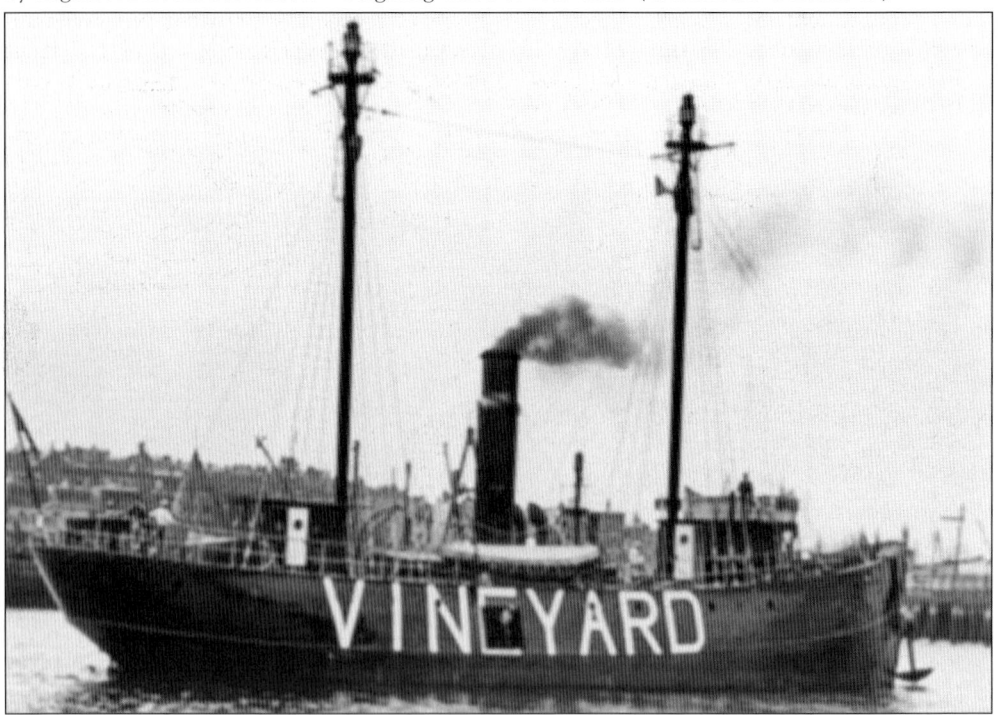

Lightships were employed in the United States beginning in 1820, and by 1909, there were 56 lightships in American waters. Of the 179 lightships built for the federal government over the years, only 15 survive today. Some were lost in storms; the Vineyard Sound lightship took the lives of 12 crewmen with it when it sank in a hurricane in 1944. (Author's collection.)

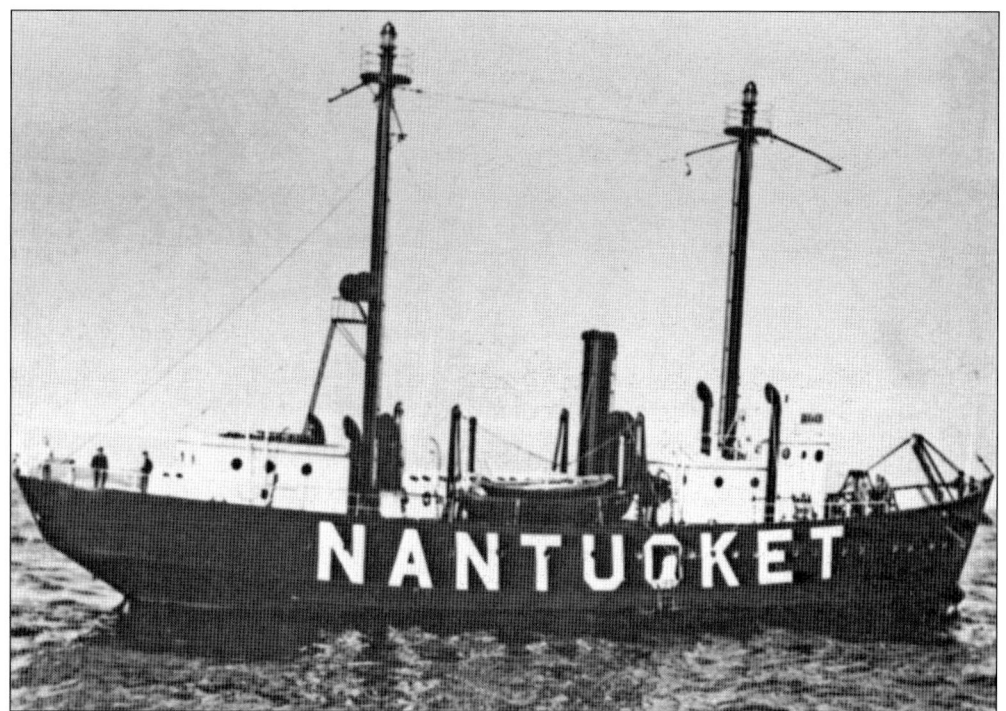

Life aboard a lightship has been described as hours of boredom punctuated by moments of sheer terror. Early on the morning of May 15, 1934, the RMS *Olympic*, sister ship of the *Titanic*, collided with the lightship *Nantucket* (LV-112) in thick fog, killing seven members of its crew. (US Coast Guard.)

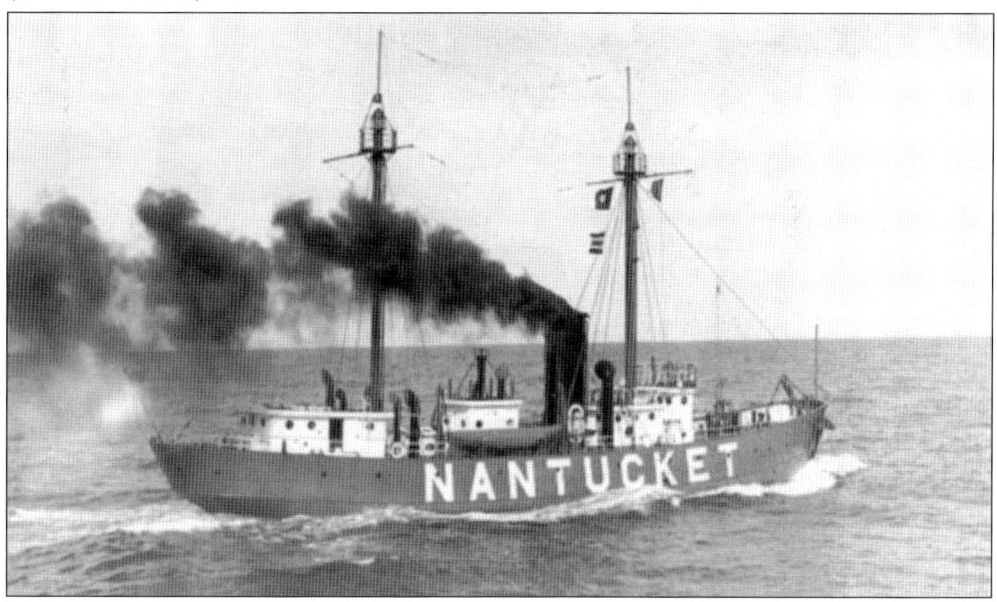

There are no longer any lightships serving as aids to navigation in United States waters. Like many lighthouses, some surviving lightships have been converted into museums. The LV-112, which replaced the LV-117 on the Nantucket Shoals, is being restored in East Boston by the US Lightship Museum. It is open for touring at specified times. (US Coast Guard.)

BIBLIOGRAPHY

Bachelder, Peter Dow. *Lighthouses of Casco Bay.* Portland, ME: Breakwater Press, 1975.
Caldwell, Bill. *Lighthouses of Maine.* Portland, ME: Gannett Books, 1986.
Clifford, J. Candace, and Mary Louise Clifford. *Maine Lighthouses: Documentation of Their Past.* Alexandria, VA: Cypress Communications, 2005.
D'Entremont, Jeremy. *The Lighthouses of Maine.* Beverly, MA: Commonwealth Editions, 2009.
———. *The Lighthouses of Massachusetts.* Beverly, MA: Commonwealth Editions, 2007.
———. *The Lighthouses of Rhode Island.* Beverly, MA: Commonwealth Editions, 2006.
———. *Lovers' Light: The History of Minot's Ledge Lighthouse.* Portsmouth, NH: Coastlore Media, 2015.
DeWire, Elinor. *Guardians of the Lights: The Men and Women of the U.S. Lighthouse Service.* Sarasota, FL: Pineapple Press, 1995.
Dolin, Eric Jay. *Brilliant Beacons.* New York: Liveright (imprint of W. W. Norton), 2016.
Gleason, Sarah C. *Kindly Lights: A History of the Lighthouses of Southern New England.* Boston: Beacon Press, 1991.
Porter, Jane Molloy. *Friendly Edifices: Piscataqua Lighthouses and Other Aids to Navigation.* Portsmouth, NH: Peter E. Randall Publisher, 2006.
Snow, Edward Rowe. *The Lighthouses of New England.* New York: Dodd, Mead & Company, 1973.
———. *The Story of Minot's Light.* Boston: Yankee Publishing Company, 1940.
Sterling, Robert Thayer. *Lighthouses of the Maine Coast and the Men Who Keep Them.* Brattleboro, VT: Stephen Daye Press, 1935.

About the Organizations

There are many organizations around the United States that are working to preserve lighthouses and their history. The American Lighthouse Foundation (ALF), based in Maine, has several chapters that care for more than a dozen lighthouses in the New England region. ALF plays a major role in Maine Lighthouse Day, a popular event that takes place in September; learn more at www.lighthousefoundation.org.

The largest lighthouse organization on the west coast, the US Lighthouse Society, offers a quarterly magazine, the *Keeper's Log*, as well as educational tours around the world; see www.uslhs.org.

And in the Great Lakes region, the Great Lakes Lightkeepers Association is a leader in lighthouse preservation and education; see www.gllka.com for more information.

There are many smaller organizations working on behalf of lighthouse preservation. The author urges caring readers to donate some time and/or money to this important cause.

Discover Thousands of Local History Books Featuring Millions of Vintage Images

Arcadia Publishing, the leading local history publisher in the United States, is committed to making history accessible and meaningful through publishing books that celebrate and preserve the heritage of America's people and places.

Find more books like this at
www.arcadiapublishing.com

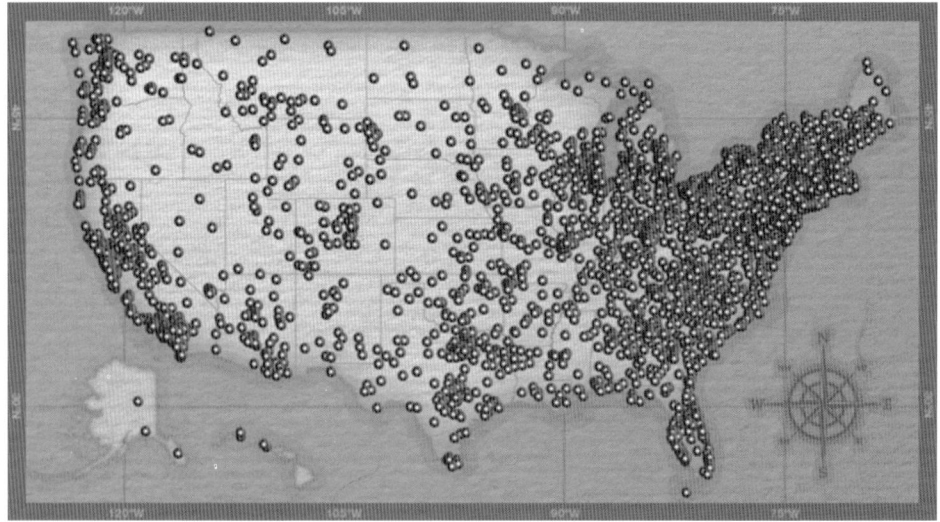

Search for your hometown history, your old stomping grounds, and even your favorite sports team.

Consistent with our mission to preserve history on a local level, this book was printed in South Carolina on American-made paper and manufactured entirely in the United States. Products carrying the accredited Forest Stewardship Council (FSC) label are printed on 100 percent FSC-certified paper.

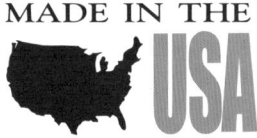